SCANDALS
OF THE RICH
AND FAMOUS

SCANDALS
OF THE RICH AND FAMOUS

BLITZ EDITIONS

Published by Blitz Editions
an imprint of Bookmart Ltd
Registered Number 2372865
Trading as Bookmart Ltd
Desford Road
Enderby
Leicester LE9 5AD

ISBN 1 85605 207 9

This material has previously appeared in *Inside Stories*.

Every effort has been made to contact the copyright holders for the pictures.
In some cases they have been untraceable, for which we offer our apologies.
Special thanks to the Hulton-Deutsch Collection, who supplied the majority of pictures,
and thanks also to the following libraries and picture agencies:
Mary Evans Photo Library, Peter Newark/Western Americana,
Popperfotos, Press Association, Rex Features, Frank Spooner Pictures,
Syndication International, Topham Picture Source.

The Author
Allan Hall is the American correspondent for a major U.K. newspaper.
He has written several books on crime, the paranormal and the unexplained.

This book was produced by Amazon Publishing Limited
Designed by Cooper Wilson Design
Edited by Graham McColl

Printed in the Slovak Republic
51729

Contents

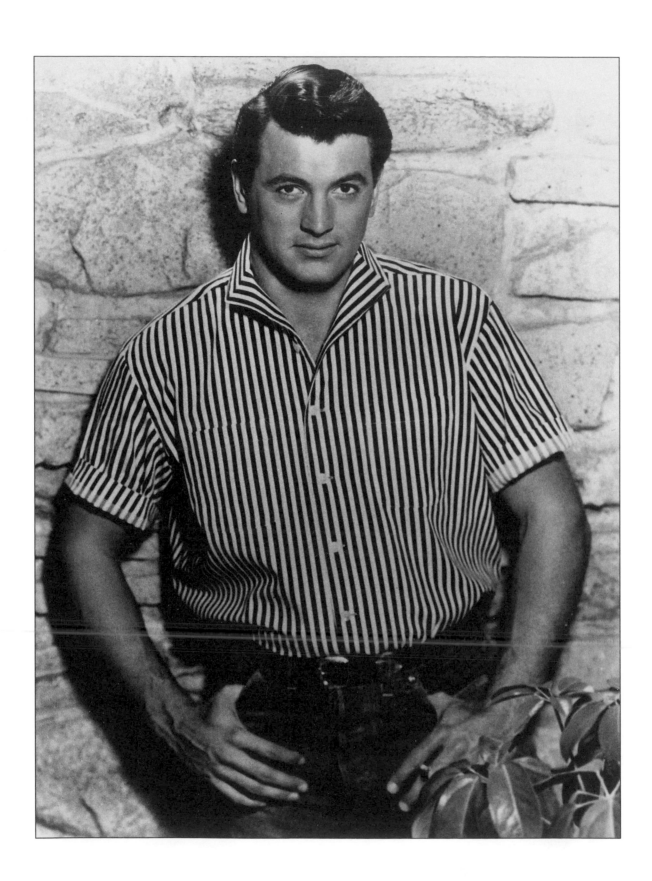

SCANDALS
OF THE RICH AND FAMOUS

Politicians, pop stars and royalty are radically different in the ways they achieve fame. But in the modern age, the differences between them are constantly blurred: some young royals indulge in drugs and sex and often appear to look to pop stars for inspiration; pop stars treat those around them with regal indifference, all the while displaying wealth and lifestyles that would be the envy of most royals; while even those politicians who are in the highest positions of power and responsibility have trouble controlling their basic instincts.

This book examines the perils of fame, money and success in the modern age. Here we have the British monarchy in trouble because of newspaper allegations of adultery involving Princess Diana and Prince Charles and the American presidency struggling to retain its dignity through revelations of corruption. There are also numerous other cases of lesser politicians and royals in trouble. Their combined exploits have helped undermine public faith in some of the world's greatest institutions.

In the world of entertainment, the struggle for success is often followed by a struggle *with* success, once fame and fortune have been earned. It sometimes appears that the difficulties that are involved in reaching the top make our favourite stars so insecure that they lose touch with the real world, never to return to their roots. Michael Jackson was able to face thousands of screaming fans, but he found day-to-day contact with adults difficult; Frank Sinatra sang of romance, but was often close to violence; the Rolling Stones seemed to rely on drugs for creative inspiration; Woody Allen was vulnerable and loveable in his films but found himself in court on child abuse charges; Freddie Mercury, James Dean and Brian Jones paid the ultimate price for their self-indulgent lifestyles.

We all need to be entertained by glamorous people and we need to believe in our leaders. What this book shows is that we should judge them by what they actually do, and not by the image that their publicists present.

SECRETS OF THE STARS

WOODY ALLEN
Troubled Genius

Woody Allen's screen persona was often that of a sensitive soul, but revelations about his real life cast him as a monster. When his partner Mia Farrow took him to court, the scenes that followed were as dramatic as any that Allen had filmed.

To millions of film fans around the world, Woody Allen was a true cinematic genius. They laughed at his sophisticated scripts, marvelled at his witty directing and admired his comic acting. Indeed, Woody Allen was almost a one-man film industry, successfully churning out a movie a year almost single-handedly for a quarter of a century.

Likewise, his lover of many years, Mia Farrow, was also highly successful. A gifted actress who starred in numerous Allen features, she was the consummate professional, a woman who had brought to life some of the most memorable characters in recent film history.

Even as individuals, Woody and Mia were icons of the industry. But together they represented a powerful film-making team that delighted and intrigued scores of movie fans in films like *The Purple Rose of Cairo*, *Broadway Danny Rose* and *Hannah and Her Sisters*.

For many years, they were also viewed as the perfect off-screen pairing as well. Both shunned the glitz and glamour of Hollywood for New York City, and seemed like caring, attentive lovers as well as being parents to a brood of children, most of whom had been adopted.

Yet together they unwittingly starred in a sordid soap opera played out to a global audience clamouring for details and dirt. The drama was more unbelievable, more sensational, more bizarre than anything Woody and Mia had ever put on celluloid – and attracted greater attention than even their most successful films.

WOODY ALLEN AND MIA FARROW STARRED IN A SORDID SOAP OPERA PLAYED OUT TO A GLOBAL AUDIENCE

Opposite: *Film-maker Woody Allen put on a brave public face as he battled allegations of sexual abuse and debauchery.*

Below: *Allen and his long-time lover, actress Mia Farrow, accused one another of heinous acts during their bitter custody battle.*

Above: *Allen with Soon-Yi Previn, the adopted teenage daughter of Mia Farrow, with whom he fell in love.*

Opposite Top: *Farrow addresses reporters. Both Allen and Farrow courted the media in their war of words.*

Opposite Bottom: *Eleanor Alter, Farrow's high-priced lawyer, with her client.*

daughter, when she was just 19 years of age. Woody, coming out of his cocoon of secrecy, openly admitted his love for the teenager, dismissing detractors by asserting, simply, that 'the heart wants what the heart wants'.

While the story caused a sensation around the world, there was an even greater outcry to come. Days later, overwhelmed with grief and embarrassment, Farrow accused Woody of molesting their seven-year-old daughter, Dylan, whom they had adopted. The damage could not have been worse. The once gentle image of a dishevelled, neurotic but lovable movie machine was drowned forever in a sea of bitter recrimination.

Suddenly Woody Allen was a corrupt, self-obsessed monster who destroyed Farrow's family in a matter of months, her lawyers would claim.

Only Allen and Farrow will ever know exactly what actually went on that day in August when he was accused of taking Dylan to an attic in Mia's Connecticut home and sexually assaulting her. But Allen announced that he would fight for custody of their three children: Moses, 15, Satchel, five, and Dylan.

A BITTER BATTLE

By launching a ferocious legal war which he had no hope of winning, he exposed the youngsters to unheard of public scrutiny. Moses, bitter at the rumours that his sister was sleeping with his father, even wrote to Allen telling him to commit suicide! 'Everyone knows not to have an affair with your son's sister,' Moses wrote. 'You have done a horrible, unforgivable, ugly, stupid thing. I hope you get so humiliated you commit suicide.'

But there were many more shocks along the way as the couple fought it out in a dreary Manhattan courtroom in a drama unparalleled in any movie. There were claims that Mia had tried to bribe Allen, demanding millions of pounds to keep the child abuse allegations private.

She counter-claimed that Woody had taken pornographic pictures of Soon-Yi, a girl he had watched blossom from childhood to womanhood. Indeed, Allen eventually admitted that he had taken some nude pictures of the girl shortly after their clandestine love affair had begun, telling her:

The first shot in a war that was to last more than nine months was fired when the news broke that Mia and Woody were going their separate ways after a relationship lasting for more than a decade. The announcement was surprising, yet no one expected to hear anything more about it given both stars' predilection for absolute privacy. Who could have possibly known the bombshells that were about to drop!

First it was learned that the 57-year-old Woody, who was famous for his relationships with young girls in his movies, had run off with Soon-Yi Previn, Mia's adopted

'Just lean back and give me your most erotic poses. Let yourself go.'

However, he steadfastly denied the pictures were 'pornographic' in nature, though an impartial opinion is impossible because they were never publicly released. Still, Mia's lawyer, Eleanor Alter, described them as 'repulsive'.

'Nobody with regard for a woman – or women in general – could have taken pictures like that,' she stormed. 'They show a contempt for Soon-Yi and for all women'.

That shocking disclosure was quickly followed by details which showed Allen's apparent nastiness towards Farrow, who had been his lover and confidante for 12 years. For a man who had made a brilliant career – and millions of pounds – exploring the pains and insecurities of personal relationships, Allen appeared, at the end of the day, as brutal and insensitive as a bar-room yob.

'Why are you getting so upset?' he allegedly asked Farrow after she had learned that he had seduced her daughter. 'Why don't we use this as a springboard to a deeper relationship?'

Mia was also held up to public scorn and ridicule. She allegedly beat Soon-Yi and locked her in her bedroom after learning of the affair, and even sent Allen a demented Valentine's Day card, which was pierced by numerous kitchen knives. Many in the press and the public also claimed she was an unfit mother, despite her many adoptions, and they even alleged that she had beaten Soon-Yi.

But her lawyer, Eleanor Alter, said that Mia was a perfect mother, yet one who was wracked by guilt because she 'felt Soon-Yi was victimised, and the horror is that she brought the person who victimised Soon-Yi into the house'.

'She cries about Soon-Yi a lot in private,' said Alter. 'She worries about what

Right: Pretty Soon-Yi was torn between her love for her adoptive mother and her love for Allen.

Below: Mia sent Allen a Valentine's Day card pierced by a large kitchen knife. Woody's supporters claimed it was proof of Mia's emotional instability.

will happen to her after Woody dumps her. I mean, this child was a virgin. And she is low IQ. She is learning-disabled. This is a kid who went to a Catholic school and never had a date.'

Still, Alter admitted that Farrow was jealous of her adopted daughter. 'Jealous? Sure,' said Alter. 'Mia loved him. She won't deny that. I mean, does anybody think she shouldn't have been jealous? It was her daughter, and those pictures! You haven't seen the pictures. I don't know what I would do if I found pictures like that of my child taken by my lover. I either would have ended up in a mental institution or killed him.'

A SERIOUS ACCUSATION

Alter claimed that Allen was so nasty that he deliberately left the pictures for Farrow to find. 'This was Woody's way of making Mia end the relationship,' she said. 'I think it was totally and utterly clear that was how he and Soon-Yi planned to come out in the open. He is a very cruel man.'

Despite the juiciness of Allen's relationship with Soon-Yi and the still-unseen photographs, the real heart of the scandal centred on Allen's bizarre relationship with Dylan. Allen insisted that Farrow had invented the allegations of child abuse to

Above: *Allen makes his point at one of his many impromptu press conferences outside the Manhattan courtroom.*

stop his custody claim, and many famous friends came forward to denounce her assertions as ridiculous. Indeed, he was largely exonerated of sexually abusing the young girl by a government-appointed panel of medical and psychiatric experts. Part of their findings was based on a video-tape which Farrow had made of Dylan describing what had happened. In one scene, Dylan recalled a particular incident in which she said Allen 'touched' her.

But the team of child abuse experts at Yale-New Haven Hospital in Connecticut said they found no evidence to back up the allegations after an extensive seven-month investigation. 'They said no child molesta-tion ever took place,' said a buoyant Allen, as he left the hospital after the three-hour meeting. 'No sexual abuse ever took place.

It was either an imagined thing or a con-cocted thing.' He claimed Farrow coerced Dylan in the video.

Although cleared, however, the report confirmed Allen's relationship with the lit-tle girl had 'sexualised overtones'. They urged him to seek continuous therapy to 'establish appropriate boundaries' between himself and his children.

One of his own witnesses during the seven-week custody trial, Dr Susan Coates, said that Allen had an unhealthy obsession with Dylan and that the relationship was 'inappropriately intense'. The psychiatrist said she was shocked by the way Allen would whisk Dylan into his arms and bom-bard her with unrelenting attention to the exclusion of his lover and his only natural born child, Satchel.

IN ONE SCENE, DYLAN RECALLED A PARTICULAR INCIDENT IN WHICH SHE SAID ALLEN 'TOUCHED' HER

Farrow said Allen used to pin the little girl to her bed at night-time, staring into her eyes until she said goodnight. In the morning he would play with the youngster in his bed dressed only in his shorts. Over seven long drawn out weeks every nuance of the relationship was dragged out in court, analysed and sent round the world. It even emerged that New York authorities broke their own guidelines by allowing the couple to adopt children when they were not married and did not even live together! By the time of their acrimonious split, Farrow had 11 – and still wanted two more.

UNCONVINCING PERFORMANCES

As the case continued, Allen tried to rise to the occasion for his most important ever role but left the witness stand with no major awards. He visibly squirmed when Judge Elliott Wilk grilled him about the ethics of going out with his children's sister. But Farrow, although often putting on an Oscar-winning display, complete with tears, did not come out unscathed. She admitted praising Allen as a 'wonderful' father as late as December 1991 when he officially adopted Moses and Dylan.

And her denial that she ruthlessly used the children in a publicity war was hard to accept. Nearly all her older children gave press interviews. Allen portrayed Farrow as a deranged, unstable and violent woman who was endangering the mental health of her children with her hatred for him.

On one occasion, the film director said his son Satchel had been brainwashed by Farrow to say nasty and hurtful things about him. He remembered his horror when the little boy said during his weekly two hour visit: 'I'm supposed to say I hate you.' Another time Allen's only natural born child also told him: 'Mommy is writing a book that she says will make you go away forever.' On another day Satchel said: 'We're getting a new daddy' and 'I wish you were dead.' Allen accused Farrow of trying to turn his children against him: 'Satchel would say these things but not act them. It was as if he was obliged to say them.'

BAFFLING BEHAVIOUR

Also, she admitted spending a night with Allen at a salubrious Manhattan hotel after

Above: *The besieged Allen tries to cover his face as he returns from a rare night out during the trial.*

ALLEN PORTRAYED FARROW AS AN UNSTABLE WOMAN WHO WAS ENDANGERING THE MENTAL HEALTH OF HER CHILDREN

---

he began bedding Soon-Yi in a bizarre effort to resolve the rift. And a former nanny who testified on Allen's behalf claimed that Farrow treated her four biological children (three by second husband, composer André Previn) better than her adopted brood, who were forced to do most of the household chores.

But the public sympathy leaned towards Farrow, especially when she tearfully confessed how she attacked Soon-Yi after discovering the nude photos. 'I wasn't proud of what I did,' she said.

Still, the all-out public relations war between the two former lovers was finally won by Mia when Allen was subjected to an intense grilling by her lawyer. It offered an insight into the bizarre lifestyle of the super-rich, and painted Woody as a thoughtless, uncaring father. Some of the more bizarre aspects included the fact that:

● Neither Moses nor Dylan – his two adopted children – or Satchel ever spent a single night in Allen's home away from their mother.

● Allen hated leaving New York so much that when they went abroad on family holidays to places such as Paris, Rome, London, Venice, Russia, and Norway he stayed in his hotel room writing.

● He admitted he never spoke to Farrow's other eight children, even on holiday, only saying 'hello' if they spoke to him.

● Allen refused to take a shower in the family's weekend home in Connecticut because the drain was on the side rather than the middle.

● He would play baseball with son Moses for no more than 10 minutes at a time because otherwise he would get sweaty and would need a shower.

● He was obsessed with cleanliness and wouldn't go near the family pets.

● When he spotted Moses' cat on the din-

> ALLEN HATED LEAVING NEW YORK… WHEN THEY WENT ON FAMILY HOLIDAYS HE STAYED IN HIS HOTEL ROOM WRITING

Below: *The happy family before the break-up. Allen holds Dylan, one of the couple's adopted children. Baby Satchel, the film-maker's only natural child, is in his mother's arms.*

ner table eating off a plate he insisted on using only paper plates and plastic cutlery from then on.

● He didn't know the names of any of the children's pets.

● He berated Farrow for not having a thermometer in the house, insisting he had to take his own temperature every two hours.

● The city-born actor always refused to sleep in a separate cottage on the family's Connecticut estate – even after Farrow had accused him of molesting Dylan – because 'there are animals out there'.

● He didn't know the name of a single friend of his three children, nor the names of their doctors or teachers.

● He had never bathed the children, taken them to the doctor's or dentist's, or attended Satchel's PTA meetings. He had only bought a handful of clothes for them.

● He did not buy the children presents himself but ordered them from a 'personal shopper' at the exclusive F.A.O. Schwartz store who made a selection for him to pick

Above: Farrow leaves the Yale-New Haven hospital after a panel of experts had reported that they could find no evidence that Allen had sexually molested Dylan.

JUDGE WILKS SAID ALLEN WAS AN INEPT, INCONSIDERATE FATHER... 'SELF-ABSORBED... INSENSITIVE'

up in his chauffeur-driven limousine.

● All the children had their own therapists from the age of two!

Finally, after a bitter seven-week trial in which their eccentric lifestyles had been bared for all the world to see, Woody and Mia arrived at the Manhattan courthouse in June 1993, to hear Judge Wilk's decision. It would not be a banner day for Woody Allen, as the Judge lambasted him as a totally inept and inconsiderate father and then awarded Mia sole custody.

But Allen refused to be daunted, immediately vowing to gain full visitation rights to his three children despite the damning loss. 'I think it's tragic for the children that their custody was not awarded to me. I will continue to fight for my full visitation rights with all of my children, which I feel is vital to the their well-being, and which I deserve. I'm committed to them totally. I could have walked away from this unscathed many months ago.'

DAMNING JUDGMENT

Allen's bravado came just after Judge Wilk had returned one of the most strident condemnations of the film-maker's character that has ever been heard. 'Mr Allen has demonstrated no parenting skills that would qualify him as an adequate custodian for Moses, Dylan or Satchel,' he thundered. Further, the Judge said Allen was 'self-absorbed, untrustworthy and insensitive' and was not qualified to care for the children on a full-time basis.

In stark contrast, he praised Farrow as 'sensitive to the needs of her children, respectful of their opinions, honest with them and quick to address their problems. It is evident that she loves children and has devoted a significant portion of her emotional and material wealth to their upbringing.'

In his report, Judge Wilk banned Allen from seeing Dylan for a period of at least six months, and after that only if it was deemed to be in the little girl's best interests and only in the company of others. He also barred the star from seeing Moses, unless Moses wanted to see Allen. However, he was given permission to visit Satchel, his biological child, three times a week for supervised, two-hourly visits. Wilk then ordered that Allen should pay all Farrow's legal costs, which amounted to a staggering £750,000.

INCONCLUSIVE PROOF

But most troubling for Allen was Wilk's severe summing up with regard to the allegations of child abuse: 'The evidence suggests that it is unlikely that (Allen) could be successfully prosecuted for sexual abuse. I am less certain, however, that the evidence proves conclusively that there was no sexual abuse.'

The day after her overwhelming victory, Farrow then announced she would try to undo Allen's adoptions of Moses and Dylan, claiming her estranged lover fraudulently adopted the two children and lied to the court. Allen's adoption was confirmed on 17 December 1991 – less than a month

before he began his underhand affair with the children's older sister.

'Had the courts known and had Moses known and had I known, and, most importantly, had the Surrogate Court known, of the relationship with Soon-Yi, they would not have sanctioned those adoptions – and for very good reasons,' Farrow declared. 'For so many, many months, my family has been living through nightmare. My children have been ripped apart emotionally. I can go back home to my children and finally we will have some measure of peace to heal. It will be a long road.' As for her wayward daughter, Soon-Yi, Farrow said she hoped they could mend their relationship. 'I do love her with all my heart and I would lay down my life for her and I just pray that she will come home.' Then she bitterly remarked that she hoped she and Allen never crossed paths again. 'I don't like him at all and I hope I never see him again,' she said. 'I cannot see anything in him to like at the moment.'

WOUNDED RIVALS

Mia returned to the solace of her Connecticut home, surrounded by the children she fought so hard to protect and keep, and Allen retreated to his Central Park apartment to lick his wounds.

In the final analysis, the vicious court battle left him bloody and bruised, forever etched in the minds of many former fans as a monster who was so self-absorbed and insensitive that he willingly destroyed his family to quench his carnal lust.

Above: *The strain shows on Allen's face as he makes yet another court appearance in the ongoing battle to clear his name and win custody of his three children.*

THE VICIOUS COURT BATTLE LEFT ALLEN ETCHED IN THE MINDS OF MANY FORMER FANS AS A MONSTER

ROMAN POLANSKI
A Life on the Run

As a boy, Roman Polanski suffered at the hands of the Nazis when they rounded up his family in his native Poland. The film director later looked for a new start in America but he would continue to experience terrible traumas throughout his life.

On 8 August 1969, as the sprawling city of Los Angeles slept restlessly through a sticky, sweltering night, a group of drugged-out misfits entered the rented home of pregnant actress Sharon Tate. She was the sexy blonde wife of Polish film director Roman Polanski. By the time a vicious orgy of blood-letting by the gang was finally over, five people in the house had been savagely butchered – their blood used to scribble several crude and threatening messages on the walls. A few months later, the world watched in horror as the maniacal man-devil Charles Manson was arrested and charged with ordering the senseless slaughter.

Almost forgotten, amid the blood, violence and horror, was Polanski, the diminutive wunderkind of the cinema who had been out of town when the Manson Family struck into the heart of Hollywood. Yet for this talented, haunted film-maker, the attack on his house would prove the most cataclysmic moment of his life... an event which propelled him on a reckless path to near-ruin and flight from the law. For behind his almost-impish visage, was a man who craved forbidden sex with girls young enough to be his daughters.

Polanski, who himself admitted in his autobiography that he is widely regarded by many people as 'an evil, profligate dwarf', knew from an early age what it is like to be a fugitive on the run from authorities. Although he was born in Paris, Polanski was the son of a Polish Jew and, throughout the vicious Nazi occupation of Poland, he was under constant threat of being identified as a Jew and taken away to the dreaded death camps – both of his parents were. (His father, a record company executive, survived his long incarceration at Mauthausen, but Roman's mother died inside Auschwitz.) In fact, Polanski himself was close to being caught – when he was just nine years of age, he fled from the Krakow ghetto shortly before it was annihilated by the Nazi brutes.

Above: *Charles Manson, whose 'disciples' murdered Sharon Tate, Roman Polanski's wife.*
Above Top: *Polanski and Sharon on their wedding day in January 1968.*
Opposite: *Polanski in 1977.*

After the war, the 14-year-old Polanski decided to become an actor – his early years were in a sense one long rehearsal – and after spending several years performing on both the stage and radio, he enrolled in the Lodz Film School, where he quickly showed a talent for directing. In 1963, that talent burst onto the international film scene when he won an Academy Award nomination for best foreign film with *Knife in the Water*, which dealt with the tense relationship between three people adrift on a small sailboat.

QUICK SUCCESS

His burgeoning talent quickly made him a star and, over the course of the next six years, he became one of the most acclaimed directors in the world. He came out with a slew of brilliant thrillers like *Repulsion* and *Rosemary's Baby*, and also

Above: *Polanski on the set of his thriller* **Rosemary's Baby** *giving some tips to a young Mia Farrow.*

Opposite Top: *A sedated Polanski is led through Heathrow Airport on his way to Los Angeles after learning that his wife Sharon Tate had been murdered by Manson's gang.*

Opposite Bottom: *A confident Polanski six months before the terrible events that would end in Sharon's death.*

took time out to film a comedy, *The Fearless Vampire Hunters*, with wife-to-be Sharon Tate, which they made in 1967, just two years before the Manson killings.

Polanski was devastated by those grim slayings. 'I was unbalanced by Sharon's death,' he conceded many years later. 'Until her death, the future seemed like some never-ending road full of surprises. After it, I came to realise that life was not eternal and that happiness was only transitory.'

After her brutal murder, Polanski even turned amateur detective, trying to find clues to the killers' identities. He bought high tech listening devices to leave in people's homes and even tested friends' cars for blood tests. His sleuthing eventually led him to suspect some of his closest acquaintances, including John Phillips, head of the pop band, the Mamas and the Papas; martial arts expert and film star Bruce Lee, who had been a visitor to his house; and novelist Jerzy Kosinski, a friend he had known since their youth together in Poland.

WICKED RUMOURS

In the wake of the Manson killings, there was also all sorts of talk about drug abuse, kinky sex, even voodoo having been practised by the victims. Although it was rubbish, it came to envelop Polanski, too, as the more sensational press scampered for even more lurid details.

'Before that (the murders) I was the toast of the town,' he revealed later. 'Then people started looking for some kind of rational connection between such a horrendous crime and the people who suffered. They concluded that the victims must have been evil. It somehow gave them more assurance.'

Although the pain never subsided, Polanski got his life back together over the course of the next few years, and returned to his first great love, movie-making. However, his struggle for peace and calm amid the ghosts of the murdered came to an abrupt halt when, eight years later, in March 1977, his whole world seemed to explode after one brief encounter at Jack Nicholson's Hollywood home. The next day, he was accused of raping a 13-year-old girl, who he called 'Sandra'. At the time, Polanski, who admits sex has always played a big part in his life, was 44 years of age! His arrest on six counts of sex and

Polanski had taken some other photographs of the girl with her mother's permission for another French publication.

But this time, according to the lengthy complaint filed against him, when Polanski took the girl to Nicholson's home, he gave her a glass of champagne and a tranquillizer, called Quaalude. When her defences were down, he allegedly raped her. Afterwards, he reportedly also coerced her into performing other kinky sex acts with him. Two hours later, the teenager went home to her mother's house, but only confided what had happened to a boyfriend. Her sister overheard the traumatic phone conversation, and told her mother. After questioning her child, the woman immediately called in the police.

STAR SUSPECTS

Armed with a search warrant, a group of officers went to Nicholson's home the following day to gather evidence. During the raid, they also arrested movie actress Anjelica Huston, daughter of famed filmmaker John Huston and Nicholson's girlfriend, on charges of possessing cocaine. She was subsequently released on bail.

Following their investigation, the police realised that Nicholson, who had starred in Polanski's detective story *Chinatown*, had not been involved in the alleged rape,

drug related offences made headlines around the world.

Polanski, who faced up to 50 years in prison, was led away by police who had arrested him at the posh Beverly Wilshire Hotel after the girl's distraught mother filed a complaint against him. In it, the woman accused the director of picking her daughter up at her home the previous afternoon for a photographic session at Nicholson's home in Bel Air.

Police claimed that the girl wanted to pose for some pictures for the French edition of *Vogue* magazine, for which Polanski was on assignment, and that she had another person arrange for the director to take the photographs. A spokesman for the Los Angeles Police Department said the teenager's mother had given permission for the girl to go ahead with the pictorial shoot, but on the understanding that she would pose fully clothed. A month earlier,

Above: *Polanski found himself facing deportation and jail in the US after he was charged with the rape of a minor.*

The following month, Polanski's attorney caused a sensation when he said that he was going to ask for an inquiry into the 13-year-old's previous sexual activity. Lawyer Douglas Dalton, who was appearing before the Santa Monica Superior Court, also hinted strongly that he would ask that the alleged victim undergo a psychiatric examination. 'The facts that we're aware of,' he said, 'show that before the events of this case, this girl engaged in sexual activities. We want to know when, where and with whom and why those people were not prosecuted.'

The judge handling the case, Laurence Rittenband, agreed with the defence request that the grand jury transcript on the case be sealed to prevent even more lurid publicity. As he walked from the court, Polanski was asked by the huge throng of reporters how he expected the case to affect his life. The director, who eight years earlier had discovered that his wife and unborn child had been slaughtered by the Manson clan, replied: 'I'm used to grief. This is a trifle.' He also repeated his claim that he was totally innocent of all the charges.

But there were too many discrepancies between Polanski's version of the events and that of the alleged victim. Later, he began changing his story to say that the girl was sexually experienced and willing – 'she wasn't unresponsive' was how he would later put it.

A SORRY CONFESSION

But Polanski's bravado soon left him. On 8 August – just one day before the trial was due to start and the eighth anniversary of Sharon Tate's murder – he appeared in court, looking nervous and red-eyed, and readily pleaded guilty to 'unlawful sexual intercourse' with the teenager – the least of six rape and drugs charges that had been filed against him. However, Polanski still faced a possible prison term of between 16 months and three years.

The plea was entered as a result of plea bargaining with the district attorney's office, which agreed to drop five other more serious counts in the indictment in return for the admission of guilt. Judge Rittenband withheld sentencing pending a probationary report on the director, who was also ordered to undergo psychiatric examination to determine whether or not he

because he was out of town at the time. Afterwards, they found Polanski in his hotel room, and immediately bundled him into custody on charges of 'forcible rape, oral copulation, sodomy, perversion and feeding narcotics to a juvenile'.

Within hours, the news of his arrest had spread around the movie capital, and soon after it was being reported in newspapers across the world. Police held him for several hours for questioning, then a court released him on about £1800 bail.

Above: *Actor Jack Nicholson on the set of* **Chinatown** *with director Polanski. It was at Nicholson's Bel-Air mansion that Polanski had sex with an under-age girl.*

should be committed to a hospital as a 'mentally disordered sex offender'.

Judge Rittenband said that the psychiatric report would help to determine whether Polanski needed treatment or whether he should be committed to a state hospital or mental health facility. He set a hearing date for 19 September.

AVOIDING EMBARRASSMENT

District attorney John Van de Kamp said the plea bargaining arrangement was reached largely at the urging of the girl's family, so that she might be spared the ordeal of having to appear on the witness stand at a sensational trial. The family's attorney, Lawrence Silver, read a letter to Rittenband asking that the state accept Polanski's plea: 'The reliving of the sorry events, with their delicate content, through the vehicle of direct and cross examination in this courtroom packed with strangers, would be a challenge to the emotional well-being of any person. The potential for harm

is even greater to one of tender years.' He also said the family was 'not seeking the incarceration' of the film-maker, only that he admit his guilt and take part in a rehabilitation programme.

Van de Kamp agreed with the family's reasoning to spare the child further trauma, saying 'We chose to provide the victim with the opportunity to grow up in a world where she will not be known as the young girl with whom Roman Polanski had sexual intercourse.'

Polanski, who has all along insisted he was totally innocent of the charges, was ordered by the court to announce what crime he was admitting: 'I had intercourse with a female person not my wife who was under the age of 18,' he said. When the district attorney pressed him as to whether he knew at the time of the incident that the girl was just 13 years old, Polanski solemnly replied: 'I did'.

Despite his plea bargain, however, Polanski still faced the possibility of deportation on the grounds he was an undesirable

ASKED WHETHER HE KNEW THE GIRL HE HAD SEX WITH WAS JUST 13 YEARS OLD, POLANSKI SOLEMNLY REPLIED: 'I DID'.

alien because of 'moral turpitude'. Under United States immigration law, aliens convicted of a crime involving moral turpitude and sentenced to more than one year in prison are to be deported immediately after the term is completed.

After the hearing, Polanski was taken to the Chino State Prison, where he spent more than 40 days undergoing a battery of psychiatric tests. His probation officer recommended that he serve no further time beyond that already spent doing the tests. But Polanski was obviously taking no chances. On 1 February, 1978, the day he was to be sentenced, he fled the country for Britain. Judge Rittenband immediately issued a warrant for his arrest. According to officials for British Airways, Polanski arrived at the Los Angeles airport without a reservation, but managed to get a seat on the only flight leaving for London. They said he waited patiently at the stand-by desk, and was given the very last seat.

Opposite Top: Polanski has always wooed beautiful young women. Here he is with 19-year-old actress Nastassja Kinski at a press conference for the film Tess.

Opposite Bottom: Another of his young conquests, Emmanuelle Seigner.

Below: After fleeing the United States, Polanski went into self-imposed exile in France.

In the crowded courtroom Polanski's attorney, Douglas Dalton, said that he did not know the whereabouts of his client, saying: 'Your Honour, I received a call from Mr. Polanski advising me that he would not be here this morning.'

'Well, where is he?' the judge demanded.

'I do not believe he is in the United States,' the attorney replied.

A spokesman for the district attorney's office said later that he did not think Polanski would stay too long in Britain, as was later proved correct: 'I suspect he is in

PSYCHIATRISTS AGREED THAT POLANSKI WAS MENTALLY STABLE AND HAD SHOWN REMORSE FOR HIS CRIME

a country where a plea of unlawful sexual intercourse would not be an extraditable offence. It could be France.'

Authorities were right – Polanski had fled to Paris, where he maintained an apartment. In the 15 years since his flight from justice, he has never returned to the United States. The year after he became a fugitive, a copy of the probation report was leaked to the media. Included in it were copies of letters of praise from such Hollywood heavyweights as Mia Farrow (who worked with Polanski on *Rosemary's Baby*) and Dino Di Laurentiis.

According to the report, all the psychiatrists agreed that the director was mentally stable and that he had indeed shown remorse for his crime. And while many people believed he should not go to prison, Judge Rittenband was intimating that he would have to serve more time than originally planned. Perhaps Polanski was upset by the probation officer's report, that set a condition of Polanski's avoiding jail 'that he not associate with children under the age of 18, except in the presence of responsible adults'.

A short while later, Polanski was heavily involved with beautiful actress Nastassja Kinski. The director flaunted the relationship – he admitted he liked 'young girls' – openly accompanying the young starlet to fashionable parties and movie premieres. It was as if he was thumbing his nose at his American accusers. Their relationship, culminated in the film *Tess*, in 1979, when Kinski was just 19 years old. It was the last film Polanski was to make for the next seven years until the big money epic *Pirates*, which flopped badly at the box office.

THEATRICAL INTERVAL

'I was working happily in the theatre,' he told an interviewer about his film hiatus. 'There you also have the same hustle, but not nearly as much.'

But when he made *Pirates*, the furore over the Los Angeles incident was dredged up yet again. Critics savaged him for the film, but some believe that it was more a blast at his sensational lifestyle than anything to do with *Pirates*. And it was often pointed out that by the time *Pirates* came out in 1986, he had already been dating 20-year-old French actress Emmanuelle Seigner for two years.

During his long respite from film-making, Polanski also decided to write his autobiography, *Roman*, in an effort to tell his side of the story. In it, he remained adamant that the 13-year-old Los Angeles girl had been a willing partner. However, he also admitted that 'overnight I'd crossed the line between decent folk and scum... now, because of a moment's unthinking lust, I had jeopardised my freedom'.

NO REMORSE

But although the psychiatrists thought he had shown remorse for his crime while being evaluated at Chino, Polanski admitted that he had lied and did not feel any guilt over the incident. 'That's what they kept asking me at the time in prison,' he confided to an interviewer. 'I knew that I had to answer "yes", but I didn't really. Let me explain. I feel I've done something wrong if I harm someone or cause grief. I didn't feel I'd caused grief here. Or any

harm, mental or physical. I don't think there was a victim in the incident.'

Still, Polanski knows that he cannot, even now, return to the United States. If he did, he would face possible arrest and imprisonment. 'I don't want to live in the U.S., I'm too European,' he says. 'But I know I have to clear this thing up sooner or later. I must do it for my peace of mind. I will go back to clear it up. I don't miss America. How could I miss a place where I had so many misfortunes? But I would go just to clear up this mess, and then come back to Europe. Maybe by now they may see it in a calmer way.'

The only way he will ever know for certain, is for him to one day return to America. But the risks are great, and may yet prove too much of a gamble even for the wild-living film icon.

JAMES DEAN
A Giant with Feet of Clay

For years after his early death, James Dean was widely regarded as one of the coolest of 1950s stars. Then a series of sordid secrets about his life began to be revealed, secrets that would smear his reputation forever.

Almost 40 years ago, Californian police officers were called to the site of a horrible car accident on a lonely interstate highway. When they arrived on the scene, they dragged the dead body of a young male from the mangled wreck of a silver Porsche Spyder. It was Friday night, 30 September, 1955. The day James Dean died.

To his millions of loyal fans, who had followed his brilliant, though short-lived movie career, which spanned just 18 months and three movies, it was as devastating as the murder of John Lennon would be to a later generation of young people. To them, the teenagers growing up in the stilted post-war years of the 1950s, the 24-year-old Dean was the rebel without a cause. With his leather jacket, dagger sideburns and a squint that spelled mischief, the farmboy-turned-actor was the leading voice of a generation who were in revolt against their parents, the clean-cut image of life in America, and a movie industry that thrived on inane comedies and happy endings. But his rebellious life came to a sudden, tragic end when his car collided into another, killing him instantly.

For almost two decades afterwards, the Hollywood studio system continued to maintain the image of the long-dead Dean as a tough, no-nonsense rebel. He became a cottage industry of sorts, spawning a host of books, television specials, t-shirts and mentions in dozens of pop songs. He was adored and regaled as an anti-hero. To hear the Hollywood press agents tell it, Dean was an all-American boy from the nation's heartland of Indiana, where he excelled as both a basketball player and a debater. After finishing school, he hitched a ride to New York City, where, after several months of near-starvation, he finally landed steady work in the burgeoning television medium and on

Above and Left: *Handsome even as a boy, James Dean grew up on Winslow Farm, Indiana.*

Opposite: *James Dean's moody features made him an icon to a generation of teenagers who grew up in the 1950s. Unknown to his countless fans, he had many homosexual encounters.*

Above: *As a teenager, Dean was a good student, with a knack for debating and basketball.*

Opposite Top: *A scene from* **East of Eden.** *Dean was nominated for a Best Supporting Actor Oscar after a fine performance.*

Opposite Bottom: *The young speed-loving star on one of his motorcycles.*

DEAN WAS MENTALLY UNSTABLE, GREEDY AND LUSTED AFTER FORBIDDEN SEX, WITH BOTH MALE AND FEMALE PARTNERS

the stage. Following a screen test, he was whisked away to Tinsel Town, where he quickly became the hottest young male actor in the world. In just 18 months of film-making, Dean had starred in three huge hits – *Rebel Without a Cause*, *East of Eden*, and *Giant*, – garnering two Oscar nominations in the process.

HIDDEN VICES

But in the late 1970s, when friends and lovers began to come forward to tell their stories about the Dean they knew, another image of the farmboy-turned-movie-idol emerged: James Dean was not only mentally unstable and greedy in his drive towards superstardom, but he lusted after forbidden sex, with both male and female partners. It was a shocking revelation to his millions of fans, but like so many other things in Tinsel Town, even Jimmy Dean was not at all as he seemed.

Indeed, Dean allegedly lost his virginity to a man when, at the tender age of just 16, he had homosexual relations with a Baptist

Minister! According to Joe Hyams, a close friend and author of the sensational book, *James Dean: Little Boy Lost*, which came out in late December 1992, the sinful relationship scarred the actor for life.

Dean was in his last year of high school in Fairmont, Indiana, when the affair began with the Rev. James DeWeerd, who confided the story to Hyams the year after Dean was killed in the auto crash. According to Hyams, the impressionable young student was mesmerised by DeWeerd, a decorated war veteran who had travelled the world and seemed so sophisticated in comparison to other people in the small town. Indeed, the minister's advice to the 16-year-old lad was that the more you experience, the better off you will be. It was a dictum the young Dean took to heart. 'In light of what was to come,' Hyams adds, 'that philosophy had ominous overtones.'

MINISTER OF SIN

The minister, who was called 'Dr Weird' by some local teenagers, loved to take young boys to a local gym and suggest that they all swim naked together. He was attracted to James from the start, and it was apparently a mutual liking.

According to *Little Boy Lost*, the unlikely companions spent many hours together on long drives through the countryside in Rev. DeWeerd's car. It was during those happy jaunts that Dean would often pour out his soul to the minister, especially the grief and guilt he felt over the death of his beloved mother, Mildred, who died of cancer when Jimmy was just nine years old. The young Dean, of course, had nothing to feel guilty about, but Rev. DeWeerd took advantage of the inexperienced, troubled youngster. As he later confessed to the author, 'I taught Jim that he was depraved and vile, that he had to seek salvation.'

That 'salvation' took the form of a lusty homosexual relationship with the minister. Once, while out driving, the minister pulled his car off the main road and drove up a lane, where he parked it by some trees. He then began regaling James about his war stories, and how he had been seriously wounded in the stomach. He asked the youngster if he would like to touch it. Later, they would eventually have a sexual relationship, which lasted many years.

As Hyams revealed, the affair was to have far-reaching consequences for Dean. 'I can only imagine,' said Hyams, 'the mixed messages that he must have received when he was seduced by a religious person, a man above moral reproach. The pattern that was to distinguish many of Jimmy's later relationships was being formulated. He was able to have sex with a man or a woman, and with ease. But he was enough of a Quaker to believe that what he was doing was wrong. As a result, he would never let anyone get truly close to him.'

After his mother's death, young Jimmy was sent to live with relatives, because his father, now working in California, could not take enough time off work to care for him properly. From a young age, he was a consummate actor, though he often angered his teachers with his many pranks. However, the dream of being an actor stayed with him.

He moved to Los Angeles, where he got bit parts in commercial and theatre work, but friends remember he was often broke. Eventually he met up with Rogers Brackett, an advertising executive and homosexual, who offered him a room at his own house. Dean, realising he could no longer afford his own apartment, leaped at the chance, and soon the two of them became passionate lovers. Brackett, who was more than 15 years older than Jimmy, was a good friend of agent Henry Willson, another homosexual whose gay clients included Rock Hudson, who many years later would die of AIDS. The parties at Willson's house were a well-kept secret among the Hollywood homosexual community. Brackett and Dean went everywhere together, even to Mexico for bullfights.

THE WILD YOUTH

When Dean arrived in New York City to pursue his dream of becoming the next big superstar, the man who did get closest to him was photography teacher Roy Schatt. It was late in 1951. Although Schatt said that he never knew that Dean was bisexual, he did think of him as a crazy, cocky young man. In fact, when Dean first came to his studio to learn about photography, Schatt didn't like him at all. 'He was a young punk,' he recalled many years later in an interview. 'He was slovenly, bent over and

squinting when actress Arlene Sax introduced him to me. He only spoke in two-syllable answers. But slowly I became sort of a father figure to him and we became close friends.'

Schatt remembers that Dean was always surrounded by young women, which fuelled his growing egotism. 'In fact, he seriously would ask me if he didn't resemble Michelangelo's David,' he said. 'I would say, "Sure you do, Jim." I admit he did have a certain resemblance.'

ROAD HOG

Besides his boastfulness, Dean was always doing crazy things, maybe for attention, maybe to bolster his own ego. Once, Schatt recalled that he, Dean and actor Martin Landau were all sitting in the photographer's kitchen eating dinner when Dean suddenly excused himself from the table. A few minutes later, they heard a lot of noise coming from outside his house. 'I raised my Venetian blind and found Dean sitting in my huge winged-back chair in the middle of the street, smoking a cigarette and holding up traffic.'

Unknown to his later fans, Dean also wore false teeth in the front of his mouth, and would love to scare people by taking them out and screwing up his face. 'He made himself as ugly as possible,' said Schatt. 'He certainly was a nut, but an

Above: *Marlon Brando, another screen idol of the 1950s. Dean always considered him to be a major rival.*

Right: *Pier Angeli, believed by many to be the only woman Dean really loved.*

'I FOUND DEAN SITTING IN MY HUGE WING-BACKED CHAIR IN THE MIDDLE OF THE STREET... HOLDING UP TRAFFIC'

interesting show-off... I always thought that what he needed was a good kick in the pants to straighten him out.'

The photographer also recalls that Dean's penchant for high-speed driving also came to the fore in his early days in New York. The aspiring star would often take his girlfriends out driving on his motorcycle, with the women always sitting on the front handle bars. 'Even when it was pouring rain, he would race around the streets of New York with a devil-may-care attitude,' he said. 'He often bragged that he had a motorcycle before (Marlon) Brando did. He was aware that Brando was his chief rival playing Hollywood's "anti-establishment" roles.'

While in New York, however, Jimmy continued to have both male and female lovers, and when Brackett moved to New York, he again offered Jimmy a roof over his head and his bed. Dean, knowing that the older man had some good show business contacts, readily agreed, although he kept the homosexual relationship secret from his close friends and other struggling young actors with whom he worked.

There were other male lovers, including another aspiring actor, Jonathan Gilmore. One night, before they had ever had sex together, Gilmore remembered Dean recalling his past homosexual affairs and the passes made at him by Hollywood chief-

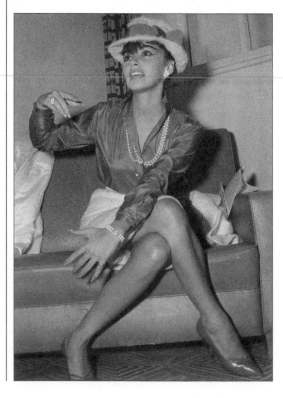

tains: 'You know, I've had my **** **** by some of the biggest names in Hollywood and I think it's pretty funny because I wanted more than anything to just get some little part,' Jimmy told him.

Gilmore later told author Hyams that Jimmy 'felt that if someone needed emotional support from a man he would probably be homosexual, but if he needed emotional support from a woman he would be more heterosexual.' Aspiring actress Arlene Sachs, who was just 17 when Dean began a torrid affair with her, remembered being at his apartment one night when a very prominent actor called him to talk about his sex life, then added that he really only wanted to bed Jimmy.

Once Dean moved to Hollywood, early in 1954, his lifestyle grew even more bizarre. Friends would recall that he disappeared for long periods, became extremely angry for no apparent reason, played with loaded guns, and of course satisfied his penchant for reckless driving.

They also remember that he became more and more involved in kinky sex: exhibitionism, leather, sadomasochism. He also dallied with everyone from starlets to petrol station workers.

MR PRIMA DONNA

He was also extremely difficult to work with. Once, he angered co-stars and producers when he walked off the stage of a Broadway hit, and further upset those around him by being continually late to work and with his hell-raising ways. He even once pulled a knife out on a worker at a theatre, because he was having one of his temper tantrums. He also refused to let the Hollywood studio system turn him into a clean-living pretty boy, which only endeared him more to his young fans.

Once, when the very powerful show business columnist Hedda Hopper met him for an interview, he was so wild that she wrote of the encounter: 'The latest genius sauntered in, dressed like a bum, and slouched down in silence at a table away from mine. He hooked another chair with his toe, dragged it close enough to put his feet up, while he watched me from the corner of his eye. Then he stood up to inspect the framed photographs of Warner stars that covered the wall by his head. He chose

one of them, spat in its eye, wiped off his spittle with a handkerchief, then, like a ravenous hyena, started to gulp down the food that had been served him.'

But despite his enigmatic ways and his penchant for kinky sex, Dean did find his one true love during the making of his first film, *East of Eden*. The young actress was Pier Angeli, who was then appearing in *The Silver Chalice*, with newcomer Paul Newman. Dean and Pier had met through Newman, and soon the two young lovers were making regular visits to each other on their respective sets.

Dean fell hard for her, and soon even began to scale back his hell-raising ways. He began to dress better, and tried his best to rope in his often lurid mouth. Eventually, it was obvious to friends that they wanted to get married, but Pier's mother, an Italian from 'the old world', didn't think much of her daughter's choice.

The young lovers were forced to meet at secret rendezvous, but eventually Jimmy decided he would become a Catholic, which he knew Pier's mother wanted him to be. But before long, Pier fell pregnant, and Jimmy demanded that she elope with

Above: *On the set of* **Rebel Without a Cause,** *with good friend Natalie Wood. The film was released shortly after Dean's tragic car crash.*

HE BECAME MORE AND MORE INVOLVED IN KINKY SEX: EXHIBITIONISM, LEATHER, SADOMASOCHISM

Above: *The movie* **Giant** *starred three of the biggest names in Hollywood: Elizabeth Taylor, Rock Hudson and Dean. But Hudson and Dean were reputed to dislike each other.*

DEAN BEDDED EVERY WOMAN HE FANCIED, INCLUDING BARBARA HUTTON, OWNER OF THE WOOLWORTH FORTUNE

---

him. She refused, and a few days later announced she was engaged to Vic Damone – whom she had met several years earlier. Dean was devastated, and sobbed often when he thought of his lost love. One night, before the marriage, Dean ran into Damone at a restaurant, and snarled: 'You might be marrying Pier, but she isn't yours, never was and never will be.'

Damone exploded, and threw a punch at Dean. But before any serious damage could be done to either star, waiters rushed over and broke up the brawl. When the wedding day finally arrived, Dean was seen sitting outside the church, on his motorcycle, wearing his familiar jeans and jacket. As the newlyweds walked from the church, he revved up the bike and sped off down the street. A friend later found him at home, rocking back and forward on the floor, weeping uncontrollably.

His aberrant behaviour grew worse. He took up with a female singer called Tony Lee, who had lost a leg to cancer. One night, the odd couple invited a friend over to Jimmy's apartment. When the friend arrived, Tony was putting make-up on Dean! Later, the friend and Tony had sex, while Jimmy looked on. Dean was also becoming more and more obsessed with his own looks, and was turning into a snob. Once, at a party, he was introduced to a struggling young actor named Jack Nicholson. Dean didn't even bother to note his existence, forcing embarrassed friends to apologise to the young Nicholson.

BRIEF ENCOUNTERS

He was also bedding every woman he fancied, including famed heiress, Barbara Hutton, who owned the Woolworth fortune. They met at a nightclub, and although she was more than 20 years his senior, they hit it off straight away. Later that night, they went back to her hotel room, and made love. Hutton later recalled in her notebook: 'It seemed the right and natural thing to do, although I couldn't help but wonder about his sexuality. He talked so fervently about men and adventure and masculinity.'

During the making of Jimmy's next film, *Rebel Without A Cause*, which was to become his most famous, he took to motor car racing, much to the consternation of his studio bosses and some of the other competitors, who labelled him a menace to himself and other drivers. At the same time, he began a close friendship with young Sal Mineo, his co-star and a known homosexual. Director Nick Ray believed Dean fell in love with the effeminate Mineo: 'He knew it and I knew it,' he later told an interviewer. 'I didn't stop it because it was helping the film.' However, before his own tragic death many years later, Mineo always denied that he and Dean had ever been lovers.

Not so Dean and Natalie Wood, the third young talent in *Rebel Without A Cause*. The two of them had a torrid affair during the filming, including one rendezvous in the back of his small sports car. Ironically, on his last film, *Giant*, he remained aloof from his many of his co-stars, including Rock Hudson, who he never liked. Not so Elizabeth Taylor, who became like a mother to him, even though she was not much older than he was.

A few weeks before filming ended, Jimmy bought himself a new car – a Porsche Spyder, and he couldn't wait for *Giant* to wrap up so that he would be able to take it for a long drive.

On 30 June, he and his mechanic friend Rold Weutherich were driving along Highway 99 just outside Los Angeles doing more than 70 miles an hour, when Dean was pulled over and ticketed by a Californian Highway Patrolman. After the officer left, Dean and his friend continued their drive north, sometimes at breakneck speeds hovering around 130mph. At around 5.30 that afternoon, Dean approached the intersection of Highways 466 and 41, just outside Bakersfield. It was a dangerous intersection, and there had been several fatal smashes there in the past.

AN UNHAPPY ENDING

An eyewitness later told police that Dean's car was doing around 110mph, when another driver, about to cross onto the intersection, appeared from the distance. By the time he saw Dean's car, it was too late. The two vehicles smashed into each other with a sickening thud. Miraculously, the driver of the other car was bruised, but otherwise unhurt. Weutherich had been thrown clear of the Porsche by the impact, and suffered several broken bones. Ironically, he would die more than 25 years later in another crash in his native Germany.

Tragically, Dean had been trapped behind the wheel. He was almost decapitated and was declared dead on arrival at a nearby hospital. The Rebel was dead, and Hollywood and the youth of America mourned not only for what had been lost to them, but for the promise that Dean had showed on the screen. Like so many other young stars of ensuing decades – Janis Joplin, Jimi Hendrix, Marilyn Monroe, John Lennon – his talent was snuffed out before it had reached full bloom.

ELIZABETH TAYLOR BECAME LIKE A MOTHER TO HIM, EVEN THOUGH SHE WAS NOT MUCH OLDER THAN HE WAS

DEAN WAS ALMOST DECAPITATED AND WAS DECLARED DEAD ON ARRIVAL AT A NEARBY HOSPITAL

Below: *Californian police look over the wreckage of Dean's mangled Porsche Spyder. The actor was said to be doing more than 100mph when he lost control of the car. He was killed instantly.*

FRANK SINATRA
Doing It His Way

Frank Sinatra made his name singing laid-back ballads and songs for swinging lovers. But this most temperamental of stars was far from relaxed when he wasn't performing, and much of his swinging was done with his fists.

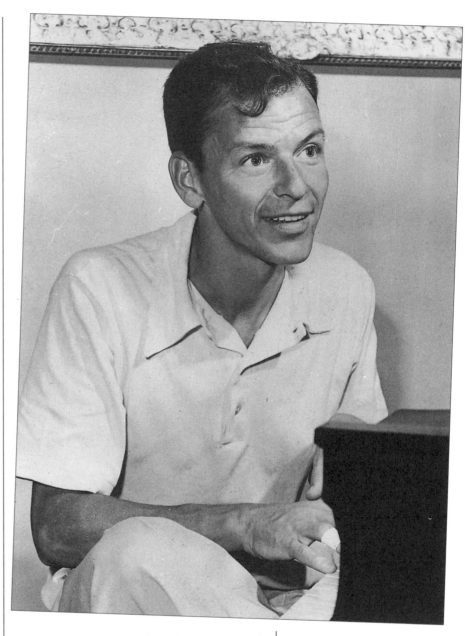

For more than 50 years, Francis Albert Sinatra has thrilled and entertained generations of fans around the world. In the 1940s, he wowed the bobby-soxers, he set new standards for cool in the 1950s and 1960s, and he later eased into his role as the elder statesman of music, all the while maintaining a hectic touring schedule that would make rock stars 50 years his junior quiver with exhaustion.

Sinatra, who outlasted every other pop icon from Elvis Presley to the Beatles, is probably the most recognisable singer of the century, a man who does do it his way, regardless of the consequences.

But with Sinatra, the music can, and often has, taken a back seat to the controversies which seem to swirl around him endlessly like a maelstrom. Along the way, he has fought and mingled with the famous, mouthed off about anything that stuck in his craw, engaged in a lengthy feud with the press and even taken to task some of today's biggest stars.

There have also been the four marriages – including one to 19-year-old Mia Farrow when he was in his fifties, the many affairs, days and nights of hard drinking, and his alleged ties to organised crime, which he continues to deny to this very day.

But 'Cranky Frankie' as he is sometimes called by his many critics, also has his warmer side. He has been a tireless worker for charity over the years – he has helped raise more than £300,000,000 for various causes – and he is said to be extremely generous with friends and acquaintances alike.

Still, it is the other side that most people see, or want to see – a cantankerous side which continues to be as blunt as it ever was. Just a few years ago, for instance, he wrote an open, scathing letter to British rock star George Michael, berating him for whining about the drawbacks of success.

Later, he then told a cheering audience that he would have liked to have kicked controversial Irish singer Sinead O'Connor 'in the butt' when she refused to allow concert organisers to play the American national anthem before one of her shows in the United States.

Today, of course, Sinatra is the grand master of the entertainment world, but it was not always the case. In fact, he struggled long and hard to get where he is today – a struggle to succeed that began dramati-

Above: *During his early career, Sinatra was the idol of 'bobby soxers', girls who swooned with his every note.*

Opposite: *For more than 50 years, Sinatra has been one of the world's best-known entertainers.*

SINATRA'S CONTROVERSIES
SWIRL AROUND HIM
LIKE A MAELSTROM

Above: *By the early 1940s, Frank was one of the top singing stars in the US.*

Opposite: *There have long been rumours of a connection between the Mafia and Sinatra. The story even found its way into the Francis Ford Coppola film* **The Godfather.**

AS HIS SUCCESS GREW, SO DID HIS EGO. HE BECAME INCREASINGLY SMUG, AND WAS SEEN WITH A STRING OF WOMEN

---

cally on 12 December 1915, in his parents' small home in Hoboken, New Jersey. Baby Frank weighed a massive 13.5 pounds, and his mother, Natalie, had an agonising delivery. In fact, the baby was so huge that the delivery doctor didn't think that the child was going to live.

Working in primitive conditions with primitive instruments, the doctor eventually managed to deliver the child, but not before accidentally lacerating part of the baby's head and right ear, leaving scars which are still visible even today. The doctor and many of the local women gathered in the room for the birth thought that the baby was stillborn, but Natalie's mother grabbed the tot and stuck it under the cold water tap. Suddenly, it began to cough, then it started to breathe.

Frank had just won his first and most important fight.

Surprisingly, given his huge birth weight, the young Sinatra turned out to be a pint-sized teenager. In fact, Frank was so thin during his early years that when he started to make it big one comedian cracked that he was 'the advance man for a famine'. But what he lacked in size he more than made up for with ambition and drive. Even when he was a young child, he dreamed of being an entertainer and, blessed with a gifted voice, he began singing professionally at local clubs in Hoboken when he was just 15 years old.

He also entered and won several local talent shows, and would slip across the Hudson River to New York City whenever he could to hear the big bands which dominated the era. He loved sitting in clubs absorbing the sounds, and he once belted a fellow customer who was talking too loud for him to hear. In his early twenties he married Nancy Barbato, and soon after he got his first big break when he landed a singing role with the Harry James orchestra. He was an instant hit – particularly with the hordes of young females who swooned and screamed at his every sigh and move, much like their children did a generation later when Elvis burst onto the scene.

After just six months, Sinatra had already become too big for the James orchestra, and in 1940 he teamed up with Tommy Dorsey, then one of the biggest names in American music. Yet despite his following among the younger crowd, Frank still hadn't made much of a dent with adults. Indeed, some of his reviews during those days were not exactly dynamite. *Billboard* magazine called him a good singer 'but nil on showmanship'.

AIMING FOR FAME

But the eager young crooner never gave up hope and simply practised harder, eventually developing that trademark timing and phrasing which was soon to propel him to superstardom. Within two years his hard work paid off, when he had a series of top hits and even replaced the legendary Bing Crosby as the favourite singer among America's college students. He and Dorsey's orchestra went on several tours, and friends at the time remembered that as his success grew, so did his ego. He was becoming increasingly smug, and was often seen with other women.

By the end of 1942, Frank was becoming too big for even Dorsey, and the young heartthrob wanted out of his contract to concentrate on a solo career. Dorsey refused at first, but finally relented when Frank agreed to a buy-out contract that would give the band leader and his manager a combined 43.3 per cent of Sinatra's future earnings! Later, it was rumoured that Frank called in some well-connected friends in the underworld to convince Dorsey to let him out of the contract. According to the story, a mobster put a gun in Dorsey's mouth and asked him to let Frank go. Dorsey readily agreed. The incident has become part of show business folklore, and was even included in Francis Ford Coppola's *The Godfather*. However, it was never known for sure if anything like that did happen, and many associates at the time believed it never did.

TOP DOG

After leaving Dorsey's band, Sinatra began a meteoric rise up the show business ladder to become America's number one singer, adored by fans of all ages. The following year, he even went to Hollywood, where he made his first film, and began being seen in the company of many stunning young women, including stunning blonde starlet Lana Turner. Meanwhile, back home in Hoboken, wife Nancy had just given birth to their second child.

Out in Hollywood, Sinatra revelled. He loved the idea of being a movie star, and his already-healthy ego got another massive boost. He became more and more demanding, and he often argued with directors over how scenes should be shot. He became so adamant that scenes should be shot only once that he was nicknamed 'One-Take Charlie'. As his power grew, so did his hold over women.

They loved him unabashedly, and, during a meeting with Franklin D. Roosevelt, even the president asked him how he made women swoon! Frank was impressed with the President, and became a committed supporter of the Democratic party. Some years later, when Republican Thomas Dewey, the New York governor, was scheduled to arrive at a New York hotel for a photo opportunity, Sinatra made sure he arrived at exactly the same time as the hapless politician. As Frank had known, the crowd quickly lost all interest in the governor!

As Frank continued to conquer Hollywood – in hits like *Anchors Aweigh* – he became increasingly convinced that he could do no wrong and he verbally sparred

with everyone from columnists to studio executives. Some movie chiefs were less than happy about his public dalliances with busty Marilyn Maxwell. They wanted Frank to retain his 'wholesome' family image. But by the mid-1940s, that was all it was – an image. Nancy had finally had enough of Frank's philandering, even though she was living in luxury given his $40,000 a week salary. They split up for a month, tried a reconciliation, but eventually they came to realise that they were no longer right for each other.

A PUNCHY STORY

As his personal life took a battering, so too did his reputation grow for being difficult on the set. He was also making some powerful enemies in the press, and he developed long and bitter feuds with the most famous columnists of the day, including Hedda Hopper, Louella Parsons and Lee Mortimer – whom he once punched at a club in Los Angeles. Mortimer suspected that Sinatra had connections with organised crime, and wrote that he had been a bag man for Mafia boss Lucky Luciano. He claimed that Sinatra had flown to Cuba with $2,000,000 in cash to give to the mobster.

Others in the media soon picked up on the alleged connections between the singer and the mob. Although it is uncertain exactly what Sinatra's connections with the Mafia have been over the years, many biographers claim he has been fascinated by them ever since his boyhood. The Mortimer incident, which occurred on 8 August 1957, came as the columnist was leaving the club. He claims that Frank hit him from behind, and that three of the singer's friends then attacked him while he was lying helpless on the floor.

Frank was arrested by police and was freed on £300 bail. There was a furore in Hollywood and New York, as columnists peppered him relentlessly for his arrogance and nastiness. As the trial approached, Frank backed down and decided to settle out of court, reportedly paying Mortimer £18,000 in damages and legal fees.

The controversies continued to swirl around Frank, and by the end of the 1940s he had hit rock bottom career-wise: he also owed thousands of pounds in back taxes to the Internal Revenue Service, and his

Above: *Sinatra and Ava Gardner in the early 1950s. Their constant bickering and fighting eventually soured their marriage.*

IN HOLLYWOOD AND NEW YORK, COLUMNISTS PEPPERED SINATRA RELENTLESSLY BECAUSE OF HIS ARROGANCE

FRANK THREATENED TO KILL HIMSELF OVER THE BEAUTIFUL AVA GARDNER, WITH WHOM HE ARGUED LONG AND OFTEN

movies were failing to make much of an impact at the box office. In one memorable review of one of his pictures, *Miracle of the Bells*, *Time* magazine wrote 'Sinatra plays the priest with the grace and animation of a wooden Indian'.

Even his records were no longer hits, and Frank complained that he couldn't find any good songs to record. Rivals like Frankie Laine and Johnnie Ray were taking over, and he was soon dumped by Columbia Records. To top it all off, he was also getting into more disputes with reporters, threatening to hit them if they continued to print 'lies' about him. It got so bad that one powerful industry man claimed that Frank was finished, and that within 12 months he would be forgotten.

A STORMY AFFAIR

It was during his plunge to the bottom that Frank met Ava Gardner, with whom he had a stormy, four-year relationship during which time he divorced Nancy. At one stage, Frank even threatened to kill himself over Ava, with whom he argued long and often. But because of their tumultuous relationship, there was renewed interest in Frank, and he began getting some well-paid stints on television and in clubs. But his bizarre relationship with Ava began to take its toll on him mentally. There was a rumour that he had tried to take an overdose

to punch photographers as they tried to get pictures of the ceremony. One indignant columnist wrote: 'If it is privacy that Frank Sinatra wants he should be kept out of the public eye permanently. Perhaps the day will come when he would like to be remembered.' Despite Frank and Ava's undeniable love for each other, however, the marriage was short lived, lasting less than two years.

Frank was in a tailspin, professionally and personally, but he persevered and, in 1953, he got his second break, when he eventually convinced producers he was perfect for the part of the tortured soldier, Maggio, in *From Here to Eternity*.

'I had to do it,' he recently told an interviewer. 'I had a personal problem with Ava (Gardner). The marriage was beginning to drift away. I think that had a lot to do with me having to be good. When I got caught up in it, I guess something came out of me that made it even more interesting to see than I even thought it would be.' He was right, even picking up the Oscar for best supporting actor, and signing a new contract with Capitol Records. When the announcement came that he and Ava were divorcing,

of sleeping pills, and reports that he was firing loaded guns. Later, famed columnist Walter Winchell reported that Frank had tried to kill himself by slashing his wrists.

Eventually, in November 1951, he and Ava were wed. Typically, Frank threatened

Above: *Frank Sinatra with Montgomery Clift in* From Here to Eternity.

Below: *With Sammy Davis Jnr (left) and Dean Martin.*

Above: *In December 1963, Sinatra's son Frank Jnr (right) was kidnapped and held for ransom.*

FRANK'S INFATUATION WITH PRESIDENT KENNEDY EVENTUALLY TURNED TO HATRED AFTER AN IMAGINED SLIGHT

DURING THE 1960S, FRANK'S ALLEGED TIES TO THE MAFIA CONTINUED TO GIVE HIM A GOOD DEAL OF TROUBLE

she sneered: 'Now that he's successful again, he's become his old arrogant self.'

Frank was again the toast of Hollywood, and he was cast in starring roles in movies like *Pal Joey*, *Guys and Dolls* and *The Pride and the Passion*. He went from strength to strength, but still controversies continued to rage about him. There were the high-living, hard-drinking Rat Pack days with Judy Garland, Joe Bishop, Dean Martin and Sammy Davis Jnr. During the rest of the 1950s, the Rat Pack were frequent visitors to Las Vegas, home of legalised gambling in America. Artists like Sinatra were paid huge money to entertain the gamblers, but Frank also owned a share in one of them, the Hotel Sands.

DIVERSE INTERESTS

During the early 1960s, Sinatra was the king of entertainment in the United States. He was incredibly successful, and owned interests in everything from movies to music publishing companies to real estate to radio stations. It was at this time that Frank became heavily interested in politics, and joined the growing band of influential Americans clamouring to back the young, handsome John F. Kennedy, who looked more like a fellow movie star than a politician.

But Frank's relationship with Kennedy resembled his romantic flings with so many women: infatuation that eventually turned

to hatred. The Kennedy clan needed the help of people like Sinatra to get themselves elected – because they could provide glamour and big money contributions. But Frank's alleged ties to some shady characters in the casinos of Nevada soon soured the relationship. Frank was furious. After all, he had worked long and hard to get John Kennedy the Presidency – urging many of his Hollywood friends to campaign for him – and now the family was distancing itself from him.

Much of Sinatra's resentment was focused on Bobby Kennedy, the new Attorney General who made organised crime his number one target. Bobby wanted to get the Mafia out of Las Vegas once and for all, but Frank kept denying the existence of the mob. (Ironically, it was Sinatra who introduced Judith Campbell Exner to John Kennedy. During their affair, she was also sleeping with notorious crime lord, Sam Giancana. Later, it was also alleged that Frank had put actress Phyllis McGurie into one of his movies because she was Giancana's girlfriend.)

BITTER DISAPPOINTMENT

The Kennedy-Sinatra relationship finally came to a bitter end in March 1962, when it was announced that Frank was going to have the President as a house guest in his Palm Springs mansion. Sinatra was bowled over by the honour, and began re-modelling his house to accommodate the President and his Secret Service escort. However, soon after the announcement was made, the White House issued a statement saying the President would not be staying with Sinatra – but with rival star Bing Crosby. Sinatra was beside himself with anger and refused to meet Kennedy at Crosby's house. Yet despite his anger, Frank was said to be genuinely distressed when the president was assassinated in Dallas the following year. It was Bobby Kennedy he really hated.

During the rest of the 1960s, Frank's alleged ties to the Mafia continued to give him trouble. While it has never been proven that he had any dealings with them, it's no secret that he knew many Mafia bosses. During those turbulent times, the Nevada Gaming Control Board, which oversees gambling in the state, revealed that Giancana had been staying at a casino in which Frank owned an interest, despite a state order that banned Giancana from entering the grounds.

Giancana, who would be murdered in the 1970s, reportedly owned a piece of the casino through Sinatra, but that was never proven. The board ordered that Frank should appear to answer questions, but he refused – initially. After a couple of weeks, he meekly backed down, and refused to contest the board's attempt to revoke his gambling licence.

His problems continued. Frank Jnr, or Frankie, had followed his famous father into show business. Unfortunately, he didn't have the old man's talent. But he had something – access to his father's fortune. In December 1963, Frankie was kidnapped at gun point! Sinatra was shocked, and issued a statement saying he would 'give the world for my son'. Frank sat by his phone for hours on end, waiting for the sensational story to play itself out.

Finally, a few tense days later, he received a phone call demanding £150,000 in ransom, which he had to personally deliver to the drop site – near some parked school buses at an abandoned petrol station in Los Angeles. Sinatra was told that the kidnappers would 'release the kid about four hours after you drop the money'. Frank did exactly as he was told – but after the deadline passed, there was still no sign of his son. Some time later, a policeman saw a young man by the side of the road. It was Frankie. A few days later, the FBI arrested the kidnappers.

CRUEL SUGGESTIONS

But soon there were reports that the whole episode had been some sort of publicity hoax, and by the time the trial started, people were openly questioning whether or not Frankie had engineered the whole thing. There was not a shred of evidence to ever support such claims, however.

A few years later, Sinatra was again making headlines – this time when he married actress Mia Farrow, who, at 19, was 32 years his junior. Again there was trouble with photographers at the wedding, and Sinatra allegedly took a swing at one of them. Like his previous marriages, this one, too, was destined to fail. They separated within a year.

Not long afterwards, he again ran into trouble when he got involved in a brawl at the Las Vegas Sands casino. He had already

AT HIS WEDDING TO MIA FARROW, FRANK ALLEGEDLY TOOK A SWING AT ONE OF THE PHOTOGRAPHERS

Below: *John F. Kennedy and Sinatra were close friends... until the president snubbed him in favour of a stay at the home of Bing Crosby.*

lost $200,000 on the tables, and he demanded some credit to continue gambling. Casino boss Carl Cohen refused, and Frank exploded. He moved towards Cohen in a threatening manner, but the wily businessman struck first, whacking Sinatra in the mouth, and dislodging the caps from some teeth. A few years later, Sinatra was again involved in an altercation with another casino executive.

A DEFIANT DEFENCE

Despite his personal problems, however, Sinatra continued to wow them in movies and on records, and even though he briefly retired, he never really lost his love of entertaining. Still, the persistent rumours of Mafia connections continued to haunt him. In 1972 he was ordered to testify before a congressional committee looking into organised crime. After some delays, Frank agreed, and when he appeared he immediately began attacking the politicians and saying they were calling into question his good name by listening to another witness who swore that Frank was connected to the mob.

Frank wrote a piece for the *New York Times* a few days later, saying: 'In my case a convicted murderer was allowed to throw my name around with abandon, while the TV cameras rolled. His vicious little fantasy was sent into millions of American homes, including my own. Sure, I was given a chance to refute it, but as we have all come to know, the accusation often remains longer in the public mind.'

He was right. When President Nixon was up for re-election, a columnist from the *Washington Post* asked him: 'Mr Sinatra, do you think that your alleged association with the Mafia will prove to be the same embarrassment to (his friend) Vice-President Agnew as it was to the Kennedy Administration?' Frank virtually ignored the question, but a few minutes later, when the columnist, Maxine Cheshire, started speaking with Barbara Marx (later to be Frank's fourth wife), he

exploded: 'Get away from me, you scum! Go home and take a bath! You're nothing but a two-dollar broad.'

There was a huge controversy, and Cheshire demanded an apology, which, of course, Frank never gave. But Cheshire wasn't the only reporter to get a taste of Frank's harsh tongue. Rona Barrett, a TV commentator, was one such victim. At a concert in New York, Frank told his audience: 'Congress should give a medal to her husband for waking up every Sunday morning and looking at her.'

And in 1974 he created an international storm when he went to Australia, and a skirmish broke out between his entourage and some reporters. Sinatra responded by publicly branding the media 'bums, parasites, hookers and pimps'. Australians reacted as one, echoing the words of a senior politician who demanded: 'Who the hell does this man Sinatra think he is?' Labour unions then joined in the fray, refusing to service the singer's private jet unless he publicly apologised.

PROBLEMS WITH THE MEDIA

Sinatra was aghast, and demanded that unless he received an apology from the journalists' union he would leave the country. Eventually, a compromise was reached, and Sinatra issued a statement saying he did not intend 'any general reflection on the moral character' of the media. However, it went on to say that he reserved the right to comment on the quality of the professional performance of the media. But while the tour went on, Sinatra continued to challenge the media, again referring to them as parasites and bums. Still, the crowds who attended his shows forgave him quickly, and the tour wound up being the biggest grosser ever in Australian history.

In the years since, Sinatra has mellowed somewhat, probably due to his age and his happy marriage to Barbara. Even today, Sinatra is still the king of entertainment in America. There can be no denying the voice has lost some of its reach, or that the famous ol' blue eyes have dimmed just a little. And yes, sometimes he even forgets the lyrics to songs he's been crooning for half a century. But Frank Sinatra, the Chairman of the Board, is still wowing them from Los Angeles to London.

Opposite Top: *July 1966, and Sinatra marries 19-year-old Mia Farrow.*

Opposite Bottom: *The Sands casino in Las Vegas, where Sinatra got into a public brawl.*

Above: *Ol' Blue Eyes today… older, greyer, more mellow, but still the master showman.*

ROLLING STONES
Outlaws of Rock

The Rolling Stones have been creating exciting music for over 30 years, and their lives have matched the drama of their songs. But the inventors of the sex, drugs and rock'n'roll lifestyle have often paid dearly for their excesses.

The Rolling Stones have withstood the test of time as no other musical group has ever done before. They have seen a succession of fads come and go, watched fellow superstars such as The Who and the Beatles rise and fall, and they have been witness to some of the most chaotic times of the 20th century.

Yet the current Rolling Stones – Mick Jagger, Keith Richards, Charlie Watts and Ronnie Wood – have withstood much more than just the ravages of time and the whimsical nature of the modern entertainment business. Collectively, and separately, they have also withstood the madcap, often dangerous, world of rock music, drug problems, sexual peccadillos, divorce, scandal, violence and even murder.

The five original Stones, who included the late Brian Jones, succeeded after his death by Mick Taylor, then by Ronnie Wood, came together in January, 1963, at a club in Soho, where they quickly gained a reputation among London's nightclub fraternity as a hip, swinging new band with their distinct rhythm'n'blues sound.

Their debut came exactly one month before the Beatles had their first Number 1 hit – with 'Please, Please Me' – but the Stones were far removed from their more genial rivals from the north. The Stones were, in essence, a band that exuded primal sexuality and anger. Jagger, who was then just 20 years old, was already gaining a name for himself as a sex symbol, and women went crazy whenever the band per-

> THE STONES WERE, IN ESSENCE, A BAND THAT EXUDED A PRIMAL SEXUALITY MIXED WITH ANGER

Opposite: *The 1967 line-up of the world's greatest rock'n'roll band. Clockwise from left: Brian Jones, Keith Richards, Charlie Watts, Mick Jagger and Bill Wyman.*

Below: *The Stones with Czechoslovakia's President Vaclav Havel in 1990.*

Above: In the 1970s, David Bowie was rumoured to be a bed-partner of Mick Jagger.

Right: A young Mick Jagger with girlfriend Marianne Faithful, who eventually succumbed to the pressures of the rock lifestyle.

another man, and Andersen also claimed Mick had had affairs with Eric Clapton and David Bowie, among others. He said that in the early 1970s, Angie Bowie caught her husband and Jagger naked in bed together, and served them breakfast in bed! Angie later recalled that she was certain the two had had sex, even though she had not actually caught them in the act. Andersen said that Mick was similarly caught in bed with Clapton. He quoted Marianne Faithfull's ex-husband, John Dunbar, as saying: 'Eric and Mick were caught in bed together, it's true.'

MUSICAL DIFFERENCES

By the summer of 1963, the Stones had been signed to a recording deal with Decca Records, and their first single, a cover version of Chuck Berry's 'Come On', made it to number 18 on the national pop charts. It wasn't exactly a huge success, but the Stones could only grow, because of their undeniable raw sex appeal and superb, energetic music. But already there were signs of dissension within the band over the direction it should take. Jagger and Richards won out – they would become the very essence of the group – and Brian Jones, who had had more experience, was virtually relegated to a back-up role.

In April, 1964, the Stones released their first album, which rocketed to Number 1 on the charts, making them the biggest act

formed. His girlfriend at the time was Chrissy Shrimpton, the sister of famed model, Jean, and their relationship was quite typical of the many that would follow for Jagger. They fought and they bickered almost constantly, but their passion for each other was undeniable.

Even then, however, there was talk about Mick's consuming lust for women, as well as men. In his controversial bestseller, *Jagger: Unauthorised*, writer Christopher Andersen claimed that a startled John Lennon once caught Jagger and Richards in bed together. According to numerous reports, it would not be the last time Jagger was linked to homosexual sex.

In fact Shrimpton herself later recalled that she found Mick asleep in bed with

in Britain with the exception of the Beatles. At the same time, Jagger met the woman who was to have a profound influence on his life and career – Marianne Faithfull, who was just 17 when they met at a party. Jagger did little to impress her that first night, intentionally spilling a drink over her and then wiping her breasts! But gradually the two became lovers, and Jagger collaborated with Richards in writing 'As Time Goes By' for her.

The incredible primal hold he and the other Stones held over their audiences was soon being played out across Europe and the U.S., and thousands of frenzied teens flocked to their concerts, where violence often broke out. Indeed, in Paris later that year, riot police had to be called into the streets to deal with a throng of bottle-throwing youths, who had been whipped into a frenzy by their musical heroes. The Stones' raunchy sex appeal was a carefully calculated marketing strategy, and Jagger issued a decree to the rest of the band forbidding them to marry! But Charlie Watts secretly married his girlfriend, Shirley, and Jones, whose growing drug problem was becoming a concern, fathered at least four children out of wedlock.

DRUGS AND DISORDER

But Jones wasn't the only member experimenting with drugs. When the band arrived in the U.S. on a second tour late in 1964, Jagger and Richards were both exposed to them, and they would be drug abusers for many years to come. Their wild excesses of booze and sex were already becoming legendary as well, as was their reputation as the bad boys of rock, which included the infamous 1965 incident, in which Jagger, Richards and Wyman urinated in public outside a petrol station. They were subsequently dragged into court for urinating in public, and were fined a few pounds each.

While Jones' slide into the drug world continued at breakneck speed, the band returned to the United States later that year, when 'Satisfaction', one of their biggest hits ever, was released. The Rolling Stones had conquered the musical world, which only fuelled their reputation for dangerous living, wild parties and no-holds-barred orgies. During the tour, Jones, who was heavily into the psychedelic drug, LSD,

caused a major stir when he ran screaming through a Los Angeles hotel lobby, convinced that he was being chased by a swarm of snakes.

But even the rich and famous wanted to meet the Rolling Stones. They were feted by Hollywood stars, authors and fellow pop singers. Back in England, Mick even became friendly with the married Princess Margaret, and the gossip columnists had a field day about the exact nature of their unlikely relationship.

Jones, too, was having his own share of problems, thanks to drugs and his increasing awareness that he was being left behind

Above: *Brian Jones and girlfriend Anita Pallenberg were tragic victims of the drug culture.*

JONES RAN SCREAMING THROUGH A HOTEL LOBBY, CONVINCED THAT HE WAS BEING CHASED BY A SWARM OF SNAKES

Above: *The 'Glimmer Twins', Jagger and Richards, leave Chichester Magistrates Court in May 1967 on drug charges.*

DRESSED UP IN AN SS UNIFORM, JONES WAS STANDING ON THE THROAT OF A MODEL SUPPOSED TO BE A JEW

By late 1966, Jagger and Shrimpton finally parted ways. Surprisingly, it had lasted longer than anyone had thought it would, given their riotous brawls and heated arguments. On 18 December she took an overdose of sleeping pills, but survived, and a week later Jagger removed all her belongings from the apartment they had lived in. With his relationship with Shrimpton now over, he became entwined with Faithfull, who had already bedded fellow Stones Jones and Richards, as well as famed black guitarist Jimi Hendrix. It would prove to be one of the wildest love stories ever in the annals of rock'n'roll.

Early the following year, Jagger and Richards again fell foul of the law when a glittering party at Keith's country estate was raided by the police. Dozens of officers stormed the house, confiscated drugs and found Marianne Faithfull naked inside a fur rug. Strangely, however, not a word appeared in the national press for a week. It was alleged that a drug dealer who supplied Richard could get corrupt police officials to forget the entire matter for some £8000, which was paid. But then the story did break, in the *News of the World*, although no names were mentioned.

in the public clamour over the sexier, more outgoing Jagger. But Jones was a notorious womaniser like his more outrageous comrade, and he began dating Anita Pallenberg, a beautiful model of mixed European descent, who would later dump him for Keith. Tragically, her relationship with Jones – he often beat her – would lead her on a spiral to drug hell.

Jones' behaviour was becoming increasingly more erratic, and Pallenberg persuaded him to pose for a photograph in which he dressed up in an SS uniform, standing on the throat of a model supposed to be a Jew. The picture caused controversy around the world and Jagger – who earlier had sent a concert hall full of German youths into a frenzy by goose-stepping his way through a tune – was shocked. He decided that Jones might have to go.

But the following month, it was announced that Jagger and Richard would have to stand trial on drug charges. They appeared in court, on 10 May, and were released on bail. But hardly had they arrived at their respective homes when the news came that Jones, too, had just been busted for drug possession in another police raid.

Two months later, a stunned, tearful Jagger was found guilty, handcuffed and taken away to Lewes prison. The judge refused to impose a sentence until Richards' trial was over. A few days later, he, too, was found guilty. The judge shocked the courtroom by sentencing Richards to 12 months behind bars, and Jagger to three months. Both rock stars were overcome by the severity of the sentence. Richards was sent to Wormwood Scrubs, but Jagger went to Brixton, where worried friends reported that he was on the verge of a total breakdown. But neither was to spend much time behind bars. Following an outcry that justice had not been done, the lord chief justice of England overturned Keith Richards' conviction and set aside Mick Jagger's prison term.

Overjoyed, the Stones returned to the studio, and came out with *Their Satanic Majesties Request*, which played up to their reputation as bad boys and purveyors of evil. Indeed, Jagger was beginning to read a lot of books on the occult, and befriended a former U.S. child star, Kenneth Anger, who was heavily involved in such matters. Anita Pallenberg was likewise a devotee.

CRAZY DAYS

As the album came out, however, Jones was in court facing his own drug charges, which had stemmed from the raid the previous May. He was given a six-month sentence. However, he, too, spent little time in prison. In fact, after just one night there, he was released on probation. To celebrate, he threw himself a drug-induced orgy, and within two days, he was in hospital after another drug-and-booze overdose. In the ensuing months, Jones became increasingly paranoid about his future with the Stones, and his heavy drug use was affecting his performances. To make matters worse, his then girlfriend, Linda Keith, tried to kill herself.

In May 1968, Jones was busted for drug possession yet again. He was by now, a virtual madman, often passing out in public and railing that everyone was out to get him. He even tried to drown himself in the moat at Richards' estate. But he received only a fine for the drug conviction, and the rest of the band thought that they could now turn to more pressing matters of recording and touring.

But a few months later, Jagger had his own tragedy when Faithfull miscarried their child. Before long, he began to see less and less of his long-time lover, who descended further and further into a drug haze. Still, it was Jones who continued to worry everyone connected with the Stones. His drug problems were critical, and his days as a member of the band were numbered. However, no-one was prepared for the shock of 2 July 1969.

That night, Jones and his new girlfriend, Anna Wohlin, were having a party at his home with friends and a work crew he had hired to do some renovations. Jones, needless to say, had taken several pills and a lot

of liquor. He decided to go swimming, and began making moves on some of the female guests of the burly work men. The workers allegedly became angry, and reportedly started shoving Jones's head under the water.

A short time later, Wohlin returned to the pool, and found Jones lying on the bottom. She and some other friends tried, in vain, to resuscitate him. When the police came, no-one told them about the party or the work-men, and Jones's death was ruled acciden-

Above: *The swimming pool at Brian Jones' estate in Sussex, where he drowned in July 1969.*

Below: *Despite Jones' death, Jagger and Richards continued to drive the Stones to new heights in the 1970s.*

JAGGER CAUGHT A
GLIMPSE OF WHAT HE
THOUGHT WAS A MAN IN
THE CROWD POINTING A
GUN AT HIM

Below: *Mick's bachelor
days came temporarily to an
end when he married
Nicaraguan beauty Bianca
Perez De Macias in 1971.*

tal. To this day, it remains a mystery as to what actually happened.

A few days later, his replacement, Mick Taylor, joined the Stones at a concert in Hyde Park, and within a week Jagger was in Australia to film *Ned Kelly*. The day Jagger and Faithfull arrived, Faithfull, exhausted but unable to sleep, took an overdose of sleeping tablets. Fortunately, Jagger managed to get help in time to save her, though it was touch-and-go for a few days because she was also undergoing heroin withdrawal.

After filming was completed, the Stones flew to America, where they put on a free show at Altamont, in California. That night, 6 December 1969, was to become a watershed for the rock'n'roll world. The innocence of the 1960s would come to a jarring, murderous halt. The Stones had hired the Hell's Angels to act as bodyguards and to help with crowd control in return for mountains of cold beer.

More than 350,000 screaming fans turned up that night, and there were outbreaks of violence as the opening acts took the stage. The Angels on duty that night were a vicious, rowdy bunch, and they attacked several patrons with lead pipes. Others were pummelled to the ground then kicked and stomped. Incredibly, Marty Balin, the lead singer of Jefferson Airplane, at one point leapt from the stage to help rescue a young man being beaten senselessly. The Angels attacked him, knocking him out, and there were urgent appeals over the public address system for calm.

By the time the Stones came on, the crowd was in a frenzy, and several tried to rush the stage, only to be savagely beaten back by the bikers. The Stones bravely tried to continue performing but, suddenly, Jagger caught a glimpse of what he thought was a man in the crowd pointing a gun at him. In reality, however, the young man, Meredith Hunter, had been attacked by an Angel, and pulled a gun at the last moment to protect himself from further violence. But before he could do anything, another biker came from behind and stabbed him in the back. The wounded man fled, only to be caught and repeatedly slashed and beaten. By the time the Stones realised what had happened, Hunter was dead. Jagger, understandably distraught, muttered that he might quit the music business.

BUSINESS AS USUAL

Of course, he did not, and he and the rest of the band soon returned to their hell-raising ways. Early in the 1970s, when the Stones moved to France because of the huge income taxes in England, Mick became involved with Bianca Rose Moreno Perez de Macias, a gorgeous Nicaraguan, who he eventually married in a circus-like atmosphere in May 1971, in Saint Tropez. At the big party afterwards, Richards passed out on the floor, and there were the usual orgies and wild carousing. It got so out of control that the local police had to be called in to

restore calm. It was a riotous start to what would be a riotous marriage.

Meanwhile, Keith and the pregnant Anita Pallenberg were busy with their own bizarre lifestyle, which they continued in their huge mansion in the south of France. Before long, locals were complaining long and loud about the weird goings on inside the estate, including drug-taking and alleged satanic rites and debauched orgies. Keith didn't seem to mind, though he was having problems with Anita, whose bizarre behaviour worried even the Rolling Stones.

WOMAN TROUBLE

Like Keith, Mick, too, was having problems with the women in his life. Bianca, who had given birth to their child, Jade, learned that he had been having affairs behind her back. When he returned to his home in France, Bianca was waiting for him with a gun. Fortunately for Mick, she didn't fire, but she did order him out of the house. They eventually reconciled, but, in mid-summer 1972, Jagger refused to let Bianca accompany the Stones on their American tour, which was again marked by violence, mass arrests and wild parties.

Jagger, who eventually relented in banning Bianca, became so worried about his own safety during the tour that he feared that he might be assassinated. But even though he had Bianca in tow, Mick couldn't stop his philandering, bedding women whenever he felt like it.

Bianca, meanwhile, was also having extra-marital romps, including one with Ryan O'Neal, the handsome American actor. Their marriage was doomed, and even though they didn't divorce until several years later, for all intents and purposes, the union was over by 1974.

In December, that same year, Mick Taylor announced he had had enough, and was quitting the band. In came Ronnie Wood, an ex-member of Rod Stewart's Faces, who readily fitted in with the bad boys of rock. As Ronnie recalled years later in an interview, he left behind the booze of the Faces for the drugs of the Rolling Stones. Indeed, the next year, when they went on a world tour, the ravages of drug abuse were beginning to take their toll, especially on Richards, who was heavily into heroin, as was Wood.

> LOCALS COMPLAINED ABOUT ACTIVITIES INSIDE THE RICHARDS ESTATE, ALLEGING DRUG-TAKING, SATANISM AND ORGIES

> KEITH WAS CHARGED WITH POSSESSION OF HEROIN WITH INTENT TO TRAFFIC — A CHARGE THAT CARRIED A LIFE SENTENCE

Below: *The middle-aged Mick settled down when he met Texan model Jerry Hall, mother of his three children.*

By 1976, Keith's life was a shambles, and completely overtaken by heroin. Then, in March, Anita gave birth to his second son, Tara, but the little tot died tragically just three months later when he choked to death. The tragedy sent Richards over the edge, his life a haze of hard liquor and heroin. The following year, when the Stones arrived in Canada to kick off another tour, Anita was stopped by customs agents and was arrested for drug possession. Police then raided Keith's hotel room in Toronto, and found so much heroin that he was charged with possession with intent to traffic – a very serious charge that carried a life sentence.

A HIGH-CLASS GROUPIE

Incredibly, however, Keith was released on bail, and soon found that Margaret Trudeau, the impetuous young wife of then Canadian Prime Minister Pierre Trudeau, had become a member of the band's growing entourage. Soon, she was allegedly having affairs with both Mick and Ron. It was at about this time that a willowy Texas beauty, model Jerry Hall, came sashaying into Mick's life. Hall, of course, is now married to Jagger, and is the mother of three of his children.

Although he himself had used drugs, Mick had stayed away from heroin, and he wanted Keith to clean up – or else. Richards, whose Canadian problems had yet to be worked out, stayed in rural New York with the rest of the band where they tried to rid him of his demons.

NEW BLOOD

It worked for a while, and it was even said that he had his blood changed in a bizarre bid to cleanse himself of the drug. Eventually, he did clean up his act, and never went to prison. Instead, part of his sentence was to play a benefit concert in Canada, which he and the rest of the band did. That year, 1979, also saw the divorce of Mick and Bianca, who eventually got more than £1,500,000 in the settlement, and custody of Jade.

Just as the headlines died down, however, Keith was back in the news, when a 17-year-old boy shot and killed himself in Anita Pallenberg's upstate New York home. He used her gun to do it. Although Keith was by now living with model Patti Hansen (with whom he would later find marital peace), it was just another controversy swirling around the Stones. Local newspapers also claimed that Anita was involved in a witches' coven, and the unsavoury past of the Rolling Stones was again dredged up by the media. However, Pallenberg was eventually fined less than £600 for having an unlicensed gun, and all the other charges related to the death of the boy were dropped.

Mick continued to shock the world while on tour, telling a British journalist that he wouldn't mind if his daughter, Jade, had an affair when she was 13 years old! 'Just as long as she didn't turn into a tramp and was having it with anyone on the street,' he said. 'It wouldn't upset me at all if she had sex at an early age. When I was thirteen, all I wanted to do was have sex.'

Meanwhile, Keith was granted a visa into the United States pending his trial, so he could get treatment for his acute drug addiction. Unfortunately, the treatment didn't work, and he was soon back on heroin. By 1978, Jagger had finally had enough.

*Above: **Keith Richards and future wife Patti Hansen tear up the town in the late 1970s.***

*Opposite Top: **Bill Wyman raised eyebrows when he married 18-year-old Mandy Smith, 36 years his junior.***

*Opposite Bottom: **Ronnie Wood, Mick Jagger and Keith Richards at the centre of another electric Stones performance.***

MATURE YEARS

When the 1980s dawned, the Stones, older and somewhat wiser, mellowed a little, though Jagger was still linked to numerous women, despite his long relationship with Jerry Hall. Their albums and tours continued to be huge successes, despite a growing friction between Mick and Keith over Jagger's wanting to issue a solo album and differences in how the Stones should continue to evolve. Moreover, Keith had never been a fan of Hall's, and did little to hide his antagonism towards her. (Ironically, as Keith became more and more of a family man, he grew to like, then champion, Jerry in her numerous public battles with Jagger.)

hers, and it was later proved so in court. 'They wanted to set me up,' she later claimed, 'because I am an American, female, famous and rich.'

Jerry and Jagger were to share many other headlines in the years following. There were the fights, the reconciliations, the births of their children, and, eventually, their marriage. But Mick, true to form, continued dallying, and caused a major ruckus when he was seen cavorting with gorgeous model, Carla Bruni.

A SCHOOLGIRL CRUSH

Bill Wyman, the band's bassist, who quit in January 1993, likewise was dragged into the public eye when he married Mandy Smith. At 18, she was 34 years his junior. Wyman had known Mandy since she was just 13 years old, and even paid for her schooling. The Fleet Street press had a field day over the relationship and the wedding, but, inevitably, it lasted only a very short time.

Even without Wyman, however, the Rolling Stones just keep on going. Battered and bruised by 30 years of drugs, scandals, women and death, they still manage to outdraw every other act in the business. To paraphrase one of their early hits, time is on their side.

The other members of the band were also getting tired of Jagger's continued antics, and Ron Wood made a point of not inviting him to his wedding in 1984.

Although they remained a group, there was no denying that the tension was getting to be too much. Each of the band seemed to spend more and more time away with their families, and Jagger continued with his solo career. In 1987, while he was in Barbados recording his second solo album, Jerry was arrested by customs officials when she opened a box with the name G. HALL on it. It contained more than £25,000 worth of marijuana. She was taken away and held, but later released on about £3000 bail. The box, of course, was not

LIZ AND LARRY
The Odd Couple

When one of the cinema's most glamorous women fell head over heels for a building-site worker, it set tongues wagging all over the world. But Liz Taylor and Larry Fortensky soon proved that their love was built on strong foundations.

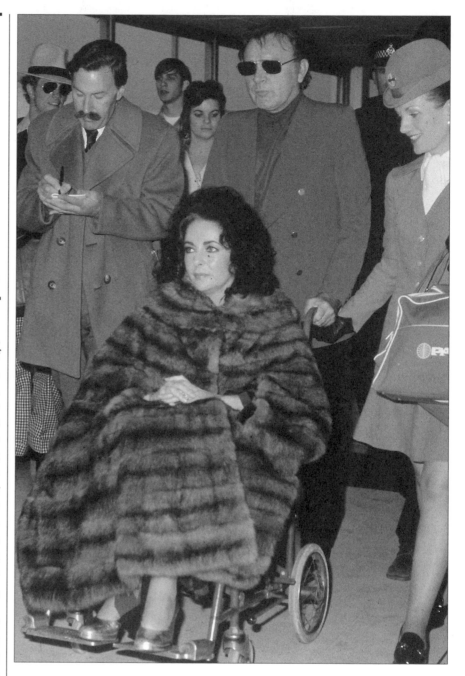

She was the queen of Hollywood, Cleopatra of the Nile, the goddess of beauty embodied in living form. Famous now for just being famous, Elizabeth Taylor still holds that magnificent essence of stardom that captivated the world, won her six husbands and an enduring place in the hearts of millions. He, on the other hand, was an alcoholic construction site worker, a sometime truck driver and all-round bad guy who got his pay cheque on a Friday night and spent it within hours on booze and shooting pool. The nearest he had ever been to Hollywood was reading the name on a postcard. Larry Fortensky was a loser – a handsome loser, perhaps – but a loser all the same.

Now he and Elizabeth Taylor are in their second year of wedded bliss, having been together for almost four years. It is the most unlikely love match in a town where sincerity is often as genuine as a studio backdrop, but Liz and Larry have defied the critics who said that their relationship would not endure. If anything, it has gone from strength to strength – possibly because they were both brought down to one level, the gutter, by booze. Although their social orbits were as far apart as the sun is from the moon, booze was the great leveller which brought them to the place where they could begin to rebuild their lives.

For Larry Fortensky, his £2,500 stay in the famed Betty Ford Drug and Alcohol Clinic was paid for by his truckers' union; a last, desperate attempt to sober him up permanently. Elizabeth Taylor had been a

visitor there before, weaning herself off booze or percodan – a highly addictive painkiller prescribed for the chronic back pain she had suffered from since childhood after falling from a horse during the filming of *National Velvet* – or a combination of both. The Betty Ford clinic operated on something called The Hazleden Method, founded at the Hazleden Clinic in Minnesota. Essentially, it was a group therapy course aimed at instilling self-worth in all patients while at the same time they admit to others in the group their terrible problems with alcohol. It is no place for fainthearts; Liz Taylor, manicured mistress of homes in Beverly Hills, Acapulco and

Above: *Screen legend Liz Taylor with the great love of her life Richard Burton, whom she wed twice.*

Opposite: *Liz Taylor and Larry Fortensky stunned the world when they announced they were getting married.*

Switzerland took out the garbage, cleaned the floors and then sat in a circle as clinic staff insulted her weakness of character. Everyone has to bare their souls, strip away the layers of disguise, of the facade that is put on for the world, until the real, unpleasant truth of what they do and why they do it is exposed. Once that point of deep truth is reached – the patients often call it being 'broken' – then the rebuilding process can begin. The idea is that a month or six weeks after entrance, the patients leave with a new self-esteem that will make them never want to touch drugs again.

Elizabeth Taylor was 57 when she moved back into the Betty Ford clinic in 1989, Larry Fortensky 20 years her junior. Here there was no star status afforded Elizabeth; in the eyes of staff and fellow patients she was just another user with just another problem. Many stars have gone to the clinic for help – Lisa Minnelli, William Hurt, Sharon Gless of TV's 'Cagney and Lacey' fame – and all have testified how they are brought to a humbling reality by the programme. It was in one of the group therapy 'encounter' sessions in April of that year when Larry Fortensky stood in front of Elizabeth Taylor and said the words that would begin his fight back to normality: 'I am an alcoholic.'

TOUGH YOUTH

Larry revealed how, as a boy growing up in the blue-collar town of Stanton, California, he had been on the road to alcoholism since he was a teenager. He told how he bought six packs of beer on the way to school and smoked marijuana. After he left school with no qualifications he began working on building sites and doing other menial labouring jobs. His money came on a Friday and it was usually gone by Saturday; squandered in all-night benders at the local pool hall and paying off fines after getting into trouble with the law over drinking and driving.

In the shark-pit atmosphere of the encounter group Larry told how his marriage to his second sweetheart, Karin Fleming, fell apart after seven years because of his chronic booze problem. In her divorce petition she had revealed: 'He is more interested in his motorcycle and going to bars than he was ever interested in

me. His greatest pleasures are shooting pool and getting drunk.'

Larry revealed all this to Elizabeth Taylor and the other poor wretches in front of him – and more. He told of the bar-room fights when pool cues were snapped across his head and shoulders; he told of the nights in the police cells when he went to sleep with his own vomit drying on him; of how the drink led him to become violent, even towards his own wife. On one occasion, as revealed in her divorce petition, 'he became extremely abusive and placed his hands around my throat, choking me'. He never earned more than £130 a week in his life and this, the Betty Ford centre, was the last stop at the end of the line.

HONEST LARRY

Elizabeth Taylor, married to rich, handsome men like Richard Burton, Mike Todd and Nicky Hilton, had complained in the past of how Hollywood had often made suitors dishonest. Here she was, a woman with a fortune estimated at over £50,000,000, hearing the most honest words spoken by a man in such a short space of time, that she had ever heard. The electricity fairly crackled between them and friends of Liz say that in that brief space of time, the woman who seemed a million miles away from Larry Fortensky's world found herself falling in love.

Californian writer James Statler said: 'In the spartan world of the clinic, away from the pressures of Hollywood and unclouded by the fog of booze that had swirled around their lives for decades, a friendship between them was allowed to grow and blossom into love. Here he was not Larry the loser who beat his wife and blew his pay packet on booze. She was not Cleopatra, the Queen of the Nile who romanced and wed some of the most eligible men in the world.

They were simply Elizabeth and Larry, two souls who had been brought low by booze and who were now getting it together again. Years of martinis and margueritas on the cocktail circuit had done it for Liz; years of beers and tequila slammers had destroyed Larry Fortensky, who was one step away from the gutter and living on social security handouts, when the Teamsters' Union paid for his entrance to

Betty Ford. It was a classic case of the Lady and the Tramp, coming together to save their lives. Instead it became the most magical of fairy tales which the world joined in to watch and marvel at.'

The first the world knew about the romance was when a fuzzy picture was published in an American tabloid magazine – known as the eternal curse of the stars – of Elizabeth being wheeled in the grounds of the Betty Ford clinic by an unknown man with a long mane of blonde hair. Insiders at the clinic – perhaps staff, perhaps patients who had left – had provided

Opposite Top: *Blue-collar Fortensky was a simple construction worker until he met Liz.*

Opposite Bottom: *Liz and Burton were the most celebrated film couple in the world.*

Below: *Burton and Liz jet off from Heathrow. Their stormy relationship caused them both a lot of pain.*

Below: *Liz with a previous husband, Mike Todd. Despite his predecessors' wealth, working class Fortensky appears to have made Liz happy.*

just enough information to whet the appetite of a curious world about this man and just what his relationship with Elizabeth Taylor really was.

Soon the news magazines, paparazzi and dozens of newspaper writers were scrambling to find out if the woman who seemed hopelessly in love with love all her life had really fallen again for someone – this time in the unlikely setting of the world's most famous booze clinic! An unknown patient who spoke with Elizabeth on the inside told one of the tabloid magazines in America just what the star found attractive in Larry Fortensky.

She said: 'Elizabeth knows he is light years away from her own world, but that doesn't matter. She says he is all man, solid, masculine, handsome. He had those hard-living qualities of Mike Todd and Richard Burton, ex-husbands who never

knew when to put the brakes on. But obviously Larry did or he wouldn't have been in the clinic with her. Here he was, putting his life in order and she admired it tremendously. She discovered in him a commitment and an honesty that her numerous other rich and famous husbands and lovers had sadly lacked.'

Two months after leaving the Betty Ford clinic, Larry moved into Elizabeth's fabulous Bel Air home, a £5,000,000 mansion decorated in exquisite taste with some of the most marvellous artworks ever produced adorning the walls – masterpieces by Monet, van Gogh, Manet and Goya. In the garage were her Rolls Royces, a Lamborghini, an Aston Martin and three Mercedes. In the wardrobes hung a couturier collection of clothes estimated to be worth over £1,000,000 – clothes with the designer labels of Christian Dior, Yves St. Laurent, Chanel, Gucci and numerous other houses of high fashion. Larry arrived in this cornucopia of wealth and style clutching a couple of shirts and a couple of paperback books. Cleopatra set about building up her new Anthony from the ground up – giving him a wardrobe and a look that would make him a walking symbol of L.A. style.

TOTAL TRANSFORMATION

Elizabeth denies any surgery or dental procedures to transform Larry from Mr. Nobody into Mr. Fabulous, but before and after pictures do suggest a *My Fair Lady* style miracle! Out went the bargain basement clothes and lanky moustache. In came enough designer suits to fill one of his old lorries, a dazzling smile and a personal hairstylist in the form of Jose Eber, Beverly Hills crimper to the stars, who has on occasions also managed La Liz's mane. Elizabeth also bought him accessories for life in this new world that must have made him feel like he had won the California lotto. He received a £12,500 Pontiac Sunbird car and was given a duplicate set of keys to her fabulous Aston Martin Lagonda, the car she cares about more than all the others.

There was talk of speech lessons so Larry would cut out the 'effing and blinding' which had punctuated his discourse on the building sites for longer than he could

remember. There is a story of how Larry was gradually eased into the glittering world of Hollywood society with a dinner one night at the home of singer-songwriter Carole Bayer-Sager, one of Elizabeth's closest friends. He allegedly used the wrong cutlery at the wrong time, shovelled in the delicately prepared nouvelle cuisine as if he was eating a pizza – and then had a hearty belch at the table! As well as etiquette courses, Elizabeth also provided two trainers from a gym on Sunset Boulevard to equip him with an exercise programme that would keep his building-site-trim body in excellent shape. What emerged was a dashing Prince Charming who looked like he had never carried a hod in his life.

SWISS BLISS

But would it last? This was the question the whole world kept asking as the most unlikely of relationships endured and endured. Perhaps the answer came when Larry flew with Elizabeth to Switzerland at the end of the year for a holiday at the Gstaad villa she had once shared with Richard Burton. Close friends of the superstar said the place was a hallowed shrine to Burton, the great love of her life.

They had met while filming the epic *Cleopatra* and burned up the screen with their chemistry, which sizzled as a steamy affair when the cameras had stopped rolling. Both were married to other people at the time; both earned the censure of the Pope because of the extra-marital activities. But theirs was a love that knew no bounds, Papal displeasure or not. And one of the places that she had kept to his memory was the Swiss villa where they had rowed, loved and rowed some more. Larry was the first man she had taken there, proving perhaps at last that the spell of Burton had been broken for good.

BEDSIDE VIGIL

Even more touching was the devotion he showed to her when she was hospitalised and literally on the brink of death from a strain of viral pneumonia. In April and May 1990 the world held its breath as she fought for life at the famed St. John's Hospital in Santa Monica, California, where ghostly-green blips on a life support

machine were often the only indication that she was still alive.

And by her side, in a round-the-clock vigil, was Larry. Elizabeth drew strength from his unqualified love for her and whispered to him through the ventilator that was keeping her alive: 'I promise you, my sweet, when this is over, I will marry you.' Beverly Hillbilly Larry Fortensky had just won the hand of the most glamorous film

Above: *Liz found Larry's unqualified love a tower of strength as she battled back from illness.*

star on the planet. And he did it simply by being himself. All that was left for him to do was to wait for the wedding, which was finally scheduled to take place in the autumn of the following year.

A DIAMOND SMILE

On the eve of her wedding, the woman who had stood centre stage in the spotlight all of her life commanded it once more. In poignant, simple terms, she told why she had chosen to go up the aisle one more time. Radiating a smile as big as the diamonds she loves, Liz said: 'I thought I would try it one more time before I die. Larry is a real man, a real guy. I love him dearly.' As if addressing unspoken concerns that some sections of the public might be tempted to believe that Larry was merely marrying her for her money, Elizabeth said: 'He is the least greedy man I have ever met in my whole life. He still works at a job in a large engine-equipment company. He does his own thing – I don't keep him. He gets embarrassed if I give him presents – and you know how I like to do that. Larry is his own man. He likes to fish. If he wants to go fishing, he goes fishing. I have been single for ten years. I have always thought knowing my nature as a marrying kind of woman that I would try one more time. This is it. I was engaged twice before but I backed down. I did not think I was going to grow old with either of those two persons, although they are very sweet and nice men. They just didn't have the potential that was important to me in a long-lasting relationship.

'Larry and I were really very buddy-buddy at the clinic. He knew I could see through him and I knew he could see through me, so it was elemental. We didn't try to get away with anything with each other. They don't like you to become romantically involved in therapy so nothing happened there. We were just too vulnerable at that stage. However, we did not wait a year to become romantically involved.'

And that love was to be sealed in one of the most bizarre ceremonies ever witnessed! The two were pledging their troth on the Neverland estate of Michael Jackson, the funfair-and-animal filled ranch outside the tiny town of Los Olivos in

Above: *Liz has been one of the most acclaimed actresses ever. Even today, as she concentrates on charity work, she still earns accolades.*

'HE IS THE LEAST GREEDY MAN I HAVE EVER MET IN MY WHOLE LIFE. HE GETS EMBARRASSED IF I GIVE HIM PRESENTS'

Northern California. Here Jackson, a child star like Elizabeth who had built his own paradise away from prying eyes, was laying on a ceremony that no-one would ever forget. The VIP guest list read like a Who's Who of Hollywood, old and new. Ex-president Gerald Ford was a guest, as was Liza Minnelli and Brooke Shields, acting as the date for host Jacko. Artist David Hockney, Rod Stewart's former wife Alana Hamilton and actor Roddy McDowell were also among the old friends paying homage to Liz on her special day.

The night before the wedding Los Olivos – also home to movie director John Derek and his beautiful wife Bo – was transformed into a fortress town. Israeli-army-trained bodyguards toting Uzi sub-machine guns provided the security for a western hoedown at the tiny town's Grand Hotel which was entirely taken over by the wedding party. Red checked tablecloths were bedecked with bleached cows' skulls and bowls of fiery chilli, and to add even more western flavour, bales of hay were strewn around the hotel's ballroom and banqueting room.

Elizabeth and Michael Jackson slipped in through a side door after being ferried from his estate four miles away in a blacked-out van, just in time to hear country and western band The Agin Brothers go through their well-worn routine of 'Tumblin' Tumbleweed' and 'Driftin' Away' as the ecstatic guests strutted their stuff in ten gallon hats and cowboy boots. Elizabeth was dressed in white cowgirl boots, jeans studded with white fake diamonds and a black blouse, while most of the men opted for checked shirts and jeans.

The rich and famous, used to eating the finest caviar and drinking Cristal cham-

ARMY-TRAINED BODYGUARDS TOTING UZI SUB-MACHINE GUNS PROVIDED THE SECURITY AT THE WEDDING

Below: *Michael Jackson is one of Liz's closest friends. She stood by him throughout the allegations of child molestation concerning him.*

pagne at £100 a bottle feasted instead on pork ribs smothered in barbecue sauce, wood-smoked salmon and cajun-spiced shrimp. There was a special buffet of char-coal-grilled vegetables for Michael Jackson, who hasn't eaten meat since child-hood. After the barbecue a convoy of limousines rolled up to take the VIPs back to the Neverland Ranch where Michael hosted a nighttime fireworks display and held floodlit rides on his funfair. As dawn broke over the ranch the weirdest wedding in history was set to take place.

MEDIA MADNESS

The road to Michael Jackson's ranch on the day of the ceremony – Sunday 6 October 1991 – hosted the biggest media circus in Californian history. Truck after truck belonging to TV stations, radio networks and newspapers choked the narrow lane leading to the wrought iron gates of Neverland where burly Jackson security chief Herbert Stubblefield warned some of

Above: *Liz is the centre of attention even amidst royalty. Here she meets Princess Margaret.*

Opposite Top: *Although now over 60, Liz still looks glamorous, especially when she dons her jewellery.*

Opposite Bottom: *Former husband Eddie Fisher spoke for many when he wished Liz happiness in her marriage to Fortensky.*

THE MOMENT THAT LARRY EMBRACED LIZ, A MAN DROPPED BY PARACHUTE FROM A CIRCLING CHOPPER!

the more veracious members of the British press: 'You guys have a better chance of getting the colonies back than you do of getting in here.'

As he spoke, the helicopters hired by a dozen news operations from around the globe were circling the 15 million pound ranch like angry gnats – trying to evade the red and white 'barrage balloons' sent skyward that morning by Elizabeth's security squad to stop them from getting too close and the all-pervasive lenses of the photographers from ruining the big day.

THE RADIANT BRIDE

Elizabeth was fashionably late when she arrived for the wedding. She and Larry had stayed in separate cottages on the grounds of the fabulous estate, with staff on hand to attend to the last minute details of dressing and hair styling. An altar was made out of orchids in the grounds where the happy couple would pledge their troth. When Elizabeth walked down the aisle she looked radiant in a figure-hugging £16,000 yellow silk and lace dress by the famed Italian designer Valentino. Larry wore a white

tuxedo and black trousers, topped off with a small green lizard brooch and a gold earring. Giving the bride away was Michael Jackson, in black denim jeans, black gloves, black shirt and silver boots!

Under the flower-decked pavilion 'new age' preacher Marianne Williamson – a love guru who has become a religious inspiration to many in the Hollywood community – waited to perform the marriage ceremony as the whirling rotor blades of the helicopters threatened to drown out her words. But soon the wedding that many had said would never happen was all over. Larry Fortensky placed a gold band on Elizabeth's hand and with a simple poem pledged to care for his bride until death. Larry said: 'With this ring I make you a pledge, that from this day forward, you shall not walk alone. My heart will be your shelter and my arms will be your home.'

Just at the moment that he embraced her a man dropped by parachute from a circling chopper! Clutching a camera, he was hired by one of America's racy tabloid magazines to take photos of the marriage that everyone in the world wanted to be in on. He landed just 25 yards from the bride and groom, a crumpled mass under the weight of 12 security men who led him away before he managed to get even a glimpse – let alone a picture – of the happy couple.

After the ceremony there was banqueting on a style and scale that would have pleased the emperors of Rome. Although recovering alcoholics Elizabeth and Larry could touch nothing stronger than grape juice, the finest wines, champagnes, brandies and liqueurs flowed like water for the distinguished guests. Caviar, smoked salmon and lobster salad, pasta in a rich white truffle sauce, medallions of veal and fresh vegetables, followed by a rich chocolate dessert – the catering was a world class affair for a world class, if not world-class quirky, wedding.

Later, when one of her ex-husbands, Eddie Fisher, saw the videotape of the helicopters buzzing the ceremony, he said: 'My God – nobody should have to suffer that on their wedding day. But Elizabeth can take it, I know. And I wish her well. This is the first time she has married a regular worker. Good luck to them both.' Those sentiments were shared around the world.

MICHAEL JACKSON
Music's Eccentric

Michael Jackson achieved stardom at the expense of a 'normal' childhood. And when he achieved massive worldwide fame as an adult he began to use his enormous fortune in a series of bizarre attempts to claw back his lost boyhood.

Michael Jackson, the chameleon man/boy of pop has defied every attempt to pin him down, label him, compartmentalise him and his enormous talent. For his adoring public he has changed his image more times than anyone can remember. He started out as the snub-nosed, afro-haired kid from the Jackson Five, hogging the limelight from an early age with a talent that could not be denied. Now, his face cosmetically altered, his hair hanging down lank like a schoolgirl's, he remains one of the world's top entertainers, ever-ready to record another magnificent album or embark upon a new world tour for his faithful fans. But just who he is... the truth may never accurately be known, except that which he wishes to give away.

Opposite and Left: *Michael Jackson's gentle off-stage image contrasts with his dynamic performances.*

Below: *The young Michael (far left) with his brothers.*

Above: *Michael's former manager Frank Dileo helped make Jackson a superstar.*

Above Right: *Jackson believed he could prolong his life by sleeping in an oxygen-rich chamber.*

What we do know is his phenomenal success. He is the highest-earning entertainer in the world, with an annual income between £60-80,000,000, depending on whether he is touring or not. He has interests in some 300 companies, ranging from health spas to grocery outlets and he owns the copyright to most of the Beatles' songs. He loves little children so much that they, apart from a few close friends, are the only ones allowed to penetrate his Neverland ranch kingdom in California where they ride on his funfair, watch movies in his on-site cinemas and revel in a land of magic where there is no adult badness to bother them.

WACKO JACKO

It has long been known that Jacko, a sensitive child, had problems growing up. He claims his childhood now makes up for the one he never had. But it is as 'Wacko Jacko' in the 1980s that he went off the star barometer and into the stratosphere. The world loves a wacky, quirky star and in Jacko they had found it. He wanted to buy the bones of John Merrick, the hideously deformed 'Elephant Man' of Victorian times. He slept in a hyperbaric oxygen chamber in his quest for eternal life. He wore disguises at Disneyworld to board the rides that thrilled him and oxygen masks in public to purify the air. What the public didn't know was that Wacko Jacko was being manipulated by a very clever army of image makers. And in 1989 *The Sun* newspaper summed it up with a headline which read: 'Why Frank Got Sacko For Putting The Wacko In Jacko!'

The story centred on the firing of Frank Dileo, the cigar-chomping manager who skilfully crafted the image of Jackson into something between a circus freak and a musical demi-god. But Dileo finally forgot one golden rule – the man he called 'Kid' was really the boss and eventually he proved it. Jackson finally realised that his Wacko image had gone too far. Dileo said: 'It was a complete shock, a nasty surprise. Michael called out of the blue and said I was fired. Then he hung up.'

Dileo had been the brains behind the *Thriller* video, a 40-million global seller that went into the record books. He was the mastermind of the *BAD* album and tour which took Jackson around the globe for 18 months. He was behind the release of Jackson in the oxygen chamber – together with the accompanying story of the quest for immortality. He was behind the closing of Disneyland in California so Michael could enjoy it in complete solitude. He was the creator of the myth that Michael had fallen for Elizabeth Taylor! No story was too outrageous, no photo opportunity so bizarre that it couldn't be tuned into the wavelength of Jacko's fame. His grand plan ensured that

Michael stayed on the front pages of every magazine and newspaper in the world.

But he broke the cardinal rule surrounding Jackson – secrecy. Jackson is a man obsessed with secrets. Even the little children who visit Neverland are sworn not to reveal its secrets. Dileo overstepped the mark when he said things like: 'He's a good kid, he's something special. I feel very protective towards him – perhaps too protective. But I am concerned about his strange eating habits.

'The Kid eats nothing but fruit, nuts, and steamed vegetables, no red meat, not even chicken or fish. He drinks nothing but fresh fruit juices and pure bottled water. He also takes massive doses of vitamins – I have seen him take as many as 50 in one day. It is all part of his longevity programme – which includes talking and playing with his deadly tarantula, a King Cobra, a boa constrictor and a scorpion. Through it all the kid is accompanied by his pet chimp Bubbles. It's bizarre, but he dresses the chimp in clothes similar to his own. He

treats it like it's human.' Michael, who had never felt more burned since the Pepsi stage disaster in which klieg lights fell on to his head and scorched him during the making of a TV advert, finally sacked him.

Not that everything that Dileo said was complete fantasy and Jackson is certainly an unusual creature. In Neverland, the ranch named after Peter Pan's kingdom, Jackson shuts out the world that, obviously, is very painful for him to deal with on many levels. Here he has planted speakers in flower beds that belt out his favourite tunes, sits in his bedroom and tears up $50,000 worth of bills and has his own fire engine and fire brigade in outfits he designed for them. We know all this because a couple ratted-on Michael, selling their story about life inside Neverland as it has never been told before.

Mark and Fay Quindoy are Filipinos who became his housekeepers at the gigantic mansion and ranch. For the lure of money they revealed all, but at the same time had nothing bad to say about their ex-

> JACKSON SHUTS OUT THE WORLD THAT IS OBVIOUSLY VERY PAINFUL FOR HIM TO DEAL WITH ON MANY LEVELS

Below: *A child at heart, Jackson once had Disneyland closed so he could play there by himself.*

ON PRIME-TIME AMERICAN TV THE MYTH OF MICHAEL JACKSON WAS SHATTERED LIKE ALICE'S LOOKING GLASS

employer. They painted a portrait of a massively overgrown child who would be far happier spending all his days in a toy-stuffed nursery or a zoo than ever venturing into the world of adults again.

Said Mark: 'The time he ripped up the money, it wasn't done maliciously. He did it because all the pieces looked like a pretty snowstorm when he threw them up into the air. He was like a naughty schoolboy who had discovered a new trick. His bedroom was just like a boy's, always untidy. He always made sure that there were new nappies on Bubbles in case he had an accident, but he didn't mind the place looking like a tip.'

The centrepiece of the estate is the million-dollar Michael Jackson museum, a shrine to himself which suggests that, for all the tomfoolery, Jackson is acutely aware of his place in entertainment history. Faye, 48, said: 'It is creepy. He drove us up to it and said: "I bring everyone here. This is my monument. I want you to see it and to love it." Man, it was weird. There were portraits of George Washington, Albert Einstein, Napoleon and Elvis Presley on the wall. But in the middle, several times bigger than all the other paintings, is a life-sized portrait of Michael. The shrine is packed with all his stage clothes, record covers, platinum albums and dolls of himself. Michael turned to us and said: "Do you like it here? Do you love me?" What could we do but say yes? But we did come to love him. As eccentric as he is he is also warm-hearted, shy and introverted. We could find nothing bad to say about him.'

THE FACADE COLLAPSES

The next time that so much would be learned about the world of Jacko would come from his own lips. It was to become the night that pop's tearful Peter Pan spoke on prime-time American TV; the night that the carefully-crafted myth of Michael Jackson was shattered like Alice's looking glass. Jackson's eccentric image had been painstakingly built over nearly two decades by Dileo and others – legions of spin doctors, PR moguls, Hollywood hype experts, agents, managers, lawyers, attorneys and record company mandarins. But in an emotionally-charged 90 minute interview in May 1993 the 34-year-old superstar finally spilled it all – or most of it anyway. It made his *Moonwalk* book seem like a biography of someone else. In many ways it also spelled the loss of the 'magic', with fans realising that the demi-god of pop is merely mortal after all.

Jackson answered many of the questions which have swirled around him like endless fog ever since his domination of popular music began.

It was long rumoured that his father abused him – now he confirmed it with heart-wrenching details of an innocence destroyed, rather than lost. He spoke about plastic surgery on his nose and how a rare skin disorder makes him appear 'whiter' than he is. He shared the sadness of his life growing up in the Jackson Five. Robbed of a normal childhood then, he indulges in it now, in the form of the Neverland ranch. He even touched on the touchy subject of his sexuality when interviewer Oprah Winfrey asked him flat out: 'Are you a virgin?' Squirming with embarrassment the gloved one – who has NEVER been romantically linked to any woman, or man for that matter – replied: 'How could you ask me that question? I'm a gentleman, I'm a gentleman. It's something that's private. It shouldn't be spoken about. You can call me old-fashioned if you want. I'm embar-

Above: *Talk show host Oprah Winfrey got the scoop of the decade when Michael spoke frankly on her show.*

Below: *Jackson picks up yet another music award, this time presented to him by Liz Taylor.*

rassed.' As if to prove it he giggled in a high-pitched squeal that seemed to come straight from the lips of a ten-year-old with Afro-hair... the boy from the Jackson Five. Even his blushing was visible.

Elizabeth Taylor, for whom he acted as best man at her wedding in 1991, was by his side doling out encouragement. During the interview Jackson's anger only surfaced once – when Winfrey settled on the touchy subject of his alleged skin bleaching. Jackson's cosmetically-altered nostrils flared as he said: 'There's no such thing as skin bleaching. I have never seen it – I don't know what it is. I have a skin disorder that destroys the pigmentation of the skin.' He said the disorder called vitiligo began after the success of his 1982 *Thriller* album and that it was passed on to him in a rogue gene by his father.

'It is something I cannot help,' he said with tears glistening in eyes unshaded by dark sunglasses. 'And when people make up stories that I don't wanna be who I am, it hurts me. I'm a black American. I'm proud to be a black American. I am proud of my race, I am proud of who I am. Using make-up evens it out. Why is that so important? That's not important to me. What about people who sit in the sun to become darker?'

Not so proud, however, of his nose, which he admits has been operated on for plastic surgery twice. He said defensively that it was a 'minor procedure' and: 'Very little. You can count the times on two fingers. If all the people in Hollywood who've had plastic surgery went on holiday there wouldn't be many people left in town. Yes, I've had my nose done. Lots of people have. But I have not done my cheekbones, eyes or lips.' Asked whether he was pleased with the results when he looked in the mirror he replied: 'I am never pleased with anything. I am a perfectionist. I try not to look into the mirror.'

MIRROR SHY

Mirrors were something he shunned as a child, too, when he was growing up under the belt-wielding hand of his father Joe. Black-sheep sister La Toya has spoken numerous times about the beatings Joe doled out. A TV movie about the Jackson Five on American TV depicted Joe somewhere between Attilla the Hun and Lindi St. Clair. Now it was Michael's turn to confess to one billion TV viewers that he didn't like his dad when he was young. 'I am sorry, Joseph,' he whispered, before going on to rubbish him on live TV. 'I love my father but I don't know him. My mother is wonderful but I don't understand

*Above: **Jackson with parents Katherine and Joe. The singer claims he was physically and mentally abused by his father.***

'I AM SORRY, JOSEPH,' JACKSON WHISPERED, BEFORE GOING ON TO RUBBISH HIS FATHER ON LIVE TV

*Left: **Jackson has said that the stage made him feel secure as a youngster: 'That was home for me.'***

Joseph. I became reclusive because I felt there wasn't anything important for me to say. There is a lot of sadness about my past life. My father beat me. It was difficult to take being beaten and then going on stage. I don't know whether he wanted a golden child. He was very strict, very hard and stern. Just a look would terrify me.

'I was scared of him as a kid and when I was older. There were times when he would come to see me and I would feel sick. And I would say: "Please don't get mad Joseph. I am sorry Joseph."' He also said his father made cruel jibes about his appearance. Plagued with pimples as an adolescent, he said: 'I was so shy I would wash my face in the dark. I wouldn't look in the mirror because my father would tease me about being ugly. Adolescence was a very difficult time for me. I think every child goes through this period because you are not the cute child you were but everyone wants to keep you that way.

'I was happy on stage because that was home for me. I was very sad when I got off stage. There were times when I cried from loneliness. I was eight or nine when we first became famous. There is a lot of wonderment in being famous. You travel the world, see people, but you put in a lot of time. I'd do my schooling for three hours and then go to the recording studio and sometimes fall asleep there. Outside the studio I'd see children playing in the park and I'd be sad and crying because I had to go to work. You don't get to do things that other children do like having friends, going to slumber parties and hanging out with friends. I never had any friends. My brothers were my friends.'

As he spoke in the living room of his mansion, set in 2,700 acres of pristine Californian wilderness, the lights of his home-made funfair twinkled in the background – the never-never world which he inhabits when away from the stage. I didn't have a childhood and I compensate for that now,' he said. 'That's why I like having children around. People used to say I was an old soul in a little body, a 45-year-old midget. But I try to do things for children, to be pure and innocent and see the world through eyes of wonderment.' Every three weeks Jackson has terminally ill children visit him at Neverland in the Santa Ynez mountains. 'We had 100 bald-headed children recently and to see those kids so happy made me cry,' he said.

LIES AND GARBAGE

Notwithstanding that it was the world's press who helped make him the phenomenon he is, Jackson lashed into what he called 'lies and garbage' written about him. He said he NEVER made a bid to buy the skeleton of London's Victorian 'Elephant Man' John Merrick and NEVER slept in a hyperbaric oxygen chamber. 'There was so much garbage written about me,' he stormed. 'Where would I put a load of old bones?' Of course, he did NOT say that it was his promotional people who planted those and other stories worldwide in a bid to build on the 'eccentric' angle which helped his mystifying image and resulted in more and more profits.

The interview cut in with views of Neverland, with pictures of him as a young man and with Elizabeth Taylor, perhaps his one true friend. She said: 'Michael is the least weird man I know. He's understanding, sympathetic, generous almost to a fault. If he has any eccentricity it is that he is larger than life.' Afterwards sister LaToya was interviewed on another programme. She claimed that Michael's interview was a calculated ploy aimed at boosting flagging record sales. 'He wants to recapture the audience he's lost,' said

Below: *Sensational allegations brought against him by a 13-year-old boy in 1993 saw Jackson threatened with permanent seclusion – or even prison.*

LaToya. For Joe Jackson, derided in front of a billion of his countrymen, all he could do was deny ever hitting his son.

In late 1993, it was Michael's turn for worldwide humiliation. A series of allegations were made that he had had sexual relationships with under-age boys. In November he flew to Britain to undergo treatment for addiction to pain-killers. It was speculated that he might not return to the USA, but he did, in early December, to face the prospect of charges of child-abuse.

FREDDIE MERCURY
A Short Sweet Life

Freddie Mercury's charisma and songwriting talent ensured that he remained at the top of the rock tree for two decades. But the king of Queen was a real-life queen, whose sexual tastes led to his tragically premature death.

H e burned as the brightest of all the stars in the firmament of rock music, and when that light went out in November 1991 the world was a sadder place for his passing. Freddie Mercury was the ultra-talented lead singer of Queen, a showman who re-wrote the rules when it came to popular music. His life was lived at a whirlwind pace of international partying, sell-out concerts and sumptuous living. It was also lived in the closet. Freddie was a homosexual for most of his life, afraid that the disclosure – despite the camp name of the group which propelled him to fame – might ruin his fame. And the lifestyle he pursued as a homosexual was eventually to be the death of him.

A TRAGIC END

It was a frail, trembling creature, unable to breathe properly, unable to even speak, who died of the dreaded disease AIDS that cold November night. Hours before his death Freddie issued a statement to silence once and for all the rumourmongers who for years had speculated that he had the disease. The statement said simply: 'I wish to confirm I have been tested HIV positive and have AIDS. I felt it correct to keep this information private to date in order to protect the privacy of those around me. However, the time has now come for my friends and fans around the world to know the truth. I hope everyone will join with me, my doctors and all those worldwide in the fight against this terrible disease.'

A few days later, Dave Clark of the Dave Clark Five, a man who had been Freddie's closest friend, revealed that Freddie had passed away from bronchial pneumonia brought on by AIDS on 24 November. He said: 'He didn't say anything. He just went to sleep and passed on. It was very peaceful. He was a rare person, as unique as a painting. I know he has gone to a much better place.'

Freddie left millions of people behind who wished that were true – that there was a heaven waiting for the superstar who started out in life named Farokh Bulsara.

He was born in Zanzibar in September 1946 to Persian parents. His early years were as exotic as his later years would become; schooling in India, holidays in some of the most romantic spots on earth and a religion as mysterious to outsiders as outer space. Freddie was brought up a Zoroastrian, one of the world's oldest reli-

IT WAS A FRAIL, TREMBLING CREATURE WHO DIED OF THE DREADED DISEASE AIDS THAT COLD NOVEMBER NIGHT

Opposite: *Freddie Mercury's flamboyance and stage personality placed him among pop's royalty.*

Below: *The ravages of AIDS begin to take their toll as Freddie draws closer and closer to death.*

ent colours and styles. He was also very interested in music, forming at first a band called Smile and then one called Queen with Brian May, a physics student at Imperial College, London, who had been musing about putting a band together for months. Roger Taylor and Tim Staffell made up the numbers, Staffell eventually being replaced by Roger Deacon on bass guitar. This was the foursome that would take the pop world by storm. Freddie took the name Mercury because he thought that, like the liquid metal, he would 'spill over the world like no-one before me'.

In 1972 they began receiving recognition on the well-worn circuit of provincial theatres and music venues. But it was in 1974, with the release of 'Seven Seas of Rhye', that Queen took off into the big time. Soon after that opening hit, a string of hugely successful singles and albums helped propel Queen to the cutting edge of popular music in the world. For Freddie Mercury, it was the key to Pandora's Box – the ingredient he needed for a life of decadent excess.

'Excess is part of my nature,' he once told a British journalist in an interview in

Above: *Freddie's elderly parents find comfort with friends at the funeral.*

Right: *An early Queen show finds Freddie camping it up.*

SUCCESS WAS THE KEY TO PANDORA'S BOX FOR FREDDIE: THE INGREDIENT HE NEEDED FOR A LIFE OF DECADENT EXCESS

gions, whose believers follow the teachings of the 6th century BC prophet Zarathustra. Life for devotees is seen as a constant battle between good and evil – some might say a metaphor for the struggle which Mercury later confronted in his decision to pursue endless sexual encounters; encounters which would eventually kill him. This mystical world of the east, however, ended abruptly when Freddie was 14 and his parents moved to Middlesex.

The drab, uniform houses and the seemingly endless grey skies were a stark contrast to his upbringing and plunged the young boy into depression. He was a fair pupil at school, but nothing exceptional. He had a flair and interest in art and at art college began experimenting with differ-

New York. He had gone there to look for success in the country that had been conquered before by the Beatles in a previous British invasion. 'To me, dullness is a disease. I really need danger and excitement. I was not made for staying indoors and watching television. I am definitely a sexual person. I like to f*** all the time. I used to say that I would go with anyone, but these days I am much more choosy. I love to surround myself with strange and interesting people because they make me feel more alive. Extremely straight people bore me stiff. I love freaky people around me. By nature I am restless and highly strung, so I wouldn't make a very good family man. I am a very emotional person, a person of real extremes, and often that's destructive both to myself and others.'

THE FAST LIFE

Freddie lived life at 100 miles-per-hour in the capitals of Europe and in New York and San Francisco. He travelled like a queen too – stretch limousines, ermine-lined gowns, £5,000 a day hotel suites, the best champagne, the best caviar – the best of everything, in fact. Nothing was too good or too costly for him and he lived life at a gallop. He developed a reputation for brilliant showmanship on stage, but it was equally mirrored offstage. Everything was fuelled by drink and cocaine – lots of cocaine that he would snort from mirrored surfaces, often up to £2,000 worth of the finest illegal Columbian that money could buy in a single evening.

But money was no object and he spent it like water. His parties were legendary affairs, even by the excessive standards of the rock'n'roll world. They cost around £50,000 each, and were replete with girls wearing nothing but body paint, boys pretending to be statues and at the centre of the orgiastic indulgences, Freddie himself, basking in the spotlight of adoration. Around him at one super-bash in his London home was a woman dancing with an exotic snake, transexuals doing strange things with cigarettes and a champagne fountain of the finest Dom Perignon bubbly that cost £20,000 to set up!

Such excesses could not be bought by a talentless one-hit wonder. Like David Bowie, Freddie and Queen remained enor-

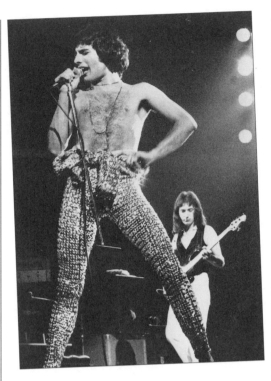

mously successful because they were versatile in changing their musical styles and images. The platform-boot-stomping Freddie of the 1970s had given way by the 1980s to a circus ringmaster look that whipped his fans into frenzied adulation. He proved this by appearing as one of the main acts for Live Aid, the concert that

EVERYTHING WAS FUELLED BY DRINK AND COCAINE – LOTS OF COCAINE THAT HE WOULD SNORT FROM MIRRORED SURFACES

Left: *Freddie openly admitted that he was 'a sexual person'.*

Below: *The stylish singer, surrounded by the other members of Queen. The band remained successful because they were willing to continually change.*

Above: *Freddie dominated the London stage at Live Aid, despite the presence of other big names in music.*

Opposite Top: *Mary Austin was both lover and friend to Freddie. She was with him when he died.*

Opposite Bottom: *Harrods, where Freddie spent a small fortune.*

MERCURY SPENT ABOUT £50,000 A MONTH, AT THE HEIGHT OF HIS FAME, ON BOTH STAGE CLOTHES AND HIS PRIVATE WARDROBE

---

shook the conscience of the world on 13 July 1985. Simultaneous live events in London and Philadelphia reached a global TV audience of two billion people as Freddie and others like Madonna, U2, Paul McCartney and Eric Clapton played for the victims of Ethiopian famine.

Freddie, by the concensus of all music critics, dominated the stage in London on that magical day, leaving close friend Elton John – one of the few who would be at his death bed just a few short years later – saying: 'He stole the show that day. He stole it from every other act there. The guy was just brilliant.' His reaction was echoed in the newspaper the next day which screamed with headlines 'Queen are King' and 'Mercury Hits Record Highs'.

Bob Geldof, the mastermind of Live Aid, said: 'Queen were absolutely the best band of the day, whatever your personal preference.' There was no getting away from it – Freddie Mercury had earned the right to party hard.

Mercury spent about £50,000 a month, when he was at the height of his fame, on both stage clothes and his private wardrobe – even although sometimes it was difficult to tell the difference.

Freddie loved luxury and quality, maintaining accounts at several Savile Row tailors for his evening wear, which later became a trademark both on and off stage. He regarded himself as a latter-day dandy, the enormous royalties and record fees subsidising his gad-about-town lifestyle.

TASTEFUL TREASURES

There was even more money spent on fine arts and antiquities. Mercury had a true artist's eye for beautiful objects together with a bank account which allowed him to turn his Kensington home into something approaching a mini-Louvre. He would think nothing of spending £1,000,000 in an afternoon on fine art, joking to friends that he wanted to be buried like the Egyptian pharaohs of old, surrounded by the possessions of this life for the journey to the next. One of his most treasured collections was of Dresden porcelain dolls. Wherever he was in the world, flunkies for the band were always called upon to seek out the best antique stores which might have new and better dolls for his collection.

He was also a patron of the finest jewellers in the world. Cartier even broke company policy to allow Mercury to shop there after hours, so that he would not be bothered by other customers.

All that glittered was gold to him and he relished it, once saying: 'All my money goes to Harrods, Cartier, Christie's and Asprey. I believe in being extravagant. Sometimes I believe that all I want in life is to make pots of money and then go off and spend it.' Mercury once said he was as addicted to shopping as he was to sex. But at least the shopping was safer for him. Sex was his dark side of fame – the dark side that would eventually kill him. The boy from Zanzibar who grew up to have the world in the palms of his talented hands was insatiable in the bedroom.

INSATIABLE DESIRES

Mercury was addicted to sex, once boasting that he liked six men in a bed at once, hundreds in a month. It was one reason why he liked to spend so much time in New York and Munich – places where gay sex was readily available at so many more places than London. After shows left him buzzing he liked nothing better than to spend the twilight hours in club after club, cruising for the young men eager to spend a night – or even just a few hours – with this legend of the pop world. He had experienced gay sex as a public schoolboy, and of course the band roadies and fellow members knew all about his sexual preferences.

But while his sexual persona may have been blurred during all the years he was with Queen, he never openly admitted his

gayness. Rick Sky, in his insightful book *The Show Must Go On: The Life of Freddie Mercury* wrote: 'In all the interviews he did Mercury never really admitted to his gayness. He referred vaguely to having tried relationships with men and women but that was as far as his revelations went. Usually he would say something like: "If people want to know if I'm gay I never tell them. Instead I say they should try to find out for themselves. People can think what they like about my bisexual image. And that's what I want them to do. I want to keep my mystique around me."'

Many of the multi-partner gay scenes that Mercury indulged in were fuelled by massive quantities of cocaine. Mercury

Left: *Freddie, always the showman, gave his all whenever he went on stage.*

Below: *A combination of fine musicianship and stagecraft made Queen's live shows memorable affairs.*

used the drug like many in showbiz – not just to obtain a 'high', but as a stimulant to keep on partying and working and partying until the machine just cranked to a stop or blew up. Paul Prenter, his former personal manager who died of AIDS three months before Mercury, revealed much about his

homosexual flings when he sold his story to Britain's biggest-selling tabloid *The Sun.* Prenter revealed Mercury became mortified with fear after learning that at least two men he had slept with had died of AIDS. It gnawed at him because, fiercely intelligent as he was, he knew that he was a high-risk candidate for the virus from which no-one has ever recovered.

In 1985, believed to be the time that he was tested positive for AIDS, Mercury made a dramatic switch in his lifestyle. Most of the partying was cut out and he stayed monogamous with one man, Jim Hutton, a former hairdresser who was to stay with him to the end. Mercury's world now centred for the most part on London and his fashionable luxury home in Kensington. But although he was sexually entwined with Hutton, one woman occupied a unique place in his life. This was Mary Austin, another devout friend who was with him when he died.

Mary and he met in 1970 at the Biba boutique where she worked. This shrine to 1960s fashion and culture was a favourite of Mercury's – he often wobbled into the emporium on his platform shoes to buy some outrageous lipstick or some wonderful chiffons for his stage shows. They lived together for several years, at first as lovers,

then, as Mercury's gayness began to consume him more and more, as friends. She accepted his lifestyle as something she could have no control over and remained his faithful, devoted friend until the end. In fact, it was Mary who eventually broke the news of his death to his parents and Mary who seemed most shattered by his end. She said afterwards: 'I feel a great sense of loss and pain and I am sure that there are lots of fans who share that loss. I never ever stopped loving Freddie and I don't think he ever stopped loving me.'

THE END APPROACHES

Rumours of the mystery illness which afflicted Freddie began circulating in the late 1980s. There were whispers that he had contracted some rare blood disease from an insect while on tour in Brazil, others that he had become bulimic, the eating disorder which plagued Princess Diana. But those who were in his close circle knew what it really was and they kept faith with the extraordinary star.

As the disease grew steadily worse so Mercury devised new ploys to disguise its ravages. He wore thick make up to hide the blotches and lesions; he padded his clothes out to make his body appear to be more nourished than it really was. And he studiously avoided all the parties, all the gay clubs and outrageous soirees that had been his favourite hangouts during the glory years. He was fiercely determined to keep the disease private, so much so that even Brian May from the band hadn't been told.

After Freddie Mercury's death, May commented: 'It was always a private thing with Freddie. We knew instinctively that something was going on but it was not talked about. He did not finally tell us until a few months ago. But he certainly knew for five years. He was living under a shadow for a very long time.'

Freddie Mercury's last public appearance was in February 1990 when Queen received a special contribution to music

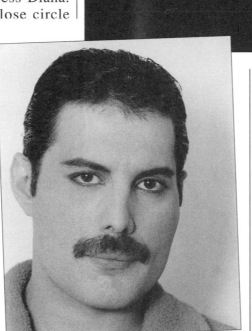

Above and Above Top: *A champion to the very end, Freddie long denied that he had AIDS – although he donated lavishly to the hunt for a cure.*

award at the British rock and pop awards. No-one who saw the pallid ghost of the great stage showman could be under any illusions about what had overtaken him. Up until the end his press and publicity people continued to lie about his condition, even going as far as to threaten libel proceedings against newspapers or broadcasters who said he had the disease.

Yet even as the denials were being issued, Mercury was instructing others in his entourage to divide up some of his huge estate for AIDS charities. In the end he decided to donate a small fortune in cash and art – Mercury amassed a museum's worth of quality art and antique collection in his lifetime – to the charities favoured by Magic Johnson, the American basketball ace who was forced to retire from the game due to AIDS which he contracted in numerous heterosexual relationships.

After Freddie Mercury died, 'Bohemian Rhapsody' was re-released, with all the profits designated for a British AIDS charity, the Terence Higgins Trust. The single which had made Queen rock legends was at Number 1 just six days later. In death, as in life, Freddie Mercury proved that he was a hard act to follow.

PATERNITY SUITS
Finding Fathers

Willing women are permanently available to most male showbiz stars. But a single night of indiscretion can lead to a man being dragged through the courts and being hit heavily where it hurts: in his wallet.

Over the years, dozens of big name stars have been slapped with paternity suits, alleging that they fathered children by fans or acquaintances. Some, like renowned Welsh singer Tom Jones, were eventually found by courts of law to be indeed the father of the child in question, while others, such as Michael Jackson, were simply accused by disturbed women they had never even met.

In both scenarios, one can see the perils of stardom. Performers, whether they be stars of screen, stage or television, are often away from home for long periods of time and, like Jones, can easily fall for the pretty fan who will do anything to meet their idol. And in cases like that involving Jackson, wealthy superstars can be prime targets for the most outrageous claims by women merely seeking money or by deranged fans obsessed with having a more personal relationship with their hero.

In July 1989, legendary ladies' man Jones was forced to pay child support to a 26-year-old shipping clerk, with whom he had fathered a boy during a wild, four-day romp in New York City. Jones, who was 48 at the time of the suit, spent months denying claims by Katherine Berkery that they had a steamy affair in 1987 which led to the birth of baby Jonathan.

Jones even refused to appear in the packed courtroom in the Manhattan Family Court, and at one stage Judge Judith Scheidlin threatened to have him arrested when his lawyer, Alton Abramowitz, dodged questions about the singer's role in the affair. She said: 'Your client has chosen not to show up in this case so I want to know pretty soon whether you intend to dispute this girl's testimony on identity or whether I will have to issue an arrest warrant and get him brought into this court.'

According to evidence presented before the court, Jones picked up Katherine at the trendy Regine's nightclub in New York on 29 October 1987. He then invited both her and her friend, Alicia, to join him and his assistant, who was identified only as Christopher, for drinks in his hotel suite at the posh Ritz Carlton Hotel. As Katherine later testified in court: 'We didn't leave the night club until 4am and got to his room, 2104, where we had drinks. I was with Tom on the sofa and then we went to bed in his room.'

Katherine, who claimed she had not had sex for a few months before the tryst with the singer, then alleged that Jones suggested kinky, three-way sex with her friend Alicia, but that she refused: 'I was a little angry with him over that. But we went into the bedroom and I had sex with him. I did not have any contraceptive protection.' The gorgeous brunette said that after falling asleep in his arms, she got up later that afternoon and went home to shower and change. That night, she was Tom's guest at a concert in nearby Westbury, on Long Island.

Later, she recalled that she, Tom, Alicia and Christopher went eating and drinking in Manhattan before going to Stringfellow's night club. As Katherine later remarked: 'Later, Tom and I were sitting around in bath robes in his suite. I was lying across his lap as he smoked a big cigar and played his own songs on a tape recorder. Then we went back into his bedroom and had more sex.' She said the sex continued again the next night.

The court heard that Jones took a blood test to determine whether the child was his, and, as the judge noted: 'The blood test showed a 99.67 return of probable paternity

KATHERINE ALLEGED THAT TOM JONES HAD SUGGESTED KINKY, THREE-WAY SEX WITH HER FRIEND ALICIA

Above: *Katherine Berkery with baby Jonathon. A Manhattan court found Tom Jones to be the baby's father after DNA testing.*

Opposite: *Tom Jones had to pay child support to a New York woman with whom he had a weekend affair.*

Above: *Jones was forced to pay out thousands of pounds because of his brief encounter.*

on Jones's part. The court finds that Tom Jones is the father, owing to clear evidence. Gentlemen, you have lost your case.'

The judge found that Katherine's evidence that she had had sex with Jones was 'totally credible'.

During the sensational hearing, Katherine also admitted that she was 'an acquaintance' of notorious Mafia boss, John Gotti, but she denied any suggestions that she had been intimate with the much-feared mobster. 'I have not seen John Gotti for several months,' she testified. 'I never slept with him or took money from him. He is someone I met.'

Katherine was also forced to deny claims by the defence that she was a prostitute, and

was in tears when she said: 'I have never been a prostitute, worked for an escort agency or lived off men.' She said that she was so broke that she had to sell off her gold Rolex watch, put her fur coat in storage and live off the charity of friends because 'Tom Jones hasn't paid a dime to me'.

Jones, who was forced to pay thousands of pounds as a result of the case, married his childhood sweetheart, Linda, when she was just 17 – more than 30 years earlier. He and Linda had one son, Mark, who is now 34 years old.

ROBERT DE NIRO

Famed film actor Robert De Niro, who specialises in playing tough characters like the young Don Corleone in *Godfather, Part II*, and boxer Jack La Motta in *Raging Bull*, had his brush with the law in 1993, in one of the strangest paternity suits ever. For over nine years, De Niro had reportedly been the father figure of a young girl called Nina, the daughter of singer Helena Springs, one of many women the actor has wooed and bedded over his superstar career.

When the tot was born, the actor is said to have accepted her as his own and, like a dutiful though absent father, regularly sent the girl and her mother cash gifts to pay for Nina's care and upbringing. According to reports, De Niro was very proud of the youngster, even once taking her onto one of his movie sets and introducing her to his fellow cast members as 'my little girl'.

However, De Niro never lived with Nina or her mother, and when Nina was five years old, Helena met and married another man. He, too, was swept away by the pretty little youngster, and asked that he be allowed to legally adopt her as his own. According to famed attorney Marvin Mitchelson, De Niro 'flew into a rage' when he heard the news, screaming 'Nina's my child!' and steadfastly refused to allow the adoption to go ahead. Unfortunately, Mitchelson later wrote in his book, Helen's new man never got over his heartbreak at not being allowed to adopt Nina, and eventually he and Helena were divorced in 1989.

Afterwards, De Niro continued to act like the father's child, sending her gifts and telling her he loved her, said Mitchelson. But then, in 1992, De Niro suddenly decided he wanted to make certain Nina was

really his child, and so he decided to have some blood tests done. The results proved negative, which shocked both the actor and Helena. Believing something might have been wrong with the tests, a second set was arranged. There was no doubt. The child was not the daughter of De Niro.

With that, says Mitchelson, De Niro 'tossed her aside like a used Kleenex', refusing to see her or even speak with her. Suddenly, a nine-year relationship had come to a jarring end. Mitchelson was hired by Helena when the actor stopped paying for the child's care, and he immediately filed a paternity suit against him. Under Californian law, if a person bonds with a child, and expresses his belief both in words and deeds that he is the father, then it can be ordered that the person is legally the father. He is therefore required to pay the necessary child support payments.

When Mitchelson filed the paternity suit against De Niro, the judge ordered that the star pay about £400 a week in temporary support while the case was played out in court. Meanwhile, another blood test was arranged, and it, too, proved negative. When De Niro was finally called to the

Above: *Robert De Niro with former boxing great Jake La Motta. Cinema's 'Raging Bull' turned ugly in a Californian trial: he denied being the father of a young girl.*

Left: *The girl in question, Nina, with her mother Helena Springs.*

THE LAWYER SAID THAT WHEN DE NIRO FOUND THE GIRL WASN'T HIS, HE 'TOSSED HER ASIDE LIKE A USED KLEENEX'

stand to offer his side of the story, he denied he had ever had a fatherly relationship with Nina. He said he never told her he was her father, and denied acting like her father.

The judge had no choice but to find in De Niro's favour, and he was allowed to

Above: *Superlawyer Marvin Mitchelson, star of the De Niro hearing, leaves court.*

THE CRAZED WOMAN BEGGED MICHAEL JACKSON TO COMMIT SUICIDE ON A CERTAIN DAY AND AT A CERTAIN TIME

discontinue paying temporary support. But Mitchelson and Helena refused to accept the decision, and filed an appeal. It was still pending at the time of publication.

MICHAEL JACKSON

Another bizarre incident involving paternity claims centred on reclusive star Michael Jackson, who wrote about the case in his huge hit, 'Billie Jean', one of many Number 1 songs from his blockbuster 1983 album, *Thriller*. In it, he sings about a girl who accused him of fathering her child.

The incident dated back to 1981, when a deranged female fan wrote to Jackson telling him about his 'son'. She even enclosed photographs of the baby and of herself. She appeared to be attractive, black and in her late teens. Jackson had never met her in his life, and ignored all her claims. For many big name stars, letters like this are just one of the perils of fame.

However, the woman refused to give up her absurd claims, and wrote to him again declaring her undying love for him and how she wanted to spend the rest of her life with him. She told Michael they would live happily ever after, caring for each other and 'their' child. Jackson was rattled by the woman's obsession, and soon began to have terrible nightmares about her, and asked aides why she was being so persistent when clearly the child was not his.

Then Michael received a package from her in the mail. Inside, there was another photograph of her – this one taken at what appeared to be her high school graduation. But there was also something else: a weapon, which Jackson and his entourage have never publicly identified. In the enclosed letter, the crazed woman begged Michael to commit suicide on a certain day at a certain time. She informed him that she would take her own life at that exact same moment – but only after first killing her child! Somehow, in the dark recesses of her disturbed mind, she reasoned that since they could not live together as a family in this life, maybe they would be able to do so in the next.

Jackson was understandably horrified, and fretted that she might one day show up at his home or at a public appearance and do something dangerous. Fortunately for Michael, however, the woman was later caught and sent away to a home for the mentally insane. The tight-lipped superstar would later admit that he wrote 'Billie Jean', in which he wails, 'the kid is not my son', about the terrifying ordeal, but refused to give any more details lest it encourage other disturbed fans to emulate the woman at the centre of 'Billie Jean'.

ERIC CLAPTON

Fellow entertainer Eric Clapton was also at the centre of a bizarre paternity hoax, this one perpetrated by a New York chambermaid towards the end of the summer of 1987. Clapton, one of the most talented musicians of the rock'n'roll era, and who had beaten both heroin and booze addictions, was named in the scam by Alina Moreni, a 27-year-old part-time singer and part-time chambermaid.

Moreni, who had a definite bulge in her stomach, broke the news to the world that Clapton was the father of her unborn child, which was due in April 1988. The stunning news sent gossip columnists into a frenzy, as the buxom beauty told all about her secret dalliance with one of the most famous men in the world. She claimed that she was a virgin when she met Clapton by chance at a Manhattan night club, and that the two immediately fell in love. She also made herself out to be a wealthy socialite, an Italian baroness who lived in a plush home on Park Avenue, where many of America's richest families have apartments.

Breathlessly, she told interviewers that 'I knew when I fell in love with Eric Clapton that it was never going to be easy. He has a beautiful heart, but not much brains. He thinks with the most intimate part of his body. But underneath all that he's just a playful, insecure child.

'That's why I have always liked him – and that's one of the things he always liked about me: my honesty.' She further claimed that after their torrid romance, she had fallen pregnant, and that the famed guitarist would come forward any day to proclaim his love for her and their unborn child. 'He makes my heart beat with desire,' she cooed. 'He is just waiting for the day when we can be together forever. He, me and our baby. It will be perfect.'

CELEBRITY GAMES

Clapton, of course, never did make an announcement, but suddenly Moreni was a household name around the world, and she was signed to sing at some of New York's most prestigious clubs, despite her large stomach. Everywhere she went, she was feted as a major celebrity. And wherever she went, she was only too willing to talk to the press about Eric and the 'special magic' that they shared together. Viciously, she also claimed that she was 'only revealing the secret of our love because he is soon to break the news to' Lory Del Santo, his beautiful girlfriend and the mother of his son, Conor. (Conor, who was born in 1986, died tragically four years later when he fell from an open window of a Manhattan skyscraper.)

Although Moreni played the pregnancy to the hilt – her stomach continued to grow – it was soon evident that something was afoot. Her manager, Lynne Robinson, noticed the growing swell in her stomach

---

MORENI CLAIMED SHE WAS A VIRGIN WHEN SHE MET CLAPTON AND THAT THE TWO HAD FALLEN IMMEDIATELY IN LOVE

Below: *A deranged fan claimed Michael Jackson was the father of her baby.*

seemed to move. As she later recalled: 'I have seen pregnant women before, and this seemed most odd. The lump definitely shifted – and when I saw her again it seemed to have moved once again.'

In early May 1988, Moreni announced that she was going away to an unnamed hospital 'to give birth to our darling child'. But her ruse was about to come undone. Investigative reporters in the United States and in Britain soon revealed that she was not Italian royalty, but rather a down-on-her luck maid who had been hired to clean Eric's New York apartment the previous year.

But during her absence to give 'birth', supporters rallied behind her, claiming that while Moreni had lied about being a wealthy baroness, she was still carrying Eric's love child. They said that she had made up the baroness story so that Eric would not be ashamed of her when the

world learned he was a new father. In fact, Moreni wasn't even Italian. Her parents were from Romania.

But despite their efforts to clear her name, the furore would not die down. Robinson said she once tried to pat Moreni's stomach, and 'she winced away as if in pain. She wouldn't let me near her. That was when I was convinced that she was a faker and that the whole thing was some kind of calculated sting against Clapton. I said to her: "You are a very, very sick girl and need help." I am a mother of three children and I know how people behave when they are pregnant. They are proud and overjoyed. They want other people to share in the joy of having a baby. There was no way that this woman was carrying anything but a pillow up her dress. I am convinced Alina has been plotting this for years. And I am certain that she is doing

> 'THE KID'S A LOSER. MAYBE SHE DID HAVE A FLING WITH CLAPTON BUT SHE SURE AS HELL WASN'T CARRYING HIS BABY'

Below: *Guitar legend Eric Clapton was at the centre of one of the most bizarre paternity cases. A woman claimed he was the father of her child – even though she wasn't even pregnant.*

it to get money out of Eric Clapton. It has got to be stopped. She became hysterical, and started screaming and shouting.'

But still Moreni refused to budge from her story. In fact, later that month, on 8 May, she telephoned her good friend Rose Genero to claim she had given birth to a healthy baby girl. She said she was naming the child Rosa Lina Clapton, and that Eric had called her from London to congratulate her. But Rosa, who knew the name of the hospital where her friend had allegedly given birth, checked with authorities at the centre.

'There was no record of her being there or indeed of a baby girl being born that night,' Rosa later said. 'I think I knew then that the real secret was not her fling with a pop star, but the fact that she had embarked on a Walter Mitty exercise that had only one ending. She was bound to be found out sooner or later. The kid's a loser. Maybe she did have a fling with Clapton but she sure as hell wasn't carrying his baby. I saw her after she said she made love to Eric. She was proudly holding up the sheet from the bed, boasting: "This is the sheet I lost my virginity on."'

BITTER TRUTH

By this time, Moreni was in hiding again, but she still maintained the veracity of her tale, adding that Clapton was on his way to America to visit her and the child. But 48 hours later the sobbing woman admitted her scam: 'I did not have his baby.' However, she still claimed that she had indeed been pregnant with the musician's child.

'I had an abortion because I saw the way he was treating me,' she said. 'When I saw his attitude towards me I knew that he had changed. I did have an affair with Eric but when I saw how he was reacting when I was pregnant I had an abortion last November. But I am a woman and I am proud. This is why I pretended for so long that I was carrying his child. It was a very upsetting time all round and now I need lots of therapy for my condition.' Moreni then expressed her remorse, saying she was sorry 'if anyone has been hurt over this, but I had to carry on pretending I was pregnant for my own self-respect'.

Clapton never did comment on the amazing hoax, and to this day it is not known whether he even knew Moreni.

EXPOSED
HYPOCRISY IN HIGH PLACES

MAYFLOWER MADAM
Sydney Biddle Barrows

Sydney Biddle Barrows' girls provided very discreet personal services to some of the highest earners in New York. And when she was finally taken to court, it was the authorities, and not Sydney, who were to end up being embarrassed in public.

New York is a city that caters to all tastes and styles; every whim, every fancy, every facet of life, both high and low. In the glittering penthouses of Park Avenue, the bistros of Greenwich Village, the ornate town houses of the Upper West Side, absolutely everything is available – at a price.

No wonder that in the cash rich 1980s, when money flowed out of Wall Street and the other financial centres of the world, prostitution went upmarket to cash in on the new-rich. In the underbelly of the Big Apple existed the street hookers, the five-and-dime tarts who would turn tricks in cars in remote parking lots or in cheap flophouse motels. But these weren't the girls that were attractive to travelling businessmen with expense accounts from the office and a loving family at home.

High-class hookers were the new money-spinning business – girls who looked like models and behaved like ladies... except in the bedroom. And no-one cashed in on the money-for-high-class-sex racket more than a woman who became known as The Mayflower Madam. Her little black book contained more secrets than a Pentagon computer, more potential damage than an arsenal of H-bombs. To this day, the Mayflower Madam has not revealed the scandals that lay within her impressive client list. The cops put her out of business. And, so far, she is the only one involved in this affair who has suffered.

The Mayflower Madam – alias Sydney Biddle Barrows – catered to the highest of high society. There were several chief executive officers of Wall Street companies. There were Arab princes, judges, a British rocker, a Hollywood film producer, a professional opera singer, a Catholic priest who smoked marijuana, an Orthodox Rabbi, bankers, brokers, deal makers, shakers and movers in the swirling Big Apple of the 1980s. And they were catered to by girls called Paige, whose father was a diplomat, and Margot, whose daddy was a judge. Sydney's skill was in matching high class merchandise to high-class payers – and it was a magic formula that worked every time. These stunning girls, dressed in

Above: *Looking more like a society hostess than a supplier of good-time girls, Sydney Biddle Barrows heads for an appointment with justice.*

Opposite: *A glass of champagne for the Mayflower Madam, the blueblood who went into history as the most famous brothel keeper in America.*

designer silk and *always* wearing stockings beneath (her strict orders) accompanied their 'Johns' to dinners hosted by men like Henry Kissinger, to United Nations balls, to ambassadorial functions and to glittering charity dinners costing £10,000 a head. In Sydney's words: 'I only ever picked the really attractive ones – and in return they got classy, attractive, successful guys. Most single women in Manhattan would have killed to go out with them.'

Sydney Biddle Barrows, the blue-blood so named because her first ancestors sailed on the Mayflower to America hundreds of years before, thought she had hit on the perfect business. 'Everyone was happy,' she said. 'The dates were so pleasant for the girls that often they were late back – having given the client some extra time for free because they were enjoying themselves so much. Often they came back and said: "I can't believe I'm getting paid for this!"'

When she was eventually busted, the question on everybody's lips was: How did this demure, single-strand pearl necklace-wearing schoolmarm get into the sleazy world of prostitution? But Sydney insists there was really nothing difficult – in a moral or business sense – to it at all. 'The American public has been fed a lot of lies. People think the girls were degraded – that simply wasn't true. The girls who worked for me never were, I made sure of it. I kind of drifted into this business, but once I was in it, found out that I enjoyed it very much. And I was good at it.'

THE OLDEST PROFESSION

Boarding schools, debutante balls, society dinners – this was the lot of Sydney Biddle Barrows before she went into the oldest profession in the world. She had completed a course in merchandising and business management at Manhattan's Fashion Institute of Technology and was working in the city in the early 1980s as a buyer for a company that shipped merchandise to clothes and fashion-accessory boutiques all over the world. 'It was quite a good job,' she said, 'but leaving it – well, I had my mind made up for me by the boss. He asked me to off-load some unfashionable handbags because he was on the take. It was a real dilemma. I knew if I didn't distribute the handbags I would be out of a job. But at the same time I was horrified and scared about getting into trouble with the police. So I quit and found myself out of a job. Then next thing I know is I am answering phones for an escort agency for $50 a night, something that was arranged through a friend. It really looked like fun, something lucrative and a real challenge.'

She became fascinated with the whole call-girl game. It struck her as odd that you could get phone sex, kinky sex in Greenwich Village, child pornography in the sleazy parlours that dotted Times Square – but nowhere was there a market for a man and a woman to get together to form a discreet liaison. She went on: 'When you think of all the dangers that street girls faced from weirdos, from disease, from danger, from being busted – when I eventually went into business there

> 'I ONLY EVER PICKED THE REALLY ATTRACTIVE ONES – AND IN RETURN THEY GOT CLASSY, SUCCESSFUL GUYS'

Below: *The Mayflower, the ship that brought Biddle Barrows' ancestors to the New World from the old. Those puritans would surely have turned in their graves at the thought of her chosen profession.*

was more chance of my girls being killed in a cab crash than meeting up with a pervert. I realised that this isn't for everyone, that ethics are in the eye of the beholder. I don't smoke, for example – to me, that's a disgusting habit. I don't gamble. Those are my moral choices. Those are my personal moral choices.

'When we went into business I found out that most of the clients worked as hard as the girls. They had to give the girls a glamorous and fun and exciting experience or they couldn't be clients. Believe it or not, that's true. And it's not true that the girls didn't enjoy it. The majority enjoyed it the majority of the time. They're just ordinary girls, articulate, fun, warm, honest, nice people with goals in life who just needed a little extra money.

'When people ask me about how I got into this business I tell them the story of a girlfriend of mine who works for a big public relations firm. She got a big promotion and called me up excitedly: "Sydney, I'm so excited! I have been offered this fabulous account with Stolichnaya, the Russian vodka." I said: "You're not going to take it, are you? You're not seriously considering it?" She said: "Of course, why wouldn't I?" I said: "You're talking about a commu-

nist product, where the money goes back into a country that is trying to destroy us. How could you possibly do that?" She didn't see it that way at all, but I would never have taken that job in a billion years. I don't care if they had offered me four times as much money as I was making. You see – people have different values.'

BRANCHING OUT

With her conscience assuaged on such difficult moral issues, Sydney and her friend who had first got her into the dial-a-girl business decided to branch out on their own. But they decided it would be strictly classy, A-list people all the way. She placed ads in such magazines as the *Village Voice* – the avant garde newspaper that served the funky Greenwich Village area of the city and which was read by newcomers to town who were looking for work and apartments – and also in *Show Business*, a magazine for those in the entertainment trade, looking for 'high-toned girls'.

Once the girls had been selected the adverts for an 'escort agency' went into such quality newspapers as the *International Herald Tribune* and the *New York Times*. Then she did some market

Above: *Sydney Biddle Barrows moved in the highest circles of Manhattan society – here she chats with her philanthropic cousins. They were totally unaware of how she made her money in the Big Apple.*

'THE CLIENTS... HAD TO GIVE THE GIRLS A GLAMOROUS AND FUN AND EXCITING EXPERIENCE OR THEY COULDN'T BE CLIENTS'

Below: *The bright lights of the big city – Manhattan, with the towers of the Brooklyn Bridge in the foreground. Such wealth meant many clients seeking sex – at a price.*

research of her own – scrutinising the pitfalls, traps and operating procedures of the other bordellos in town. Calling herself Sheila Devin, she traipsed around escort agencies on the pretext of getting a job – but really honing her skills about the game, deciding what she would and wouldn't do when it came to running her own stable of luscious, willing young things. And she was in business – as simple as that.

The girls, whose maximum age was 25, were instructed on how to behave, how to dress, how to deport themselves, how to get past hotel security guards (dress like a young business executive carrying a briefcase – with the case containing the credit-card machine that they would need to take a client's money) and even what lingerie to wear. The girls were instructed to be courteous at all times, demure, coy and charming.

It was entirely up to them what sex acts they got up to – although there was a sliding-scale of fees depending on any particular client's 'preferences'. And she also told them how to check for certain types of sexually transmitted diseases, if they were at all dubious about going to bed with a customer. Sydney said they were housewives, college kids, models, students and aspiring actresses. And they were all spellbound by their new madam's sales-pitch that they were going to be the *crème de la crème* of night ladies about to take Manhattan by storm!

HIGH DIVIDENDS

The operation was run out of an apartment on the Upper West Side of town, the ritziest neighbourhood for what many still say is the lowest profession. Soon the calls were coming thick and fast. Because Sydney operated on a grapevine network – clients telling other potential clients – there was always an element of risk when the agency started, in 1981, that it might take some time to really get going. But in her case, the well-chosen women and 'discretion at all costs' began to pay high dividends.

Soon high rollers, particularly men from the Middle East, began shelling out thousands a night for girls. 'Those guys would order girls like they were pizzas,' she said.

'They'd have several in one sitting and still come back for more.' As well as receiving a percentage for each 'trick' booked by Sydney, there were lavish gifts heaped on them by the grateful men they satisfied – everything from costume jewellery and perfume to expensive watches and gems by Rolex and Cartier.

An interesting sideline to the nocturnal activities of the Mayflower Madam only emerged after her arrest on prostitution charges. For five years she had been seeing a psychoanalyst in an effort to make herself 'like myself better'.

She explained: 'It was nothing to do with the business I was in. My father left us when I was four. He is some guy that everyone says is my father but I just never knew the man. I'm sure that had a lot to do with my being unhappy and having negative images about myself. It's one thing for parents to be divorced, but my father's attitude was that if he wasn't married to my mother anymore then the kids didn't exist either.

'I mean, how do you explain to someone who is four years old that your own father doesn't call for your birthday or Christmas? We were from the only broken home I knew about. I told my therapist all about it but he wasn't bothered about it at all. In fact I was rather proud of what I was

Above: *Dancing in Stringfellows nightclub with William Novak, her biographer.*

Right: *Tom Bird, another eligible bachelor, dances with the celebrated madam after her arrest.*

SHE DENIED THAT SHE WAS SOMEHOW TAKING REVENGE ON MEN BY GETTING GIRLS TO CHARGE THEM FOR SEX

---

doing. I got a lot out of it professionally and personally.' She denied allegations, levelled later, that she was somehow taking revenge against men by getting girls to charge them for sex – a scheme concocted because of her father's departure.

She scoffed at any psycho-babble explanations of her work. 'I simply enjoyed it and was good at booking the best for the girls,' she said. Was she never tempted to go on to the shop floor, as it were, herself? 'Absolutely not,' she said. 'After all, Lee Iaccoca ran Chrysler and he never made a car on the production line!'

The money continued rolling in at an impressive rate of knots for the Mayflower Madam – her girls charged $1,000 (approximately £750) – for sex with clients, and more for 'extras,' which might include kinky sex, or overtime. Quite how much she earned has always been shrouded in mystery, but it's believed that she kept over £100,000 of her immoral earnings, profits after she was arrested.

Sydney was 32 in 1984, and her prostitution business was two years old, when she was finally arrested. Out of the hundreds of

they could not go after me. They made this big publicity splash about me and all the Mayflower connections.'

She was arrested and led away in chains in a night-time bust. The press had been tipped off and they had a field day – never had they seen the proprietor of a whorehouse so demurely dressed in a grey flannel business suit with a petite figure and a ready smile. Instantly she was recognised as something different from the usual madam busted by the city's vice squads. But it was not so much her personal appearance or the number of girls she controlled that interested the press – it was *who* the girls had been with that set tabloid newspapers in the Big Apple clamouring for the secrets of the little black book with all the names. A source in District Attorney Robert Morgenthau's office said: 'It's dynamite. She's got the A-team of commerce, foreign royalty and showbiz in there.' Bids for the names soared into six figures, then over $1,000,000. But Sydney's own code of morals protected – and continues to protect – those 'gentlemen' who sought out her girls. She says: 'I could never, ever reveal who they were. They were men buying a service, that's all, a service that happened to be sex. I couldn't ever betray that trust.

Above and Right: *Sydney was never a shrinking violet – preferring to defend her trade in flesh, and always insisting that her girls enjoyed the line of work they were in.murder.*

streetwalkers, the dozens of bordellos, the innumerable back street cat-houses, hers was the one that was chosen – because of the neighbourhood it was in and due to her irate landlord.

He became concerned at the number of girls coming and going from the premises each night – the girls bringing back their credit card receipts to the 'madam' and picking up fresh instructions of where to go, or merely to be inspected to make sure they matched up to Miss Barrows' high standards of dress and deportment. She says angrily now: 'In order to get the police to move in this the landlord had to exaggerate. He had to make me sound so big that

'I think the prosecutors expected me to throw myself upon their mercy or something but I wouldn't give them that satisfaction. They tried to get me to feel bad about the girls – saying that I had corrupted them. But I told them that just as there can be people who drink socially and not become drunks, so there can be call girls who are call girls with no ill effects. It's a personal, moral decision. I told them: "Why shouldn't sex be for sale if a girl wants to do it?" It's not the oldest profession for nothing and what do these so called experts know anyway? I held my head up high when I was arrested.'

Friends threw defence-fund money-spinning balls, eager to help out with her soaring legal bills which would mount by the day and eventually top out at something over $300,000. She was facing numerous felony counts which could have put her in prison for up to seven years.

A SPLENDID VICTORY

The case rapidly became an embarrassment to the city as massive media interest from around the world made the whole investigation something of a laughing stock. The police were castigated for booking a madam in a city where there are routinely between 15 and 20 murders a night – wouldn't their time be better spent in getting their priorities right, it was argued?

Eventually, nine months later, her case was plea-bargained down to a single count of promoting prostitution – what the defence would later term a 'kiss on the wrist' punishment – and she was fined just $5,000. The deal saved her from prison – and also saved the lucrative book and TV deals which she would have been banned from pursuing had she been behind bars. All in all, it was a splendid victory for her.

Life after scandal has been kind to the Mayflower Madam, but the tag which ensured her continuing success as a scarlet woman is now one she would like to put behind her. Not for any reasons of shame or disgrace – just that she wants to move into writing, or designing or, more recently, lecturing. But there are never any regrets.

She said: 'Would I do it all again? Sure, of course I would. What happened that was so bad? I got busted? So what? Am I dead? Blind? Don't I still have both my arms?

Have I lost any friends? Doesn't my family still love me? Don't I still have a wonderful future ahead of me? I can't find one negative thing to think about it, not one.

'They were heady times. It was like a sorority house. It wasn't some sordid, weird, grimy business. There was an esprit de corps that was just marvellous between me and the girls. One thing I always liked was taking them to wonderful stores in New York, like Saks Fifth Avenue, where I would buy them wonderful outfits. It really uplifted my heart to see them kitted out in glamorous clothes, the kind they only ever

Above: *Two V for victory signs from Sydney after she learns that there is no prison cell awaiting her.*

'WOULD I DO IT ALL AGAIN? SURE, OF COURSE I WOULD. WHAT HAPPENED THAT WAS SO BAD?'

used to dream about. It was like summer camp and college all rolled into one. No, like Edith Piaf, I have no regrets.'

In the years immediately following the scandal Sydney wrote a book, and enjoyed a career as a £2,000 a night speaker, travelling around America giving lectures on business success and tips on etiquette – combined, of course, with the lurid tales of when she was America's most famous madam. 'I guess I will never entirely shake it off,' she said. 'If I died today my headstone, I am sure, would read: "Sydney Biddle Barrows – Mayflower Madam". But I hope that I might also be remembered for other things as well. I have achieved other things in my life, so everything is not all negative, not all just the "Mayflower Madam".'

She rolled her show out to places like Peoria, Illinois, Omaha and Kansas City – true small town America where audiences blushed, giggled and winced at her tales of the high life. One of her most successful stories was telling the audiences what the successful hooker never left home without – make up, a spare pair of knickers, shower cap, pen and paper, cab fare home... and an aspirin in case of a headache while on the job!

TV FAME

In 1987, Candice Bergen, the famed Hollywood actress, played Sydney Biddle Barrows in a sanitised made-for-TV movie about her pimping success. Sydney also went on to write another book, this time an etiquette guide, most of it based in or around the bedroom. But even though she still has her Upper West Side apartment and all America knows – and remains intrigued by – her personality, a long term companionship still seems to evade her. Men don't want to date her, she said. 'I would never have thought the supply would dry up. But it's not worth it for men to get involved with someone so high profiled, I guess.'

Society too – the connections which allowed her to trade on the blueblood Mayflower connection – wants little to do with her. The Mayflower Society, a snooty sect of social climbers in New York, has barred its door to her and she finds that the invitations to show up at the kind of high-class affairs that her high-class girls went to have also evaporated. The Social Register, a kind of who's who of American elite, dropped her and her mother after the scandal broke. And her grandfather, Donald Byers Barrows, said of her shortly after the arrest: 'I have a great many grandchildren, and had them all over to visit several years ago. But Sydney's attitude was very poor then. Always has been. I am not really interested in seeing her after what she has done. I just dismiss her ongoing notoriety as an unpleasant thing in my mind.'

Love her or loathe her, approve of her or damn her, she remains right about one thing – 'Here lies the Mayflower Madam' could well end up as the epitaph on Sydney Biddle Barrows' tombstone.

JEFFREY ARCHER
An Identity Crisis

When a British newspaper printed a story about an alleged encounter between the Conservative Party chairman Jeffrey Archer and a prostitute, he fought back fiercely. The country held its breath as the sordid allegations were dragged through court.

It was quite the most extraordinary scandal to rock the British establishment in many a year.

Jeffrey Archer, boyishly handsome deputy chairman of the Tory party and beloved standard-bearer of the faith in the shires and the counties – who rallied the troops on behalf of his faithful prime minister Margaret Thatcher – had, quite simply, been caught at the centre of a scandal involving a prostitute. Although totally innocent of ever having met the woman in question – let alone having slept with her – Archer did the decent thing by immediately resigning his position.

But his decision to step down in October 1986, and his statement that he had never met vice-girl Monica Coghlan, did not spell the end of the matter. Instead, libelled by a national newspaper that he had indeed known her, his fight to clear his name went to the highest court in the land – and with it unravelled one of the most intriguing stories ever heard in a British court.

At its end Jeffrey Archer, now Lord Archer, was totally vindicated and the *Daily Star* newspaper was poorer to the tune of £500,000 plus costs – the biggest libel damages award in British history. And it had all happened because Jeffrey Archer, in being a thoroughly decent chap, had tried to help a woman pleading on the phone to him, and had become embroiled in a plot that involved a vice girl, a dubious witness to an encounter that never happened, and a Sunday newspaper.

The world awoke to the scandal on Sunday 26 October 1986. On the front page of the scandal sheet *The News of the World*, and on further pages inside, there unravelled an extraordinary story of how an associate of Mr. Archer – a man named Robert Stacpoole – had gone to platform three at Victoria railway station in the heart of London to hand over money to a waiting prostitute.

The prostitute, Monica Coghlan, was taking the money to 'go away' on holiday for a while. Long range cameras supplied the photos of the cash being handed over while inside the pages of the newspaper were curious tape recordings, allegedly made between Monica – calling herself 'Debbie', the name she used when 'working' – and Mr. Archer. The conversations, which will be examined later in the context of the amazing court case which was to follow, apparently had Mr. Archer offering to set up money through an intermediary to pay for her to go on holiday. *The News of the World* did NOT say he had slept with a prostitute, or that he had known her. It did, however, print sections of conversations between Coghlan and him in which she said she was being 'pressured' by a third party to 'spill the beans' on an alleged night of love between her and Archer – something that he vehemently denied.

UNANSWERED QUESTIONS

The world was left with the curious, unanswered question as to why a man at the pinnacle of public life in Britain would arrange for a prostitute to go away on holiday if he had never met her. For Archer, who resigned his job on the day of the scandal, the answer was an easy one. It was clear that someone was trying to implicate him with this woman and that she was in trouble. In order to get her away from the third party he would pay her expenses for a holiday.

His statement said: 'I have never, repeat never, met Monica Coghlan, nor have I ever had any association of any kind with a prostitute.' Yes, he might have been guilty of foolishness. Yes, his marriage would survive. But his career was in tatters and there seemed little left for him to do but to go back to writing his extremely successful novels and plays and retire from public life.

Opposite: Jeffrey Archer, a favourite of Mrs Thatcher's, was caught up in the maelstrom of a wicked plot that ended in his resignation.

Below: Mrs Thatcher, who valued Archer beyond words.

HIS FIGHT TO CLEAR HIS NAME UNRAVELLED ONE OF THE MOST INTRIGUING STORIES EVER HEARD IN A BRITISH COURT

Above: *Mary and Jeffrey Archer sip champagne in the garden of their Cambridge home after their victory.*

Right: *Lloyd Turner , the silent editor of the* **Daily Star***, who refused to go into the witness box to give evidence during the trial.*

CALM AND COLLECTED, MARY SHOWED TRUE COURAGE AS SLUR AFTER UNSUBSTANTIATED SLUR WAS LEVELLED AT HER HUSBAND

But a week later the *Daily Star* newspaper, under the supervision of its editor Mr. Lloyd Turner, printed a page one story under the headline 'Poor Jeffrey!' It was the story of a friend of Monica, talking about how Monica had told her about the encounter with Jeffrey Archer. And that was the *Daily Star*'s fatal error which would land them in court and cost them such massive damages.

The News of the World had been meticulously careful NOT to draw any such link. It provided its readers with tape extracts, photos and a diary of events leading up to the pay-off at Victoria Station. Nowhere was there a mention that he had ever known her for the simple reason that they could never prove such a thing. The *Daily Star* could not prove it either and it would cost them dear.

When the story broke, Jeffrey Archer discussed it with his brilliant and loyal wife Mary at their home near Cambridge and decided that resorting to law was the only course open to them. It would be painful, it would mean putting themselves up to scrutiny in the highest court in the land. But he was innocent – and he was determined to clear his name.

It was not until July the following year that Archer vs the *Daily Star* and Lloyd Turner was finally heard at the Law Courts in the Strand, the venerable high temple of justice in Britain. It was theatre of the highest order, the court case of the year that had queues lining up as dawn broke over

London trying for a few public seats in the pathetically small court, to witness the spectacle. And it would prove to be a shining victory for Archer, a humiliation for Fleet Street and a rout for Monica Coghlan.

Arriving with Archer that first day was wife Mary – the hitherto private woman whose courage in coming forward to stand by her man earned her the respect of the nation. Calm and collected, she showed true courage as slur after unsubstantiated slur was levelled at him.

The only time she ever looked at all pensive or worried was on the first day of proceedings, Monday 6 July 1986, when the tape recordings were played to a hushed court. Afterwards, Archer denied having met Coghlan in Shepherd Market in September. He also denied going with her to a hotel called the Albion where they had sex and denied that he had ever met her. Archer hired the most brilliant libel litigator in Britain, Mr. Robert Alexander, Q.C., who said that Archer had paid her money for two reasons.

One was that he needed time to stop an 'evil man' spreading lies about him, and the second that he genuinely felt sorry for the prostitute who was beginning to become hounded by the press.

These are the sensational extracts from the tape recorded conversations between Coghlan and Archer that were played on

the first day of his libel trial against the *Star*. The first was recorded on 25 September 1986, and the reader should bear in mind that Mr. Archer has no idea that Monica Coghlan is in cahoots with *The News of the World* as she makes the calls.

TAPE A: Extracts from their telephone calls on 25 September 1985.

COGHLAN: I don't know if you remember me, this is Debbie here...

ARCHER: Who?

COGHLAN: Debbie...

ARCHER: No, I'm sorry, have you got the right number?

COGHLAN: Well I met you in Shepherd Market a few weeks ago and we went back to Victoria, there was a gentleman there when we was leaving. He's giving me a lot of hassle. He's telling me who you are and he's been offering me money. I don't want anything to do with this. I just want this guy off my back. I've got a two year old son you know, I live up North...

ARCHER: I'm sorry, you must have the wrong number. Who do you think you are speaking to?

COGHLAN: Archer, Mr. Archer...

ARCHER: Yes you are but...

COGHLAN: Well he told me who you were, right, and he put a proposition to me about money, but I don't, I don't want to know any of this, I just want this guy off my back.

ARCHER: Well, I'm awfully sorry but I don't know who you are and I don't know who he is, but of course if he was saying that I would tell the police straight away.

COGHLAN: You would tell the police...?

ARCHER: Of course I would, because it's not true and I don't even know who you are. I'm awfully sorry, but I've never met you and I don't know who you are.

COGHLAN: He said he recognised you, right?

ARCHER: What's his name?

COGHLAN: It's like a foreign name, Kurtha, or something like that. He said that he thinks you recognised him. He just won't leave me alone. I'm really frightened.

ARCHER: Well I'm awfully sorry, I don't know you. I don't know him. It's a ridiculous suggestion and I suggest you go to the police.

COGHLAN: To the police...?

Above: *Lord Justice Caulfield, the stern but fair judge who presided with equanimity and fairness over the libel trial.*

ARCHER: I certainly would if anyone suggested it was me. I wouldn't hesitate to go to the police.

COGHLAN: All my family, they don't know what I do. They think I come to London on business. I just want this flaming guy off my back. He said he knows you very well.

ARCHER: Well, I'm awfully sorry, it wasn't me on that night, whenever night it was. 'Cos I don't know you at all.

COGHLAN: I met you in Shepherd Market. You approached me. You said you'd rather get your car and pick me up and in the meantime this other guy came up to me and I... I... told him how much it is and everything. I got into his car and then when I came out of the hotel with him, you was parked outside.

ARCHER: Well, I'm sorry, that's not me. It may well have been someone who looked like me. But it certainly wasn't me. And I'm very sorry you've made a bad mistake.

COGHLAN: He's shown me a picture of you and, you know, as far as I'm concerned it was you. Can't you just sort of make a call and get this guy off my bloody back?

ARCHER: Well, if you give me his name

'IT MAY WELL HAVE BEEN SOMEONE WHO LOOKED LIKE ME. BUT IT CERTAINLY WASN'T ME'

Below: *Monica Coghlan, the prostitute at the centre of the scandal, on holiday in Spain with her young son.*

'I AM JUST TRYING TO HELP YOU. GET HIS NAME AND I WILL GET HIM OFF YOUR BACK'

and telephone number I will try.

COGHLAN: I haven't got his number with me, I left it at home. If I can give you his number could you just bloody get him off my back?

ARCHER: I certainly will, 'cos I shall put it in... I, I certainly will...

COGHLAN: Thank you very much. OK, I'll get back to you then.

TAPE B: Extracts from their telephone conversation on 2 October 1986.

COGHLAN: Is that Mr. Archer?

ARCHER: Speaking.

COGHLAN: Yes, this is Debbie here.

ARCHER: Oh yes.

COGHLAN: I spoke to you last week.

ARCHER: Yes you did.

COGHLAN: I've actually been staying with some friends in Manchester because I'm too scared to go to the house because there are reporters there.

ARCHER: If anyone says anything to you, stay very firm and say: 'I made a mistake. Now I have seen the picture more carefully, it wasn't him,' and that will be all right.

COGHLAN: But it was you, I've seen the picture, look...

ARCHER: I assure you, it was not me.

COGHLAN: Well, the picture they showed me was definitely...

ARCHER: Well, I'm sure it looked like me but it wasn't me. And you don't want to...

COGHLAN: Look, I don't want nothing from you or anybody else, right? I just want to be able to go home with my son, you know, and forget this whole bloody thing.

ARCHER: Well how, how can I help you?

COGHLAN: Well, can't you sort of meet me or something, or arrange something to get this guy off my...

ARCHER: You said you were going to tell me his name.

COGHLAN: But I can't get in the bungalow to get the number or his name.

ARCHER: I don't know what to do about it because it's really nothing to do with me and I am just trying to help you. Get his name and I will get him off your back.

COGHLAN: As far as I'm concerned I'm an innocent party, apart from my job.

ARCHER: I believe you totally and I also believe you wouldn't talk to anyone. And I admire you for that too.

COGHLAN: So you want me to ring you

when I get...

ARCHER: If you can get the name of the person who's been bothering you...

COGHLAN: But he has got a picture... and it's outside, the car's parked outside the hotel. I've seen the picture with my own eyes.

ARCHER: Well, I assure you it's not me. But I would just say to you, if you speak, then they will print it.

COGHLAN: Yes.

ARCHER: Whatever you do they will print. Uhm, and if they catch you they will offer you a lot of money.

COGHLAN: Yeah.

ARCHER: You realise that?

COGHLAN: Well, I know, they've offered me money already. I don't want the money.

ARCHER: I think that's very good. I think you're a very honest and good person.

COGHLAN: Well, as soon as I can get the number I'll do what you said anyway.

ARCHER: And in return, I'm afraid that you'll have to say very firmly that you made a mistake. It certainly wasn't me and, uhm, don't tell them you've been in contact or there'll be more trouble.

TAPE C: Extracts from their telephone conversation on 23 October 1986.

COGHLAN: Hello, I spoke to you a couple of weeks ago.

ARCHER: Yes, you did.

COGHLAN: Apparently this Aziz Kurtha... uhm, he's made some kind of statement.

ARCHER: Yup.

COGHLAN: And he's going absolutely crazy to get hold of me.

ARCHER: Well, I think it's quietening down.

COGHLAN: It's quietening down?

ARCHER: I hear from the people who have been in touch with me that it is. But I think that you will have to stay out of sight for a bit more still.

COGHLAN: Well, I was going to go back to work, because, you know, I need the money now.

ARCHER: Yeah, of course.

COGHLAN: I've had my phone changed.

ARCHER: Well done, well done. And I'm sorry you have been through all this inconvenience

COGHLAN: Well, I just, I thought if I went away altogether then nobody could get to me. But according to my neighbours, they're there every day.

ARCHER: I'm surprised. I thought they weren't. But if you say nothing – I admit they will try to trick you – but if you say nothing they can't...

COGHLAN: But I mean, can't you do anything for me?

ARCHER: Yes I will. Now I've got the man's name I can do something. K-U-R-T-H-A. I will do everything in my power to see that he doesn't bother you again. You are being very brave and I admire you.

TAPE D: Extracts from their telephone conversation on 23 October 1986 – the second telephone call.

COGHLAN: Hi, did you...

ARCHER: Yes I did. I got a real grip of it today. Did you go to Tunisia on holiday?

COGHLAN: To Djerba...

ARCHER: Do you, I mean do you have friends out there?

COGHLAN: I just took a holiday.

ARCHER: Well, I am sorry for what you're going through. They may still try to talk to you but I have done two things today which will frighten them.

COGHLAN: What's that?

ARCHER: I can't tell you but I can assure you that it's been done.

COGHLAN: I just want these people off my back.

ARCHER: Well, that's what I worked on today.

COGHLAN: You're telling me that you have done something today, you're not telling me what.

ARCHER: Well, I have spoken to two newspapers as well. Do you want to go abroad again?

COGHLAN: Go abroad again?

ARCHER: Uhm...

COGHLAN: Well, it'd make things easier for me, of course.

ARCHER: What I'm saying is, if a friend of mine helped you...

COGHLAN: A friend of yours...?

ARCHER: ...helped you financially to go abroad again, would that interest you?

COGHLAN: Well, look, I'm not trying to hassle you.

ARCHER: Debbie, I realise that.

COGHLAN: I'm a prostitute, that's how I earn my living. I'm very good at it, right?

ARCHER: Right.

COGHLAN: If by me going on holiday

again you could get things sorted out in between or whatever, yes, I would do that. This has taken me, you know, since this happened with you and I, it's been seven weeks and for them seven weeks I've just, you know, things... I just can't go back home.

ARCHER: I understand what you're saying Debbie, I'm trying to help you.

COGHLAN: You sending me away for two more weeks, what difference is that going to make? I need some guarantees.

ARCHER: I can't guarantee that, hard as I am trying to do my end. Well, I'm telling, I'm saying now if a friend of mine supplied some money for you to go abroad...

COGHLAN: Who is the friend?

ARCHER: Well, it doesn't matter. He'd come and give you the money and that's

Above: *Robert Alexander QC, the brilliant lawyer for Jeffrey Archer. His penetrating questions and unstinting quest for truth won the day.*

'THEY MAY STILL TRY TO TALK TO YOU BUT I HAVE DONE TWO THINGS TODAY WHICH WILL FRIGHTEN THEM'

Above: *Mrs Mary Archer leaves the High Court after another gruelling day of testimony.*

that...

COGHLAN: I think you know what a person I am. I know that you've met me, right, and you know that I looked after you, there was no hassle of anything like that. You know that guy told me that day we was going in, he told me who you was and if I really wanted it out for you I would have looked for different distinguishing marks or whatever, but I didn't...

ARCHER: Debbie, I know...

COGHLAN: As far as I'm concerned, I've sacrificed what I have for you, right. I've not asked you really to do anything for me.

ARCHER: I accept that totally.

COGHLAN: It's Kurtha that really worries me.

ARCHER: Well, I will tell you after today he will be a very frightened man.

COGHLAN: All right, you say you're going to sort it out or you can deal with people.

ARCHER: Where will you be tomorrow?

COGHLAN: The station.

ARCHER: My friend will never find you...

COGHLAN: I just feel scared...

ARCHER: He'll just pass you an envelope and go away.

COGHLAN: You must know somewhere in Victoria?

ARCHER: Some part of Victoria Station... the number, a platform on Victoria Station would be easy.

COGHLAN: A platform...

ARCHER: Platform number three.

COGHLAN: What, on the station or the underground?

ARCHER: No, the station.

COGHLAN: ...the entrance.

ARCHER: At 11 o'clock.

COGHLAN: Well, how will he know me?

ARCHER: You'll be standing there.

COGHLAN: I'll have a green...

ARCHER: ...leather suit?

COGHLAN: Yeah.

ARCHER: Now, how long do you think you can stay abroad?

COGHLAN: Well, if you tell me, you know, you tell me what you want me to do.

ARCHER: Right. Well, if you'll tell me from abroad and tell me you've got there safely, and when you ring on this phone please don't ever speak to anyone else.

After such electrifying recordings, playing in the serene calm of the court, pressmen and observers alike began to get an idea of the plot that had taken place around Archer. Monica Coghlan, a street prostitute, had been in the pay and protection of *The News of the World* and was ringing up Jeffrey Archer in a bid to get him to admit that he had slept with her – something he never did. Instead, in a show of charm and courtesy, he offered to help her away from the man Kurtha who had obviously, it seemed to him, been blabbing all over London his lies that he had seen him with her.

Mr. Alexander told the jury that the whole background of the conversation was one in which Archer was determined to clear his name. But he admitted that it had been a mistake for him to offer the prostitute money. 'That was clearly, looking back on it, a very foolish thing to do,' said Alexander. 'Because it was easy to be misconstrued by those who wished to misconstrue it.' He said Archer had been taking Coghlan at face value and had been trying to stop a very wicked story being circulated about him. He also thought he could help her out of trouble. In referring to the *Star* story – the crux of the case, not *The News of the World* one – he said: 'The story sought to totally destroy Mr. Archer's career. They were saying that Mr. Archer would have sex with a prostitute whose speciality was perversion.'

IN THE WITNESS BOX

On that same first day Mr. Archer stepped into the witness box to give his reasons why he had paid money to someone he had never met. He said: 'It's not unusual for me to receive lots of calls from people who cannot handle their life, or who say that there is something wrong with their life. So it was not a total surprise when something like this happens.

'It did worry me if someone was going around London saying that I had had a relationship with a prostitute. It struck me I should find out who this person was and the only way I could do this was if the person who had phoned me was to tell it to me. She had said that she would find the name and address of the person spreading these stories. I confess to not having taken it wholly seriously and assumed that if she saw the police it would die because there was no truth in it.'

It was assumed that on such an electrifying first day that any testimony to follow would by nature be mundane. But on Friday 10 July Monica Coghlan, perhaps the real star of this show, wearing a light grey suit and white shirt, appeared in court, pointed nervously from the witness stand towards Mr. Archer, and unwaveringly said: 'That's him'.

Asking her about the night of 8 September the previous year, when she is alleged to have had sex with Mr. Archer, the Star's QC Mr. Michael Hill told her to detail what happened. She said she went into a hotel with a client, London solicitor Aziz Kurtha. Afterwards, outside the hotel, she claimed Kurtha saw her talking to a man. 'He told me that it was Jeffrey Archer, the well-known author, and he said something about him being an MP,' said Monica.

A TAWDRY MATTER

Later, she said she and Archer went into room 6A of the Albion Hotel where they had sex at an agreed rate of £50. She told the hushed courtroom: 'I told him if he took some time and I took my time and made it a bit longer it would be another £20. He agreed and gave me another £20 note. Then he got undressed. He commented on how lovely I was.' She said sex took about ten minutes. 'Because it was over so quickly I suggested that he relax for a while and then we could try again,' she said.

Former Cambridge don Mrs. Archer did not look at her nemesis when she took the witness stand, but she did take copious notes of what she had said. At one stage, there was a famous quote from Monica Coghlan that she remembered that her client had had a 'spotty back'. And, later on in the trial, in an equally famous quote, Mrs. Archer defiantly said that her husband's back was quite free from blemish.

In the end, after two weeks of evidence, it emerged that only the story told by Mr. Archer was the genuine one. His claim that he was having dinner at the exclusive Le Caprice restaurant on the night of his alleged sexual encounter was corroborated by his dinner partner and no witnesses provided by the Star, including The News of the World team which had actually set up the bugged telephone calls, could prove that he had slept with Monica Coghlan.

It was easy by the end of the case to see which side the Judge was coming down on. He made a memorable summing up, one in which he referred to the 'fragrance' of Mary Archer, and one clearly designed to leave the jury in no doubts about where he stood in the whole tawdry matter. The jury saw it his way too, and when they filed back into the court a little after two hours, Mr. Michael Hill breathed into the ear of Star editor Mr. Turner and said: 'We've lost'.

It was the size of the loss that stunned the Star – the biggest libel damages in history, plus costs, which boosted the bill to something approaching £800,000. Outside the court Jeffrey Archer emerged with his wife Mary into a sea of supporters and pressmen, clamouring for a shot of the victor.

His reputation had emerged intact in the nastiest brush with chequebook journalism in many a long year. Now Lord Archer, he can look back on the case as one that was worth fighting, no matter the agony at the time.

> IT WAS EASY BY THE END OF THE CASE TO SEE WHICH SIDE THE JUDGE WAS GOING TO COME DOWN ON

Below: *Jeffrey Archer, vindicated. It had been an emotional roller-coaster, but he had won back his good name.*

DUKE OF DRUGS
Jamie Blandford

Many wealthy people have dabbled in drugs at one time or another. But the Marquess of Blandford went a step further and became a fully-fledged junkie. That eventually led to the man who was heir to a vast estate being confined to a prison cell.

The noble Marlborough family has produced many fine Englishmen during its time. The 8th Duke of Marlborough, for example, was a hero of empire during the latter half of the 19th century; and Winston Leonard Spencer Churchill was a cousin of the Marlborough clan who became Britain's saviour in World War Two. The Marlborough family was one of immense wealth and privilege, Englishmen who put duty before self and honour above everything.

In fact, there are two-and-a-half whole pages about the family in Debrett's Peerage, the bible of the aristocracy in Britain. But perhaps there was something in the family motto which betrayed an underlying misery, a clue perhaps to the tormented nature of the tribe which was a bedfellow to its privilege and wealth. 'Faithful Though Unfortunate' is the motto – and nowhere does it apply more accurately than to the Marquess of Blandford, commonly known as the Junkie Earl in tabloid headlines.

Nowhere in British society is there to be found a more striking portrait of a man who truly had everything... only to be brought down to the gutter by that great leveller of modern day society; drugs. Jamie Blandford is a parable for our times.

The medieval philosopher Francis Bacon wrote: 'As for nobility in particular persons, it is a reverend thing to see an ancient castle or building not in decay; or to see a fair timber tree sound and perfect. How

Opposite: *Jamie Blandford has squandered a fortune and his family name through his drug addiction.*

Below: *The splendid family home, Blenheim Palace, symbol of wealth and good breeding.*

Above: *Jamie's father cutting a celebration cake with his bride, Tina Livanos, in 1961.*

Right: *Sir Winston Churchill, whose family is related to the Blandfords.*

HIS WAS AN ARISTOCRATIC BIRTH, CHILDHOOD AND UPBRINGING — EVERYTHING TAILORED FOR HIS UNIQUE AND ENVIABLE POSITION IN LIFE

oldest and most respected families. He was born on 24 November 1955 to the then 29-year-old Marquess of Blandford – the current Duke of Marlborough – and his first wife Susan Hornby, of the W.H. Smith bookshop family. His was an aristocratic birth, childhood and upbringing – everything tailored for his unique – and most would say enviable – position in life.

CHILDHOOD TRAUMA

Blandford's parents divorced when he was five. Jamie, as he was universally known both then and now, seemed to have weathered the break-up badly; he fell back in later life to blaming the childhood trauma of divorce for some of his mammoth problems. But there were those who believe that it affected him more deeply than even he knew. The English gift for a stiff upper lip in the face of adversity can be a double-edged sword – it also stifles emotions and feelings that would best be gotten rid of through expression. Blandford would later recall the time he said goodbye to his father when he went to live with his mother in the Oxfordshire village of Little Coxwell: 'He drove me to prep school and I remember distinctly leaning over the side of the car to kiss him goodbye. But he said: "No, no, no – we don't do that anymore." The conse-

much more to behold an ancient noble family, which hath stood against the waves and weathers of time!' The Marlborough clan undoubtedly wished it were the case with them. But the ravages of 20th century pursuits, particularly that of drug addiction, have brought sorrow to the ramparts of their stately homes.

Charles James Spencer-Churchill, the Marquess of Blandford, is in line to inherit the title of 12th Duke of Marlborough. He also becomes the Earl of Sunderland, Earl of Marlborough, Baron Spencer, Baron Churchill of Sandridge, a prince of the Holy Roman Empire as well as Prince of Mindelheim in Swabia. With those titles comes a fortune in the region of £100,000,000, a seat in the House of Lords, Blenheim Palace, 12,000 acres of land and the historical luggage of one of Britain's

quence of this was fear of rejection, which from then onwards, up to this very present day, scarred my mind. And that's why the relationship as such between us has broken down. I don't blame my father – that's how it was in those days. He, in turn, was brought up by my grandmother with a rod of iron – literally.'

At Harrow, the public school attended by so many of England's statesmen and aristocrats – including his cousin Sir Winston – he was an unremarkable pupil who nonetheless is remembered as cheerful and adept at athletics. His former master Geoffrey Treasure said: 'It's sad what became of him, but it didn't have to be so. There was never any question of him being removed from the school. I think his problem later on was through having a very difficult home life. Certainly the impression I got was that he was rather out on a limb – not at school, though; at school he was gregarious and happy.'

There was a famous occasion that his schoolchum Harry Baden-Powell, a fellow member of the school's cross country running team, well remembers. He said: 'When addressed by a bossy schoolmaster one day he is rumoured to have replied: "You can't tell me what to do – I am going to be the Duke of Marlborough." I think he understood that school rules were pretty irrelevant for someone who is worth more practically than everybody else put together.'

ARISTOCRATIC CONFUSION

At 18, dashingly handsome and eminently suitable for marriage, Jamie Blandford was headlined in the newspapers as the most eligible bachelor in the kingdom. But like Prince Charles, he suffered from a lack of sense of purpose and direction. He knew that the glittering prizes of an aristocratic birth were always there waiting for him and they seemed somehow to weigh him down more than spur him on. He has said in interviews: 'I do feel confused about my destiny and I have always resented having my life mapped out for me. I really don't know what to do with my life...'

As a young man on the threshold of adulthood, he tried many things. He enrolled at the Royal Agricultural College in Cirencester for a brief period, intent on studying farming with a view to devoting his life to becoming a gentleman landowner. He later went to Australia to herd sheep on a cattle ranch in the outback, an experience that he thoroughly enjoyed for a short while. Upon his return he tried to get into the army, but failed, and pulled strings on the old boy network from Harrow to get a job in the City of London as an insurer. The City offers magnificent opportunities to men as well connected as the Marquess, but there was something lacking in the character of Jamie Blandford; something which made him reject the disciplines of hard work and conformity. As if living up to the family motto, he truly became unfortunate.

He plunged into society life in London, a heady world of endless socialising and massive alcohol intake. But soon that wasn't enough for him; he craved satisfaction in something else – and found it in drugs. From marijuana, to cocaine to –

HE PLUNGED INTO SOCIETY LIFE IN LONDON – A HEADY WORLD OF ENDLESS SOCIALISING AND MASSIVE ALCOHOL INTAKE

Below: *The boater-hatted boys of Harrow. Even such a privileged beginning as this was not sufficient to keep Jamie Blandford upon the straight and narrow in life.*

lected driving offences the way some people collect stamps; once he had the dubious distinction of being banned twice in one week. Always there were the sage comments from the bench about a misspent life, the waste of talent and privilege, the comments that he had been dealt every advantage in life, and yet had managed to turn them all into the most appalling burdens. There did, indeed, seem to be no end to his downward spiral.

worst of all – heroin, he tried to seek new experiences. All these drugs were taken along with copious amounts of booze. At the peak of his drug problem in the early 1980s he was spending up to £1,500 a week on drugs – drugs which he hid in toilet cisterns, cocktail cabinets and under stairways as he tried to maintain the facade of a 'casual' user: one who handled drugs in social settings only. In reality, he was a slave to the mind-bending drugs and it is necessary in this chronicle to give just the briefest details of his descent into hell.

Both his father and his late stepsister Christina Onassis, of the hugely wealthy Onassis clan, tried to force him into rehabilitation clinics when they realised that the drugs had completely taken over his life. They paid for him to enter an expensive £1,000 a day Parisian clinic – which he escaped from by breaking out of a window. At another clinic he burned down a potting shed. Back on the streets he was prey to the dealers and the scumbags once more.

PROBATION AND PRISON

It was inevitable that such a degrading lifestyle would run headlong into the path of the law. In 1985, Blandford was fined and put on probation for breaking into a chemist's in his desperate search for drugs. Within six months he was in court again, then sentenced to three months in prison. In 1986, he was released, only to receive another suspended sentence for the possession of cocaine. On top of all this he col-

Above Left and Above: *The world of the junkie is a depraved, dispiriting one, where the 'fix' is the only priority in each waking hour. It has led Jamie Blandford to ruin.*

But in 1987 he met a beautiful, understanding and loving woman named Rebecca Few Brown, a blueblood who counted the Duchess of York among her friends. Rebecca had a stabilising influence upon him. She selflessly devoted herself to trying to help him conquer his appalling addictions. Like Princess Diana, she was a kindergarten teacher before she found herself in the unwelcome spotlight of publicity; unlike Diana, she was the target of newspaper cameramen and reporters because of her relationship with a junkie, not the heir to the throne of England.

She was not on the same social scale as Blandford, but she was acceptably 'society' enough to be known on the circuit in London and the Home Counties. One of her former classmates at the Hampden House School in Great Missenden, Buckinghamshire, was Antonia de Sancha, the sometime actress who would later find infamy from her relationship with the Tory cabinet minister David Mellor.

'Rebecca was pleasant enough,' recalled a friend, 'but she got pushed around a bit. She was a bit pathetic. The school was not the kind to turn out brain surgeons and High Court judges – and in that she did not disappoint. Our school, basically, was filled with its share of rich thickos from broken homes in the shires.'

Ski-mad Becky took to the slopes of the swish European alpine resorts where 'the set' routinely holidayed during the winter season. She went into business with friend Cess Morrison, catering for ski-parties with wholesome food and plenty of fine wines. At one stage she was feeding former world motor racing champion Jackie Stewart at his luxury villa overlooking Lake Geneva in Switzerland where Prince Philip was an occasional visitor.

Her first proper relationship was with Princess Margaret's friend Ben Holland-Martin, and it was he who first brought her to the chalet called The Gay Gnomes, owned by Paddy McNally, the sometime racing entrepreneur who was romantically linked with Fergie for some time before her romance with Prince Andrew.

BACHELOR PARTY

Before meeting Blandford, Rebecca had a fling with McNally as he sought solace over the break-up with Fergie. The relationship was bumpy – he was, after all, old enough to be her father – and while she was looking for something permanent, insiders in the set say he was merely enjoying a fling. When they finally split, bachelor girl Becky met bachelor Blandford at a party during one of his less crazy periods and he became spellbound by her. A friend at the time told noted author and journalist Christopher Wilson: 'Jamie became obsessed with her, like he did with all his women. They got together, broke up, got together, broke up – it was that sort of rela-

tionship. The minute she said she didn't want to know him any more, Jamie decided that's when he wanted to marry her and that's when he popped the question.'

The wedding was in 1990. A healthy, beaming Marquess of Blandford appeared in the newspaper looking nothing like the shell of a few years earlier when his most famous appearances had been behind a mahogany rail in magistrates' courts. The nation rejoiced, too, in his marriage; the British do not like to see a man down forever. But the same cannot be said of his rigid, austere father, who, it is believed, was angry that his son had married beneath him. He was also said to be upset at the choice of best man – none other than Paddy McNally, Rebecca's former lover. McNally gave the newlyweds a top-of-the-line Range Rover car, worth over £35,000. One guest observed drily: 'It was almost a thank

Below: *Jamie Blandford walks in a London street shortly after one of his cocaine suppliers was jailed.*

Above: *Jamie as a cheeky five-year-old pageboy at a 1961 wedding.*

A YEAR AFTER THE MARRIAGE, BLANDFORD AGAIN FOUND HIMSELF BACK BEHIND BARS — FOR DRIVING WHILE BANNED

tence for driving while banned. Six months after that a son, named George, was born to the happy couple and friends once again presumed that the daughter of a chartered surveyor had done what the finest public schools of England and all the wealth and privilege that was his birthright could not: reform a weak character who was incapable of reforming himself.

IN TROUBLE AGAIN

The happy pictures of Blandford and Becky with their newborn son, however, were papering over the cracks in a crumbling facade. Behind her back, Blandford had plunged into the partying piranha pool again. He had also taken London apartments for the purposes of entertaining women and was soon back where he had started. Three years after they had married they separated, and Blandford was once again in trouble. In January 1993 there was the most extraordinary attack on Blandford by Lord Spencer-Churchill, his uncle, who told of how exasperated everyone who was ever close to Jamie had become, including his own father who knew that one day he was obliged to pass on the magnificent estate and lands to him.

He said: 'All I know is that without having James certified mad, my brother cannot stop him inheriting the Dukedom. I don't think James is prepared to listen to anyone. He is acting like a befuddled megalomaniac. He insults people. I think he behaves despicably. I know what traumas my brother is going through. After everything my brother has done – and he has done a remarkable job at Blenheim – it must be an awful worry to him that when James inherits, everything is going to crumble.

'The family is deeply concerned for his health. It would be better for James if he seeks medical help but it seems difficult for him to realise that he needs such help. His father is deeply fond of James, as we all are. We are a very united family. I think my brother feels deeply let down by him and there has been a lot of suffering in the family. We have tried to help him out, my goodness how we have tried.'

At the time of his outburst Becky had taken George to her mother's home in Cottisford, not far from the Blenheim estate, while her estranged husband galli-

you for Jamie for taking Becky off of his hands. It was frankly way over the top. We all looked in the opposite direction.'

But while she had achieved miracles in turning Blandford around from his drugs self-destruction, there was already trouble in the marriage before the honeymoon was over. Rows were witnessed in hotel corridors by guests in San Tropez. On one occasion, Rebecca was seen in tears as a result of her husband's verbal bullying. Upon their return to Britain they moved into The Lince, a beautiful Georgian House on the Blenheim Estate that Blandford is one day destined to inherit. Nearby, an army of workmen toiled around the clock to carry out improvements to the £1,000,000 Wooton Down Farm, the 12-bedroomed Cotswold farmhouse set on 850 acres of prime land that his father was giving to him as a wedding present. A year after the marriage, Blandford was back behind bars, serving 37 days of a three-month jail sen-

Above: *The Marquess of Blandford marries Becky Few Brown in February 1990. The marital bliss was to be short-lived.*

vanted around London, often with numerous pretty young things on his arm. Becky was certainly not missed by Blandford's father – she revealed how he had branded her a 'dirty little scrubber' after appearing scantily clad in the top people's magazine *Tatler*. 'Everything's your fault,' she claimed he said. 'I never want to speak to you again.'

BLANDFORD'S AGONY

Experts believed that it was the thought of responsibilities as a father which plunged Jamie off the deep end once more. As mentioned, he had a bitter childhood, in which he believed he was starved of love and attention. Dr. Sebastian Kraemer, a child psychologist at London's respected Tavistock Clinic, said: 'If you have never been loved, or have been neglected as a child, it creates a considerable obstacle when it comes to your turn to be a parent. Good parenthood is something that we learn from our own parents. Blandford's

agony at not being able to see his child will be no different to anyone else's in the same situation. It is the worst pain any father can experience, but he is quite right to blame his drug and drink dependency on his cool upbringing. Most addicts we see are like big babies – they haven't been able to grow up and accept the responsibilities of adulthood because of something missing in their childhoods. Many come from difficult backgrounds. But it is not good enough for him to just say: "Oh, well, I can behave badly because I had a difficult childhood." It's a reason, but it's not an excuse.'

A court ruling was put on Blandford early in 1993 to stop him from pestering Becky and his baby son. Lord Spencer-Churchill sided with her as friends rallied round to give her solace. He said: 'Becky has behaved like a perfect lady. I think she has conducted herself in the most exemplary, dignified way, bearing in mind the harassment she has been through. The irony is that there are some cases of people who have no money at all but are very

'HE IS QUITE RIGHT TO BLAME HIS DRUG AND DRINK DEPENDENCY ON HIS COOL UPBRINGING'

BLANDFORD WAS EXPOSED AS A 'CRACKHEAD' — SOMEONE WHO GETS HIGH ON THE CHEAPEST FORM OF COCAINE THERE IS

Below: *New Scotland Yard – hardly a fitting place for a noble to end up, but Blandford has become familiar with police stations and policemen throughout his life.*

happy. I think that power corrupts and money corrupts and if you don't know how to use it, and you don't know how to behave with it, this is the way you end up. But luckily the majority of people are more level-headed and more sophisticated when it comes to money and power.'

CRACK REPORTER

To show how far and how hard Blandford had fallen the Sunday newspaper, *The News of the World*, sent a reporter to gate-crash a drugs party where Jamie Blandford extolled the virtues of dealing crack on the street. It was in March 1993, and showed that, far from being on the road to recovery, he was still in the grip of the drug. The party was held at a £300,000 flat of a wealthy female friend in Chelsea – with Blandford cycling to make the rendezvous because of his driving ban. Blandford was exposed as a 'crackhead' – someone who gets high on the cheapest, most dangerous form of cocaine there is. Crack is an import from America, where whole inner city

areas have been laid waste by the drug as it has destroyed families, communities and basic human decencies. Essentially it is cocaine mixed with other ingredients into small white balls – crack rocks. These are heated by the user in a glass pipe or other smoking implement. There is a little smoke which the addict inhales for a massive, instant high. There are numerous reported cases of first-time crack users dying as the jolt from the drug hits their hearts like a kick from a mule. Those who survive become pathetic slaves to the substance – and will sink to any levels in a bid to get more and more of it.

The dossier compiled by *The News of the World* was handed to Scotland Yard, who confirmed they were investigating it. But here is part of the transcript of a taped conversation with Blandford, together with explanations of some of the drug-world terms as written by reporter Chris Blythe.

'He phoned a drug-dealing partner to complain about some undersized crack rocks they had been sold. The drug-crazed conversation, recorded on tape, went as follows: "Is the dude da? Yeah, where are you? We need to sort them things out. They're too small, them things, or we're going to lose customers. You slipped me another one of those yellow bellies." (Impure crack.) He put the phone down and retreated with the girls to a side room. Twenty minutes later they returned to the front room with bulging eyes and dilated pupils after a drug fix. Blandford – in jeans and a brown leather jacket – sat on the sofa and began jabbering intensely. He said: "As from tomorrow I'm getting some weights the size of a calculator. They're smaller than this, yeah, and they weigh to .01." (His reference to electronic scales accurate enough to measure within 0.01 of a gramme.)

'He went on: "So from tomorrow every-thing is going to be absolutely spot. I mean you probably lose out on stuff in the end... But I mean, what you lose out in weight you gain in customers." (The scales are so accurate it will be impossible to short-change junkies – but that will also make them trust you more.) He then spoke to the girls about our reporter and said: "Does he want to talk to me or what?"'

BLYTHE: I could definitely do some (drugs).

BLANDFORD: Well, let me tell you something – the more you buy, the better the deal is. You realise that, you know.

He then began advising our reporter on the tricks of his trade. He claimed £500 would buy an ounce of crack in the shape of a disc, which had been moulded in the bottom of a cut-off Lucozade bottle. The discs are made by heating the cocaine with another substance and adding cold water so the mixture solidifies.

BLANDFORD: For 500 quid you could get a disc. Like the bottom of a Lucozade bottle.
BLYTHE: Five hundred notes?
BLANDFORD: That's an ounce. An ounce of powder washed up. If you can get it for 500, let me know where.
BLYTHE: So you're talking about a grand for that really?
BLANDFORD: Oh yeah, absolutely. You know what you've got to understand, right, is that if you buy 500 quid's worth – you cut it, you should be able to make 500 on top.
(By cutting it he meant either breaking a crack disc into rocks or diluting cocaine by mixing it with another white powder.)

BLYTHE: You reckon?
BLANDFORD: Certainly 250.
BLYTHE: Well, that's reasonable in that case.

In further drug conversations Blandford smoked crack through a biro pen case, introduced the reporter to a drug-dealer who handed over £280 worth of crack-cocaine to him and spoke about how the 'sensible people' smoke 'within their capabilities.' The crack that Blythe purchased was analysed by chemist Jeremy Wooten at a laboratory in South-East London where he declared: 'It is reasonably pure cocaine. We shall pass this to the relevant authorities.'

Scotland Yard acted on Blythe's dossier and the chemical report to stage a series of raids on a housing estate in London where several crack dealers were arrested. Blandford was not arrested and there were no legal complaints either to the newspaper or to the Press Complaints Commission. Blandford remained at large, a rebel without a cause. In May 1993 he was arrested and thrown in jail for failing to pay Becky thousands of pounds in maintenance money. He was released on appeal. His liberty was probably fleeting.

'WITH BULGING EYES AND DILATED PUPILS AFTER A DRUG FIX, BLANDFORD SAT ON THE SOFA AND BEGAN JABBERING INTENSELY'

BLANDFORD SMOKED CRACK THROUGH A BIRO PEN CASE AND INTRODUCED THE REPORTER TO A DRUG DEALER

Below: *It appears to be too much for Jamie Blandford as he leaves yet another court after yet another appearance.*

MONACO MADNESS
The House of Grimaldi

Prince Rainier and Princess Grace of Monaco were universally regarded as royalty's most distinguished couple. But when their three children began looking for independence, the dignity of the House of Grimaldi soon became seriously threatened.

Monte Carlo; the very name conjures up nights of elegance and excess. Fortunes gambled on the casino tables, beautiful women on the sun-kissed beaches, a walk on the elegant corniche before dinner at any one of a hundred elegant and fabulously expensive restaurants. Monte Carlo is the main city of Monaco,

the 12th century principality which, along with Liechtenstein and Andorra, has remained time-locked in a Europe which has seen vast change.

Monaco has a ruling royal family called Grimaldi, which was saved from decay and maybe even extinction by the marriage of its ruler, Prince Rainier, to the glamorous Hollywood actress Grace Kelly in the 1950s. The marriage of the potentate to the

Opposite: *Prince Rainier of Monaco (standing centre) on the 25th anniversary of his reign, with (clockwise from top right) Prince Albert, and Princesses Stephanie, Grace and Caroline.*

Below: *Monaco – home to roulette wheels and yachts.*

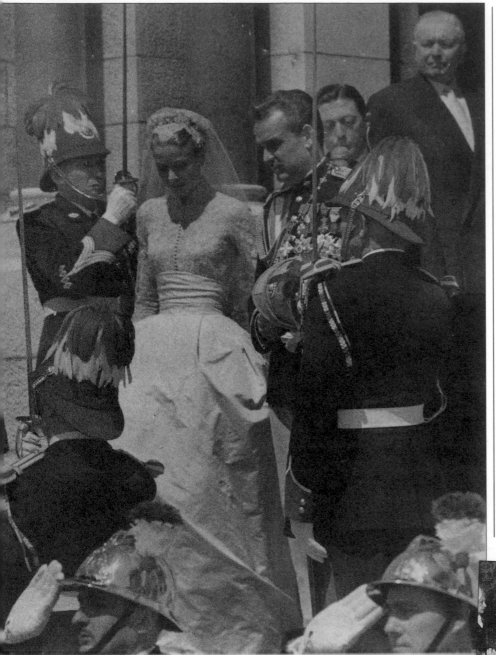

Princess Caroline was the golden child, the first born into the new dynasty, on 23 January 1957. Grace Kelly had arrived just the previous year and the birth of a girl into the old dynasty was celebrated throughout the world. 'All seemed under control,' wrote a newspaper, 'until the children started to grow up.' Princess Caroline had an upbringing where she wanted for nothing. A sheltered education in the palace under the tutelage of governesses was followed by several terms at the dignified St. Mary's girls' school in Ascot. She was a distinguished scholar whose beauty was apparent at a very early age.

THE TOPLESS PRINCESS

But she was guaranteed a place in the scandal hall of fame – and an eternal following of photographers around the world – when she became, at 21, the first princess ever pictured topless. It was at the Monte Carlo Beach Club, haunt of much of Europe's rich, handsome and famous, and it sent her parents into a frenzy of anger. They tried confining her to the palace. They tried cutting off her allowance. But Caroline was a girl whose will was not to be tamed. She had begun, shortly after her topless episode at the beach club, an affair with French playboy Philippe Junot. Her parents strong-

actress turned Monaco into a veritable Disneyworld-sur-mer and the spotlight has rarely been off of this tax-free paradise ever since.

But the royal children spawned in the marriage between Rainier and Princess Grace have frequently failed to give the ruler the kind of solace that he would have liked to have found in his autumn years. The Princesses Caroline and Stephanie, and the heir Prince Albert, have led lives rich in scandal, embarrassment and personal tragedy. It's no wonder that Prince Rainier is often referred to as 'Grey Head' by his citizens – the antics of his children have done little for his nerves or his hair colour!

Above: *The fairy tale begins – the wedding of movie star Grace Kelly to Prince Rainier in 1956. She would give celebrity status to the backwater monarchy of Europe.*

Right: *The couple sit solemnly in the throne room of the palace in Monaco before exchanging vows.*

Left: *Prince Rainier and Grace, flanked by Albert and Caroline, attend a Red Cross Ball in Monaco.*

Below: *Princess Caroline and Philippe Junot in Monaco after their 1978 wedding.*

ly disapproved of the liaison and did their best to keep them apart. Ultimately, because she had reached the age at which she did not need parental consent to strike out on her own, she decided to marry him, with or without their consent.

There was a full state wedding in 1978 to Junot, but the marriage was doomed from the start. Princess Caroline, back from her cruising honeymoon off the French Riviera, found out that her playboy catch had actually made approaches to the more lurid publications of Europe in a bid to sell topless poses of his new bride that he had snapped on honeymoon. In her grief she confided to her mother – a woman who had always been appalled by him.

'Leave him or marry him,' her mother had said when Caroline, before the nuptials, had railed at her domineering mama's dislike of her lover. 'I did it to spite mama,' she later told friends with regard to her decision to marry Junot. 'It was a very bad mistake.' The marriage lasted precisely 831 days, although relations between the two had been destroyed long before the end.

The divorce was a painful affair to Prince Rainier because of the staunch Catholicism in his family. Caroline applied for a Papal annulment to the marriage, which was eventually delivered 12 years later. Junot later complained that it was

Prince Rainier and his wife who had driven the wedge between him and his bride. He said: 'They did everything in their power to avoid our being alone, even for a minute. I was given no opportunity to sort out our problems as any other couple would have been able to do. Caroline was taken away from me, our home in Paris locked up and all communication, even by telephone, was made impossible. All this created a deep well of bitterness inside me which took years to overcome. Perhaps we had life too easy… we saw each other within a sort of cyclone which made our lives go round so quickly, and ultimately made us unhappy.'

THE PREGNANT BRIDE

Caroline, however, found both happiness – and pregnancy – within what some say was an indecently short time after she broke up with Junot. She met and fell in love with the son of an Italian industrialist named Stefano Casiraghi and she was pregnant when she married him in a civil ceremony in 1981. Caroline was deeply hopeful that her children would be recognised by the Catholic church – which was rather doubtful, because the offspring of a divorced woman in the faith are usually deemed illegitimate. 'I put my trust in the church's charity,' said Caroline, although it would be many years before the kind of charity she was seeking would be forthcoming.

Above: *Caroline looks blissfully happy upon her engagement to Italian businessman Stefano Casiraghi.*

Right: *The couple evade the cameramen as they speed off for a romantic holiday before their wedding.*

Opposite: *The beautiful Princess Stephanie on a trip to New York to promote her album.*

Her friends say that the marriage was not a passionate one. Casiraghi had a long affair throughout it, with the daughter of a famous European aristocrat, and he certainly had troubles of another kind: massive debts. He became a construction magnate in Monte Carlo, reclaiming land from the sea for further development in the cramped principality. He also owned yachts and a helicopter service, with 12 craft, each costing £1,500,000. But it was a house built on sand – the empire was owned by banks who loaned him the money and they came calling for their cash. Caroline was forced to put up £1,000,000 worth of her late mother's jewels as collateral to the banks to stop them foreclosing on his businesses.

Shrewdly she contacted an old flame, Roberto Rossellini, son of Ingrid Bergman, who worked on Wall Street and asked him for the best way to salvage what was left of her husband's dwindling empire. But as she became more and more involved in his business enterprises she was seen less and less in Monaco: locals grumbled that her absence cost them 50 per cent in tourist revenues in one year, a massive amount as there is no income tax in Monaco and the tourist cash is all-important. She spent more and more time in France, enrolling her children in schools instead of frittering her time away at balls and the Grand Prix.

SPEEDBOATING TRAGEDY

In 1990, however, the sympathy of the world reached out to Caroline with the loss of Casiraghi in a speedboating accident. Eight years earlier she had earned global condolences for the death of her mother in the car crash; now she was experiencing the full weight of grief once more. She took to wearing black, lost 25lbs – at one time it was suspected she was suffering an eating disorder – and retreated from public life. It was to be almost two years before she found happiness again with Vincent Lindon, a French actor who she met at a discreet dinner party at the chateau home of an aristocratic count.

Lindon, 31, was shy, sensitive and self-effacing – a dramatic difference to the playboy types that Caroline had traditionally found herself falling for. A former lover of the daughter of French prime minister Jacques Chirac, Lindon is the son of a rich

engulf her, particularly after she moved to America where she tried to become an actress and singer. The lovechild which she was to have by her bodyguard in 1992 was said to have aged Prince Rainier by another 20 years overnight. Time will tell whether she will yet mature into a dignified, graceful beauty like her elder sister.

Stephanie was in the car that day her mother ran off the road and many say the deep scars have never totally healed. Those looking for a reason to explain her wayward behaviour have been fond of quoting that as a possible explanation for some of her more extravagant mistakes. Whatever the reason, Stephanie still seems intent on going her own way, no matter what her father or the world may think of her. The most widely photographed young woman in the world next to Princess Diana, she still commands centre stage wherever she might be.

As a child there was intense rivalry between Caroline and Stephanie. Certainly Caroline was blessed with the more classic looks of her mother while Stephanie's square jaw and masculine shoulders marked her out as a tomboy during her teens.

industrialist who may yet end up taking Caroline down the aisle a third time. It could also be a church wedding again, as the Vatican granted her an annulment for the marriage to Junot, decreeing that the marriage never existed. But Lindon has been told by Prince Rainier that he will inherit no titles and have little access to her children should the marriage end in divorce. It is yet to be seen whether those are conditions he wishes to abide by.

SEXY STEPHANIE

If Princess Caroline was a headache to her father, then Stephanie was a living nightmare. Beautiful, sensuous, she was a child of her age who cared little for the pomp and circumstance of her regal birth. With an allowance topping out at over £30,000 a month, the fleshpots of the world were hers to enjoy. Scandal after scandal seemed to

Insiders say Caroline teased her constantly, leading the younger princess to become ever more impish and impudent in her behaviour. Princess Grace once remarked of her: 'I gave up punishing her when she was only seven. I could have hit her like a gong and it wouldn't have done her any good! She got very bossy and exhausted a long line of nannies in her time.'

Unlike university-educated Caroline, Stephanie barely made it through a strict Roman Catholic high school. She was almost expelled once for putting frogs underneath the wimples of the nuns who taught her! But it was when she reached 18 and the boyish looks had given way to a taut, shapely sexiness that made her a top fashion model, that the trouble really began.

REBEL BELLE

Soon newspapers all over the world were splashed with photos of Stephanie exasperating society or the authorities wherever she happened to be. She was topless on beaches where it wasn't allowed; she was in the arms of men that her father deemed to be beneath her; she was seen lurching from all-night discotheques, the accumulated effects of too much champagne and too little sleep showing clearly upon her face.

That she was a very independent woman became clear to her father after she moved to America semi-permanently in 1988. A paparazzi photographer snapped her at a chemist's in Hollywood as she bought dozens of contraceptives!

There was a furious missive that followed from her father, threatening to cut her allowance, but Stephanie ignored it. She had recently broken up with Anthony Delon, son of the heartthrob French film actor Alain Delon, lived briefly with a playboy called Mario Olivier – who had a criminal record for sexual battery – and had taken up with Ron Bloom, a Jewish record producer who was working furiously to make her a star.

The man's religion was as much a bugbear to the Prince back home in Monaco as anything else. The House of Rainier is a strictly Catholic dynasty with rigid rules about the offspring of the principality's partners. Rainier is certainly not anti-semitic but he was adamant that she should settle down with a European blueblood.

A PAPARAZZI PHOTOGRAPHER SNAPPED HER IN HOLLYWOOD AS SHE BOUGHT DOZENS OF CONTRACEPTIVES!

Opposite Top: *Happier, more innocent days. Caroline (left) and Stephanie having fun during a 1977 skiing holiday in Switzerland.*

Opposite Bottom: *Stephanie in Los Angeles, where she increasingly spent more time during the 1980s.*

Below: *A guard of honour at Stefano Casiraghi's funeral after his death in a powerboating accident.*

Above: *Comforted by her father, Caroline pays her respects to her husband at his funeral.*

STEPHANIE GAVE LEFUR
£40,000 WORTH OF
PERSONAL GIFTS AND
SPENT £5,000 ON HIM AT
FLASHY RESTAURANTS ALL
OVER EUROPE

But there was to be no permanent romance with Bloom. From him Stephanie moved on to movie star Rob Lowe – whose videotaped sex romps with an under-age schoolgirl in a hotel room in Atlanta sent the Prince into further paroxysms of anger!

In 1990, however, Stephanie took up with a man with a very dubious past – something far more sinister than someone who took sexy videos of himself performing in the bedroom. Jean-Yves Lefur was a smooth-talking French businessman who swept her off her feet after they met at a Parisian ball. Here was someone that the ultra-conservative Prince Rainier definitely approved of.

But Lefur, 27 at the time, had a secret past. In 1985 he was prisoner no. 2567843 at Fleury-Merogis prison outside of Paris where he was doing time for business fraud. Far from being a blueblood, he was the son of a man who lived in a council house who earned a living fitting out butcher shops in the capital.

It was Prince Rainier who eventually came to the rescue of Stephanie as he saw her frittering away a fortune on him. She paid the £2,500 a month on a Paris apartment they shared together. She paid for a £35,000 engagement party in Paris at the height of their love affair. She gave him £40,000 worth of personal gifts and spent £5,000 on him at flashy restaurants all over Europe.

DETECTIVE WORK PAYS OFF

Prince Rainier decided to get private detectives to run a background check on the man leeching off her daughter – and when confronted with the evidence that she had been duped she kissed him and said: 'Thank you, papa. I loved him so much I would have married him. Now I never want to hear his name mentioned again.'

After she broke up with him Stephanie plunged back into the world of singing, trying to revive a career that had never gone anywhere. But in 1992 she found herself booed off stage in Belgium by concert goers who winced at her voice. A planned South American tour was cancelled because of pathetic ticket sales. And her album *Stephanie* performed so miserably in France her record company refused to

going bad when his daughter was snapped in a sensational series of photographs, naked around a pool, cavorting with a man named Daniel Ducruet, the man hired to be her bodyguard.

Ducruet, 33, was a former Monaco policeman that Prince Rainier dubbed 'street trash' after he learned that he was doing more than merely protecting his daughter. And he hit the royal rafters when the double blow landed – one that his daughter was pregnant by him; the second that he had dumped his own girlfriend Martine Malbouvier, who had a four month old son by him, to join Stephanie's million-dollar lifestyle.

Left: *Grace the beautiful – her daughters inherited her amazing looks.*

Below: *As she is remembered by the world, a study in glamour and elegance before her untimely death.*

allow it to be released in England. 'I am not surprised that this album hasn't sold,' said Pierre Louis Berlatier, a Sony Music official in charge of promoting Stephanie's album sales in France. 'She is very nice but it would be a good idea for her to try acting instead.'

Stephanie hoped to become the next Madonna. One of her albums, *Hurricane*, had sold more than five million copies in France five years previously. But record moguls didn't have the heart to tell her that it was so popular because it was a curiosity item – bought because of who she was, not what she could do. Jerry Greenberg, a Sony Music spokesman in Los Angeles admitted that Stephanie was a total flop in America, saying: 'It just didn't happen. It went totally unnoticed.'

Stephanie turned once again to romance in a bid to cure the wounds of failure – but admitted that in affairs of the heart she had often been less than successful. In a rare moment of public candour she said: 'I guess I have been unlucky in love. Even if I have given my all, I haven't always gotten my share back. But I am not the first young woman to have had that experience.'

Prince Rainier hoped that the next one she fell for would be Mr. Right. In his eyes, however, he turned out to be the worst of the lot! Prince Rainier knew things were

'I hate them both,' fumed Martine, whose tragic story of betrayal made newspaper headlines around the world. 'They have ruined my life. It hurts and it hurts bad. When my baby cries I'm the only one who puts him to bed. There's no-one else to take care of him. I am just a working girl and Stephanie is rich and powerful. I only make £140 per week and it's rough to pay a babysitter on that salary but I have no choice.'

Prince Rainier is alleged to have raged to a friend: 'How could Stephanie do this to me? I have forgiven her for much of her wild behaviour, but this is too much. That baby will be no grandchild of mine. That man will never be part of this family!'

Stephanie's son was born in November 1992 amid much acrimony in the royal household. Prince Rainier immediately cut off her allowance, there was little contact between him and his daughter, and he refused to see the child. But he remains devoted to his daughter. And the depth of love between them was demonstrated by an extraordinary police operation just weeks after the child was born when Stephanie inadvertently found herself at the top of a Mafia death list.

A COCAINE DEAL

For years she had run with a crowd that bought and used massive amounts of drugs – cocaine being the favourite – which fuelled the long nights of partying and the sun-soaked yachting holidays. The police came to Stephanie and made a deal with her; she would supply information about a drugs lord in return for immunity from prosecution. Prince Rainier threw his hands up in resignation and urged his daughter to co-operate. She did – but her confessional sessions with the forces of law and order plunged her into danger.

Labri Dahmane, the ruthless cocaine baron who had initially identified Stephanie and her pals as being among his clients, was himself linked to the cocaine cartels of Colombia and Sicily's mafia. A police source leaked the Princess's name to the press and the mafia godfathers were furious. Stephanie had spilled the beans on one Giovanni Felice, a ruthless drug runner who for years had supplied the rich and powerful – including her – with their potions and powders.

Above: *Prince Rainier in London with Albert in 1968 after visiting the Post Office Tower together.*

Opposite Top: *Lady Helen Windsor, the British royal who briefly captured Albert's wandering heart.*

Opposite Bottom: *Albert and his father wave to the Monaco crowds. Caroline is next to Albert, standing behind her three children Andfrea, Pierre and Charlotte.*

> STEPHANIE RECEIVED SEVERAL THREATENING PHONE CALLS, ONE OF WHICH PROMISED HER THAT HER SON WAS TARGETED

Once the mafia knew that it was Stephanie that had informed, she became the target for assassination. Prince Rainier moved swiftly to take her and her child back under his wing. Her luxury penthouse apartment in Monaco was transformed into a fortress with gun-toting bodyguards watching over her around the clock. Six more guards were posted at Monaco's Princess Grace Hospital where she was receiving regular check-ups after the birth of her son. And a special armoured limousine was provided for her whenever she left the refuge of her apartment.

In all, 12 drug dealers were fingered on Stephanie's evidence. Nathalie Nottet, a French police spokeswoman, said: 'It is true that a certain young princess was involved in the operation and all the arrested individuals have been co-operating with the police.' Stephanie received several threatening phone calls, one of which promised her that her son was targeted, but so far both have remained healthy. But Princess Stephanie remains a constant worry to Prince Rainier – he wonders, as does the world, when the next scandal may surface to strike him.

THE HEIR AND SUCCESSOR

Prince Albert, as the male in the line, is considered to be the heir and successor to the House of Grimaldi, but his behaviour gives little solace to his father. Empty headed, he has lived his life as if it was one long champagne-soaked party. Always on his arm there have been bevies of beauties, ranging from Brooke Shields of Hollywood fame to Lady Helen Windsor to Princess Astrid of Belgium and countless minor royals in Europe. His nights were spent in clubs and casinos, his days soaking up the sun at poolsides and aboard million pound yachts floating lazily along the Côte d'Azur. The only thing he seemed to excel at was sports and at one time he was the captain of the Monaco bob sled team at the winter Olympics in 1991. His team came in 43rd and 23rd in two separate events.

Prince Rainier could tolerate his son's 'wild oats' spree, as long as it didn't bring disgrace upon the family name – but that is exactly what happened in November 1986 when Albert fell head over heels in love with American porn star Teri Weigel. Weigel, 29, has appeared in some of Hollywood's most shocking triple-X rated movies and met the debonair prince at a Monte Carlo party attended by Princess

Caroline. 'He lifted up my skirt and exposed me to Caroline,' said Weigel in a kiss-and-tell with an American magazine some years later.

'She was very shocked. Later he took me back to the apartment that he keeps solely for entertaining women and we made love. It was a great experience.' A livid Prince Rainier threatened to bring in legislation that would make Caroline and not Albert heir to the throne of Monaco, but Albert managed to convince his father that the affair was only fleeting.

Albert has been thoroughly tested by the antics of his three children during the past decade and a half. Those trials, added to the pain that was obvious to a watching world at Grace's funeral, have ensured that he has had widespread sympathy from those who have followed the goings-on at the House of Rainier during that time. Albert can only hope that, as his children reach maturity their behaviour begins to reflect their position and status as members of one of Europe's most glamorous royal families.

THE WINDSORS
Britain's Troubled Royals

A series of revelations concerning the excesses of the British royal family's private lives sickened the recession-hit British public in the early 1990s. After a century of living it up at the public's expense, the Windsors appeared to be living on borrowed time.

Her Majesty the Queen summed up 1992 in a Latin phrase; quite simply, it was her '*annus horribilis*', the year in which scandal seemed to dog the House of Windsor at every turn, culminating in the decision of the Prince and Princess of Wales to part, plunging the very future of the monarchy into doubt. But scandal is no stranger to royal households. It has been a bedfellow of the bluebloods of the British realm for as long as they have ruled. The House of Windsor certainly seems to have had more than its fair share of such torment, however, as the following delicious, decadent and debauched romps of the royals will show only too clearly!

It was the age of beauty and decadence, of languid summers and holidays by the sea. It was the *belle epoque* in France and the last fling of the old order in Britain before the conflagration of World War One would sweep away everything that was accepted as custom and practice. For the Prince of Wales it was the age of love and devilment – both fulfilled in his passions for a woman who became known as 'The Jersey Lily'.

Bertie, as he was known to his friends, was the jocular, life-loving hedonist who would later become King. His was an ordered world of game shoots and naval reviews, state banquets and informal dinner soirees amid London society. And a world where one took a wife for duty – and a mistress for pleasure. The great country houses of England have long echoed to the foot-steps of the admiral off for an assignation with the cleric's wife; the general off to meet the diplomat's betrothed. So it was for the aristocracy and royalty. The only rule of the game was that everything was known – but nothing was said.

BERTIE THE BONKER

Possessed of an enormous sexual appetite which the brothels of Europe could do little to satisfy, Bertie took to bedding the wives and mistresses of friends – and later used to regale the cuckolded husbands and lovers with tales of the pleasure he took! He lost his virginity when he was 19 to actress Nellie Clifton, while he was stationed at Curragh Military Camp outside Dublin and never looked back. Queen Victoria was most definitely not amused by her son's

Above: *Edward the Caresser, Prince of Wales, dallied with one of the most brazen women of his day.*

Opposite: *The happy family of the House of Windsor upon the marriage of Prince Charles to Lady Diana Spencer in 1981.*

LILLIE LANGTRY'S RELATIONSHIP WITH BERTIE SHATTERED THE CLAY FEET OF THE BRITISH MONARCHICAL FIGURES FOREVER

Above: *Queen Victoria at her most stern. She ruled an empire upon which the sun never set – and spawned a bloodline with roving eyes and unfaithful hearts.*

VICTORIA LOVED HER SON, BUT REMAINED CONVINCED THAT HIS SHENANIGANS HAD BROUGHT ABOUT THE DEATH OF HER BELOVED ALBERT

continuous courting of scandal, but there was very little she could do to contain him. She loved her son, but remained convinced throughout her later years that his shenanigans had brought about the death of her beloved Albert, who died in 1861. 'That boy,' she wrote. 'Much as I pity I never can, or shall, look at him without a shudder.'

PRINCE OF SCANDAL

Victoria nurtured the idea that he might change his scandalous ways with his marriage to Princess Alexandra of the royal house of Denmark in 1863, but she was to be proved sadly wrong. Although Alexandra was reared in the finest tradition of European royalty, groomed for the high office she would someday command, and was pretty, witty, intelligent and charming,

it would never be enough to satisfy the roving eye of Bertie. Soon, after a blissful honeymoon, he had slipped back to his bachelor ways – ways which included gallivanting across Europe to places like Monte Carlo and Biarritz, and bringing back an interesting selection of society friends to his London home, Marlborough House, for dinner parties, all-night card games and general debauchery.

The first taste of the scandal that was to come occurred when he was hauled into court as the witness to a gambling debt. The second was when he was named in a divorce case by Lady Harriet Mordaunt, who insisted that he was one of her many lovers. The establishment of the British monarchy rallied around Bertie, as did his family, and the case was dismissed in the end because of the unstable nature of Lady Mordaunt's mind. But it rocked Bertie and many of his fellows in society who believed he was heading for much stormier seas. The tempest occurred in the shape of Lillie Langtry, an actress and celebrated beauty of her age whose relationship with the Prince of Wales forever shattered the clay feet of the idols who were the British monarchical figures.

Lillie was born Emilie Charlotte le Breton in Jersey in 1853 to a highly sexed church official known among parishioners as the 'Dirty Dean'. It was rumoured that his dalliances had been so numerous on the island he had to break up his daughter's first puppy love affair when she was 17 – because the boy in question was a bastard who he had fathered in one of his numerous illicit dalliances.

A VOLUPTUOUS TEMPTRESS

Jersey, her father knew, would always be a place too small to contain such a beauty and firebrand as his daughter. She was voluptuous and desirable from the age of 15 onwards, and she knew it; revelling in the attentions of the local lads before she always broke their hearts. She knew that her destiny lay in society and after a trip to London – where she was particularly captivated by a trip to the theatre – her father knew that there would be no holding her.

Luckily, the escape route came in a fashion that even she thought would never happen. She snared the affections, in 1874, of

Edward Langtry, who was the witless heir to an Irish shipping fortune, when he docked his private yacht on the island in the search of hedonistic pleasure. It came his way in the shape of Lillie, who won him over with her beauty.

'To become the mistress of the yacht, I married the owner,' she would later say with wicked delight, and thus earned her passport, at the age of 21, out of Jersey. Soon she was the toast of London society, the must-have invitation for all the correct balls and dinner parties. The Countess of Warwick, who was also to enjoy Bertie's bed during his ladykilling period, remarked after meeting her at one such function: 'We were magnetised by her unique personality. How can words convey the vitality, the glow, the amazing charm that made this fascinating woman the centre of any group that she entered?'

Such vitality and glow would soon come to warm the cockles – and much else besides – of the heart of the Prince of Wales. Lillie had met the renowned portrait painter George Francis Miles at a London party. He asked her to pose for him. Soon the delicious portrait he painted was

Above: *Lillie Langtry, the actress who captured the heart of a future king.*

Left: *A stern-faced Edward VII and Alexandra at Sandringham in 1864.*

'TO BECOME THE MISTRESS OF THE YACHT, I MARRIED THE OWNER,' LILY SAID WITH WICKED DELIGHT

Above: *Sarah Bernhardt, another actress from the days of the Belle Epoque, who captured the heart of Bertie.*

WITHIN THREE WEEKS IT WAS PILLOW TALK AS THE FATHER-OF-SIX FELL HOPELESSLY IN LOVE WITH HER

built her a house in Bournemouth which was used for country trysts, hired an apartment in Paris for continental trysts and used the lodgings of a friend in London for capital trysts. Abroad, in places like the famous Maxim's restaurant in Paris, he brazenly flirted with Lillie, once even going as far as a full-mouthed kiss in front of all the other diners. Such actions could not escape the attentions of the newspaper writers abroad, but in Britain the press played a game of self-censorship which effectively gave sanction to his cavortings.

Such infidelity on a grand scale was more than the wretched Edward Langtry could bear. After he learned that Bertie had brazenly introduced his mistress to the Queen and Princess Alexandra he plunged into a vortex of alcohol abuse from which there was neither redemption nor escape. He died penniless, cadging drinks from anyone who wanted to hear the stories of how he had lost his beautiful wife to the next King of England.

THE COMMON TOUCH

Like the modern-day Princess of Wales, the Jersey Lillie was becoming very popular with the ordinary people. She was cheered and waved at in public, and her dresses were instantly copied. If she wore a dress to Ascot or Sadler's Wells one week, it was guaranteed to have been copied for the fancy West End stores by the following week. Edward had achieved one small victory over hypocrisy in that he flaunted his mistress. But the power of Victorian morality repressed any public 'crowing' over such a dubious triumph and his wish for her to be fully recognised by the royal family as his 'official' mistress for all public functions was never granted.

It was only natural for a man like Bertie that his roving eye would take him elsewhere. He passed on Lillie to Prince Louis of Battenberg, father to Earl Mountbatten, while he took his pleasure with the French actress Sarah Bernhardt. The affair with Lillie had lasted almost four years and there was no acrimony on either side when it ended in 1880 when she became pregnant and was forced to go to France to have his illegitimate child in secret. Upon her return she was no longer the society dame she had once been. Lillie yearned for the public

appearing on greetings cards which sold all over London. Prince Edward saw one of these cards and, by royal command, ordered it to be arranged that he too should get to meet the lovely lady about whom all London was talking.

In May 1877, a dinner party thrown by a bachelor friend of the Prince had Lillie Langtry – and her somewhat gormless husband – in attendance. From the moment he clapped eyes on her, Bertie schemed to have her. Lillie, too, was now skilled in the art of secret lovemaking, having had several 'menfriends' since persuading her husband to bring her to London. At the dinner party it was small talk between Bertie and Lillie. Within three weeks it was pillow talk as the father-of-six fell hopelessly in love with her.

Bertie seemed to go out of his way to flaunt his new mistress, forever testing the boundaries by which his life as prospective monarch of the realm was governed. He

limelight that she had once enjoyed so much and found it in the theatre.

She called upon Bertie to pull some strings with the West End crowd and was rewarded with a part in a play called *She Stoops To Conquer*. The Prince of Wales and many other distinguished members of society were there to cheer her on at opening night – even though reviewers in the newspapers were not so kind the following day. One said: 'As a novice, she should first learn the art of acting.' Lillie didn't care about the negative press and set about touring Britain with a repertory company she formed before sailing to America where she captivated the people. In 1892 she visited the town of Vinegaroon in Texas where Judge Roy Bean was so smitten by her he ended up changing the town's statute to permanently name it Langtry!

Lillie returned to Britain and married baronet Hugo de Bathe in 1897, moving with him to France where she spent the best part of the next two decades. She died in 1929 and was buried in St. Saviour's churchyard in Jersey, the island where she was born and from which she had longed only to escape. She had been to the funeral 19 years earlier of a man the public used to nickname Edward the Caresser. History knows him better as King Edward.

Above: *Lillie Langtry, the 'Jersey Lily', who inveigled her way into London society.*

Left: *The boudoir where Lillie's trysts with Edward took place.*

THE PUBLIC USED TO NICKNAME HIM EDWARD THE CARESSER. HISTORY KNOWS HIM BETTER AS KING EDWARD

EDWARD AND MRS SIMPSON

While King Edward VII's fling with Lillie Langtry could be dismissed by some as mere philanderings which placed no strain upon the fabric of monarchy or British life, the future King Edward VIII's swooning love affair with an American divorcee called Wallis Simpson did exactly the opposite. His infatuation with this woman would not only cost him his crown – it would drive the nation to the brink of its gravest constitutional crisis in centuries.

At a time when the empire and the commonwealth were needed most at the side of the Mother Country – when the storm clouds of war were gathering over Europe – this ineffectual, weak man's love was stronger for him, and more necessary to him, than any instinct to obey his call of duty. Edward was a weak man governed by a strong woman – a woman who, in the end, did not get her wish to be Queen.

ABANDONING THE THRONE

Before it broke upon the British public and the world in a storm-tide of publicity, Edward had been nurturing the secret of his plans for months. In his heart he had already chosen to abandon his throne for the woman he loved – now it was a matter of choosing the right moment to do it and under what circumstances. A court Press far more restrained than the tabloid gossip-mongers of today, and a code of silence among the echelons of the aristocracy, worked in his favour to keep the affair silent. But it could not last forever.

Edward VIII was King of England for 326 days before he abdicated for the woman he loved. The love affair had gone on for three years – an amazing length of time to keep a secret from a world that devoured news about the greatest surviving monarchy with alacrity. He had met Wallis Simpson in 1931, a 34-year-old American divorcee who people regarded as witty, if a little plain, and charming, but endowed with a tart tongue when she chose to use it.

She had had an upbringing as far removed from the House of Windsor as it would be possible to get; her father was a businessman from Maryland who had died when she was five and she had been raised in Baltimore by her mother. As a young

EDWARD VIII WAS KING OF ENGLAND FOR 326 DAYS BEFORE HE ABDICATED FOR THE WOMAN HE LOVED

Above: *The Duke and Duchess of Windsor. She could never be queen, so he gave up his throne.*

lady she was always stricken by the sight of men in uniform – and in 1916 married a naval pilot, admitting to friends that she found the sight of his dress uniform and medals 'irresistible!' She was also drawn to a particular kind of lifestyle – one of parties, champagne, ballgowns and dances – like a moth to a flame, even though she had experienced none of it while growing up. She was, in fact, a social climber of the highest order.

Her marriage to Earl Winfield Spencer was short lived. The salary of a naval pilot was hardly enough to keep her in the manner to which she wanted to become accustomed and they parted in 1922. Her second marriage followed in 1928 to an Anglo-American businessman named Ernest Simpson who headed the London office of his wealthy family's shipping company.

For Wallis, the combination was thrilling – wealth and London, the society capital, rolled into one.

In 1929, she arrived to settle in the capital permanently, leaving behind forever the low social order of her formative years. In London she became something of a hit on the social circuit, recognised as a competent and amusing hostess who was never anything but charming to her guests.

She moved among lords and ladies, marquesses and duchesses – and she did it with a style which suggested she was a natural! But while she soared up the social barometer, her own marriage to the staid workaholic Ernest was headed for poor weather. Rows over his dullness and her champagne-soaked extravagances drove a wedge between them.

In December 1930, a dinner party that was to have extraordinary consequences for all concerned was hosted by Wallis Simpson at her splendid London home. The guests were Benjamin Thaw, new first secretary of the American embassy in London, his wife Consuelo and her sister Thelma, Viscountess of Furness. Lady Furness was described as a vampish figure who fancied herself as a cross between a Hollywood actress and a music hall queen, a woman of ravishing beauty and a stunning secret. For she was the current mistress of the Prince of Wales, the future King of England. Eventually a friendship blossomed between the three women and Wallis was soon privy to the secret affair being conducted by Thelma.

THE PRIZE CATCH

Eventually the Simpsons dined with the Prince and Wallis was spellbound. Because she knew of his intimacies, his likes and dislikes, his manner and his substance, she was able to perform as the most perfect guest. But in her heart she had started scheming to take this prize catch away from Thelma. Landing the Prince would take her out of the mainstream of high society into the stratosphere – and that is exactly what she planned to do.

Soon she and her husband were regular visitors to his country retreat and he reciprocated, increasingly without Thelma, at the Simpsons' flat off of Oxford Street in London. In January 1934, with Thelma still

unaware of the predatory ambitions of her new 'friend' she said to Wallis: 'I am off to the United States on a trip. Please will you look after the Prince to make sure he isn't lonely?' She looked after him all right – so much so that by the time Thelma returned in the spring, they were lovers.

Edward was a weak man, someone who looked for a maternal, strong streak in a woman – and he found it with Wallis Simpson. She doted on him because he was the entree to a world she had only ever dreamed about. But he genuinely needed her, needed her love and attention and strength the way a child needs its mother. It would forever remain a lopsided relationship, never a true partnership in the sense that most healthy relationships should be.

Below: *Edward's marriage to Simpson, a divorced American, shook the British establishment to the core.*

It was nothing new – indeed, seen as nothing wrong – for a member of the royal family like Edward to have affairs. It was the maintenance of secrecy which was all important. A small clique of his friends rapidly knew about the affair, even though they found the chemistry between the two strange to say the least. Love letters released many years later, after Wallis's death at the age of 89 in 1986, showed that he was infantile and pleading in his need for love and affection.

She was stern, admonishing, sensible. This showed through in their day-to-day attitudes towards each other. He was completely and utterly captivated by her. His friends said they could never recall a time when he looked so happy or so sad in equal amounts. A look from her could trigger euphoria like a drug or plunge him into the darkest moods. Slender, sophisticated and witty, as opposed to his shy, awkward, fumbling demeanour, it seemed as if she was the one who had been born into this lineage, not him.

DANGEROUS LIAISONS

Soon the discretion which was supposed to govern such dangerous liaisons of the heart was shed as the Prince, like a proud schoolboy showing off his latest toy, took her around the watering holes of Europe on whirlwind tours. Paris, Rome, Budapest, Monte Carlo – soon even the British Press was having to take note as their foreign rivals filled columns of newsprint every day with their glorious partying.

But the implacable British press barons like Rothermere and Beaverbrook, men committed to the notion of a solid and trustworthy establishment, kept the shenanigans from the readers of their newspapers, believing that trivia would only damage the crown and ultimately the country. Better, they believed, that the man in the street did not know of the strange frenzy of love that was gripping the future king. In America, there was no such hesitation among the Republicans. 'Queen Wally' screamed one newspaper headline as it delved into lurid details about the sleeping arrangements between them during one tour in Yugoslavia and Greece.

In January 1936, Edward became king, taking on all the rights and responsibilities

which the highest office demanded of him. His affair was known in the highest reaches of society – but it remained just that; a dalliance, a whim, an amusing diversion. No-one suspected that Edward would suggest anything as absurd as marriage to Wallis – something that would never have been sanctioned because, as head of the Church of England, he was forbidden to marry a divorced woman.

ROCKING THE ESTABLISHMENT

Some weeks before the death of his father, which placed him upon the throne, Edward had spoken with Prime Minister Stanley Baldwin, informing him of Wallis's intention to proceed with divorce from her husband. Baldwin was horrified. He knew that the Press turned a blind eye to his dalliance with a married woman – but a divorced one! The shock for the establishment would be too much to bear. He begged Edward to get Wallis to reconsider a divorce, but Edward told him: 'It would be wrong for me to attempt to influence Mrs. Simpson just because she happens to be a friend of the King. I have no right to interfere with the affairs of an individual.' Baldwin, for his part, was amazed at the self-delusion that Edward seemed to be stricken with. It was as if he fully expected to be allowed to 'carry on' with her as always and expect people to ignore it. But the conspiracy of silence ended months after his accession to the throne. There was an eight-day period after it when Edward wavered between duty and love – and history records which won in the end.

The silence ended when the Bishop of Bradford, Dr. Blunt, chastised him for his 'carefree' lifestyle which was out of keeping with the economically-hard times and the teachings of the church, which he represented. The newspapers could no longer ignore it. The British establishment, so pliable at times in turning away its face in matters of discretion, now met the crisis full on and the matter was splashed over the newspapers. Edward had fully expected the British people and the establishment to come over to his side in the matter. He wanted to marry Wallis and place her upon the throne next to him. The very suggestion

Above: *The newspapers at first held off the crisis, then enjoyed a field day.*

Opposite Top: *Wallis Simpson, found by the noble family of the realm to be altogether unsuitable to wear the crown of queen.*

Opposite Bottom: *Stanley Baldwin, whose government kept the lid on the crisis until it could no longer be contained.*

EDWARD WANTED TO MARRY WALLIS AND PLACE HER UPON THE THRONE NEXT TO HIM

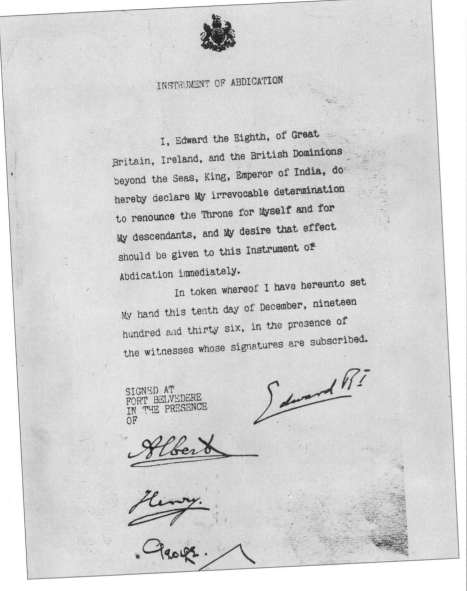

INSTRUMENT OF ABDICATION

I, Edward the Eighth, of Great Britain, Ireland, and the British Dominions beyond the Seas, King, Emperor of India, do hereby declare My irrevocable determination to renounce the Throne for Myself and for My descendants, and My desire that effect should be given to this Instrument of Abdication immediately.

In token whereof I have hereunto set My hand this tenth day of December, nineteen hundred and thirty six, in the presence of the witnesses whose signatures are subscribed.

SIGNED AT
FORT BELVEDERE
IN THE PRESENCE
OF

Above: The abdication letter in which Edward VIII relinquished the crown over Wallis Simpson.

Right: Edward caused a great deal of controversy when he met Adolf Hitler in 1937.

THE MONARCH, LIKE KING CHARLES AGAINST CROMWELL, WAS ON THE LOSING SIDE

threw his mother Queen Mary into apoplexy. There was an emergency council of war at Buckingham Palace which was attended also by Baldwin.

When he announced to Baldwin his intention to marry, the PM replied: 'We will not have it, sir. People are talking about you and this American woman. I have had so many nasty letters from people who respected your father and who do not appreciate the way you are going on.' Edward, baffled, became convinced that there was some kind of conspiracy aimed directly at him. All he could mumble was 'poor, poor Wallis'.

She, meanwhile, became the target of a fearful campaign of hate in which bricks and stones were hurled through the windows of her London residence and children sang outside the door: 'Hark the Herald Angels sing, Mrs. Simpson's Pinched our King!' She packed her bags the first night of the 'crisis' and fled to the South of France on the first night train. Edward stayed behind to wrestle with the establishment and his own conscience. He set about trying to lobby the high and mighty, who might sway opinion in his favour.

THE GREAT DEBATE

One curious ally was staunch monarchist Winston Churchill – perhaps because his mother was American too. One anecdote recalls a lunch he enjoyed with playwright Noel Coward in which Churchill said: 'Why shouldn't he marry his cutie?' To which Coward replied: 'Because England doesn't want a Queen Cutie!'

An idea proposed by Esmond Harmsworth, of the *Daily Mail* publishing empire, seemed to offer the best solution of all. Esmond said that he might try wooing his mother with the idea of a morganatic marriage, the compromise whereby she would be his wife but would have no claim to any titles within the British royal family, and neither would her children. The Queen would not accept it. The cabinet would not accept it. It had become a battle of wills between constitutional rulers and the constitutional monarch. The monarch, like King Charles against Cromwell, was to end up on the losing side.

The King was hopelessly and irreversibly in love with Wallis Simpson. Duty

Bahamas during the war years and the couple settled afterwards in Paris in a splendid white chateau for which they paid a peppercorn rent. They married in a simple ceremony in the Loire Valley and remained as exiles from the House of Windsor for the rest of their days. He died in 1972 at the age of 77; she died 14 years later.

There was a certain bitter irony at Edward's funeral, which was held at St. George's Chapel, Windsor. Wallis was there for the occasion, confronting the heirs to this contradictory, somewhat cold, often hypocritical family. She was allowed to stay one night at Buckingham Palace before journeying back to Paris and obscurity. On her dressing room table she kept a message written by Edward which read: 'My friend, with thee, to live alone, methinks were better than to own a crown, a sceptre and a throne.' Truly, if nothing much else was worthy in his character, Edward did possess and nourish a love that was Olympian in its magnitude.

PRINCESS MARGARET

Affairs of the heart have plagued the House of Windsor in the same way some families inherit genetic disorders. But perhaps none was sadder, or more poignant, than that between Group Captain Peter Townsend and Princess Margaret, the relationship which started as a schoolgirl infatuation and went on to develop into a deep and abiding love. Ironically, Princess Margaret won the kind of backing and public support for her forbidden romance which was denied to King Edward VIII – but it still did her no good. In the 1950s, Britain was still a place where the order of things was dictated by tradition and conformity. Even though the swinging sixties, free love and sex before marriage was just around the corner, for Princess Margaret they might as well have been on the moon.

Margaret was a beautiful 14-year-old schoolgirl when she first met the dashing flier Townsend. The 29-year-old war hero, his uniform bemedalled for valour in the Battle of Britain and other airborne conflicts, was assigned to Buckingham Palace as an equerry to King George VI. Townsend was the epitome of a young girl's romantic ideal. He was tall, good looking, charming, brave and sensitive.

became an alien word to him. Everything he was brought up for, nurtured for, was scattered and destroyed by that strongest of emotions. In the end, after having discussed it with Wallis, he decided to abdicate, to forfeit his inalienable right to rule for the woman he could not rule without. Later, in her memoirs, Wallis wrote of how she wept when she heard the abdication speech on the wireless on 11 December 1936. She said: 'I was lying on the sofa with my hands over my eyes, trying to hide my tears'. The King had told the nation and the empire that he could not rule alone.

He left for France and did not return to live in Britain again. Wallis and Edward, now given the courtesy titles of Duke and Duchess of Windsor, caused a furore in 1937 when they were seen as guests of Hitler, but they did not disgrace their country by choosing to live in Germany during the war. Edward became governor of the

Above: *The happy couple on their wedding day in France.*

WALLIS AND EDWARD CAUSED A FURORE IN 1937 WHEN THEY WERE GUESTS OF HITLER

*Above: **Princess Margaret, a royal beauty without peer. But her love for Group Captain Townsend (right) led to a disastrous romance.***

*Opposite Top: **Princess Margaret with the Governor of Mauritius, Sir Robert Scott, on the African tour where her love for Townsend grew stronger every day.***

*Opposite Bottom: **A beaming Princess Elizabeth with Prince Philip of Greece, the man who became her fiancé. The course of true love was not so easy for Margaret.***

To a young woman aware of her own sexuality just beginning to blossom, he was an idol and she worshipped him as such. It was 1944 and the war was not yet won, but the royal family had garnered massive public affection during the worst of the blitz for refusing to leave London. Princess Margaret was turning into the most beautiful of the King's daughters and her adolescent life fascinated the royal watchers of the Press. Soon she would really give them something to write about.

Townsend was given a house in the grounds of Windsor Castle where he lived with his pretty wife Rosemary. Margaret sought him out as often as she could, asking him advice on any subject under the sun. Of course, it was all done merely so she could get breathlessly close to the man she was beginning to hero-worship.

A LONG SEPARATION

In 1947, at 17, she set sail with her sister, Princess Elizabeth, later to become queen of a tormented household, on a tour of South Africa. The tour, a three-month long marathon, was planned as a test of the love that Prince Philip of Greece proferred for Princess Elizabeth. He had been courting her for some time and the King felt that a long separation would test the feelings of both of them. But where Elizabeth felt only sadness at such an enforced separation, there was joy in Margaret's heart because Group Captain Townsend was accompanying them. And Rosemary was staying at home. Later a royal aide would recall: 'A smile of pure joy crossed Margaret's face when she heard that Captain Townsend was to join the party. She could not believe her luck.'

On the ships, on the verandahs of the African hotels, with the southern stars twinkling above them, Margaret drifted off into a romantic dream world as she stayed up late listening to the wit and wisdom of the cultured Townsend. A shiver began running through royal ranks that there was a replay of the abdication crisis of 1936 fomenting itself, but the King, who was close to both his daughters, believed that it was nothing more than a girlish infatuation for a handsome, decorated warrior.

But Margaret was obviously scheming for something much, much more than passing affection from her hero airman. In

sive 'establishment' would doom them as it had doomed others before.

Once they were caught in an act of frolicking in Buckingham Palace itself. Townsend was carrying Margaret up a staircase, like a groom crossing the threshold of a honeymoon hotel with his new bride, when the King happened to come across them. He was flabbergasted at such intimacy, even though Margaret blurted out: 'I told him to do it papa, I ordered him!' Another time they were caught kissing by a footman in a drawing room and on another occasion were seen embracing by staff in a stairwell. Soon the affair was the talk of the palace.

Townsend had risen to the rank of Deputy Master of the Royal Household and knew that he was probably on borrowed time. But he used his position to arrange cosy weekends at country houses where he would be present with the Princess and they never, ever, displayed affection in public.

Their trysts were arranged within the palace but they never left it together. They

1951, having spurned many society suitors who would have given their right arms to squire around the beautiful, eligible bachelor girl at town and country balls, she saw her chance to develop a relationship with Townsend. He parted with his wife when the strain of long separations due to royal duties became too much for her to bear. Rosemary vanished from the house she shared with Townsend in Windsor Castle's grounds to move in with a lover. Townsend, who was now becoming as close to the princess as she was to him, said: 'We were not right for each other. We married in wartime and now in peacetime the marriage is over.'

The duo were riding through the grounds of Balmoral, Queen Victoria's favourite Scottish retreat, and it was then that she told him of her love for him. He returned it back with all his heart – but, wiser and older than her, perhaps knew it was doomed from the start. She was intoxicated by the twin drugs of youth and love – he knew better and believed that the all-perva-

Above: *Group Captain Townsend in Brussels, where he was stationed as air attache.*

THE ROYAL FAMILY KNEW CONCLUSIVELY ABOUT THE RELATIONSHIP BUT DID NOT MOVE TO BREAK IT UP

THE ESTABLISHMENT BELIEVED THAT MARGARET AND TOWNSEND'S RELATIONSHIP WAS SCANDALOUS

drove away in plain cars – often alone, for this was in the days before global terrorism – and spent precious moments at locations which are secret to this day. But they were like a modern day Romeo and Juliet – unable to live without one another, yet becoming increasingly aware that their romance was doomed.

Soon the whisperings of 'cradle snatching' began to pervade society, then the palace. Prince Philip, curmudgeonly patriarch of the post-war reign of the House of Windsor, was one of the biggest objectors. He regarded Townsend as nothing more than an 'employee' of the family firm and implored Elizabeth to work against the relationship. Margaret, who has a streak of determination running through her that is every bit as fierce as that belonging to her future brother-in-law, was determined to bring her affair out into the open – and get the 'establishment' to support her. It was not to work out.

She met with Sir Alan Lascelles, the Queen's private secretary, to enquire whether a divorce on Townsend's part, for admitted adultery by his wife, would stand in the way of their future happiness. Lascelles said, wrongly, that he could see no problem as long as a suitable period of time elapsed between the decree absolute and the publication of their burgeoning relationship. The royal family now knew conclusively about the relationship but did

not yet move to break it up. It was, after all, still contained within the walls of the palaces and houses of the Windsor tribe. But that all changed at a certain ceremony at Westminster Abbey.

It was the Coronation of Queen Elizabeth, her sister, in 1953, the most glorious of royal spectacles and the first one ever to be filmed by television cameras for those at home and those abroad in the remains of the empire and commonwealth. A keen-eyed Fleet Street reporter happened to glance at Princess Margaret leaning forward to brush off a speck of dust from the uniform of Group Captain Townsend as her sister moved regally up the aisle.

It was interpreted – correctly – as an act of love by a woman for her man and the information travelled around the world. Captain Townsend doubly confirmed the reporter's suspicion when he looked longingly into her eyes. Society columnists pulled in favours from aristocratic tipsters and informants and, sure enough, the story of the forbidden affair was given as much play the next day as the Coronation itself.

Even though Britain was slowly becoming a more liberal society, with more rights for women and class barriers being torn down, there was no such moral relaxation for the watchdogs of the establishment. They believed that Margaret and Townsend's relationship was scandalous, akin to the constitutional crisis of 17 years

Left: *Queen Elizabeth II at her coronation in Westminster Abbey. Margaret's act of brushing a piece of fluff from the suit of Group Captain Townsend during the ceremony set tongues wagging.*

earlier. It was nonsense, of course, especially as the divorce rate in Britain was soaring that year.

Margaret and Townsend's love affair could hardly be held up as tearing apart the moral fibre of the nation. But Churchill – the man who had held such kind words and thoughts for the lovestruck Edward all those years before – felt duty-bound to put the age-old honour of the monarchy before individual rights and dreams. He packed Margaret off on a tour of Rhodesia with her mother while Group Captain Townsend was exiled to the British Embassy in Brussels as air attache.

The affair continued, however, despite the obstacles placed in their way. It was conducted in secret love letters, in expensive international telephone calls and at out-of-the-way hotels and homes of friends. But just before Princess Margaret's 25th birthday her sister Elizabeth, as Queen and Head of the Church of England, told her that Winston Churchill had communicated the feelings of the cabinet to her. Those feelings were that Parliament would never, under any circumstances, sanction a marriage between her and Townsend. She

was faced with either dumping Townsend, or going off into social Siberia with him, exiled like the Duke of Windsor had been so many years before.

In October 1955 it came to an end. There was an enormous amount of public sympathy for her, but it was not enough to break the back of the establishment's power. Crowds had begun gathering outside

Below: *The end of the romance nears as Group Captain Townsend is quizzed by a reporter in Belgium about the affair.*

Below: *Prince Andrew, another royal who chose an unsuitable companion – Koo Stark.*

Clarence House, her London residence, screaming: 'Marry him! Marry him!' Editorials in some down-market newspapers begged for her to go her own way. But the pull of duty was ultimately stronger. She was not as foppish, or as weak, as the former King Edward. Margaret ultimately knew that her duty lay with the monarchy.

On Monday 31 October, she issued this statement: 'I would like it to be known that I have decided not to marry Group Captain Peter Townsend. I have been aware that subject to renouncing my rights of succession it might have been possible for me to contract a civil marriage. But mindful of the church's teaching that a Christian marriage is indissoluble, and conscious of my duty to the Commonwealth, I have resolved to put these considerations before any others.

'I have reached the decision entirely alone, and in doing so I have been strengthened by the unfailing support and devotion of Group Captain Townsend.' She went on to marry Lord Snowdon, a marriage which floundered in 1978 and finally ended in divorce. No man, say those who really know Margaret, ever lived up to her dashing war hero.

ANDREW AND FERGIE

The course of true love has never run smooth for Prince Andrew, the 'playboy prince' who of all the Queen's sons became the most dashing, daring and handsome. Unlike Edward, who cares not at all for the action-man life, and Prince Charles, who is keen on subjects like architecture and the environment, Prince Andrew revelled in the hurly burly of military life and was never happier than flying his beloved helicopters, or carousing in the mess with his warrior chums. And when it came to the 'fillies' as he was fond of calling them, none was more contentious, or would cause a bigger stir, than one soft-porn actress named Koo Stark.

Kathryn 'Koo' Stark was a gorgeous young woman of wealthy parents and a budding future as a film actress or photographer – she seemed to show promise in both fields. But she had erred, just once, in her judgement while trying to make her way to the top. She had made a movie called *Emily*, a soft-focus romp with well-endowed men and women getting into more positions than a Rubik's Cube. And that was why she could never, ever, be acceptable to the House of Windsor.

A DOOMED AFFAIR

British gossip writer Nigel Dempster claims that the duo were introduced at his home in London in 1982 during a party and that they corresponded with each other during the Falklands War. It was said from the early days that she possessed the wit, sophistication and sensitivity which he seemed to lack. Anyway, the chemistry between them was definitely there – even though the affair was doomed to die.

But not at first. Koo was a hit with the Queen and Queen Mother when introduced to them at Balmoral while the Duke of

Edinburgh – always one with a keen eye for the ladies – was entranced by her. It was only when the details of her foray into soft-porn began to seep out little by little that the pressure was increased on Andrew to end the affair.

Andrew was besotted with Koo, of that there can be no doubt. They wrote passionate love letters to each other, and they planned a future together. But that big D word among the Windsors – Duty – reared its head and, under direct orders from the Queen herself, Andrew was told to end the relationship forthwith in 1983. He did so, in a particularly cool and calculating manner.

Nigel Blundell and Sue Blackhall, in their authoritative work *The Fall of the House of Windsor* wrote: 'Their intense 18 month relationship ended in 1983 when the Queen and the Duke of Edinburgh became alarmed at the continuing furore over her soft-porn cinematic credits. Loyal at least to his mother, Andrew cut the poor girl dead. Without having the decency even to telephone her, he ordered the Buckingham Palace switchboard not to put her calls through to him.

'It was a callous, though perhaps royally predictable way of ending what had been an amazingly passionate love affair with a hugely loving and supporting young lady.'

But if the Queen and Prince Philip had known of the titanic convulsions within the royal family that one Sarah Ferguson would ultimately cause, then Koo Stark might well have seemed an almost ideal partner for their son.

It is generally believed that Andrew and Sarah Ferguson, his future wife and Duchess of York, who had known each other from their earliest childhood days because of Sarah's father Major Ron Ferguson's managership of Prince Charles' polo team, married on the rebound of true love – he for Koo Stark, she for a former racing driver and society dandy called Paddy McNally. After engineering an invitation to the palace in 1985 – aided and abetted by Princess Diana, her friend – the spark between Andrew and the red-haired

Above: *Koo Stark in the soft-porn film* Emily *for which she was ever damned in the eyes of the royal family.*

'IT WAS A CALLOUS, THOUGH PERHAPS ROYALLY PREDICTABLE WAY OF ENDING WHAT HAD BEEN AN AMAZINGLY PASSIONATE LOVE AFFAIR'

senting her as he did so with a splendid oval ruby surrounded by ten diamonds. Soon the nation was gushing over a new royal love match as the potteries began to turn out commemorative plates and jugs and other assorted paraphernalia.

A REGAL SPECTACLE

On 23 July the same year he led her up the aisle of Westminster Abbey as 500 million TV viewers around the world witnessed the spectacle which some say only the British can pull off with such majesty and panache. There was a lingering kiss on the balcony at Buckingham Palace, an open horse-drawn carriage ride through London and a helicopter to the royal yacht Britannia for a honeymoon in the Azores. This, thought the British public, was a match made in heaven. Never did two more vivacious, headstrong yet likeable people pledge their troth to join the ranks of the Windsor dynasty. Yet it was all going wrong before it started. Physically they had it all – their displays of affection for the press on public engagements and at photo-

Above and Below: *The Duchess of York was taken to heart by the British public in the days before her marriage. But her PR image soon began to spin badly out of control.*

beauty known as 'Fergie' to all her friends seemed to glow and intensify.

Their courtship was carried out at the country homes of discreet friends, places where details would never be whispered to the scoundrels in the tabloid press. At one such place, Floors Castle in Scotland, Andrew dropped to one knee on 19 March 1986 and proudly proposed to Sarah, pre-

Left: *The royal couple were unable to escape the cameras on their honeymoon.*

Below: *A visit to the races. But Andrew's shipboard service meant that Fergie was soon looking for solace.*

calls while on holiday were causing eyebrows to be raised in the Palace. They seemed literally incapable of keeping their hands off each other. But physical love is never enough in a relationship, let alone a marriage. In short, they had little to talk about once the lovemaking was over. He was still a sailor in love with the sea; she was intent on rising through the highest ranks of society. Somewhere down the road it seemed inevitable that their interests would not converge.

Fergie tried to play the dutiful wife, first by learning to become a helicopter pilot, which she believed would give her 'something to talk with him about when he comes home in the evening'. Unfortunately for her, he wasn't coming home all that often. Andrew truly loved the service life and in 1987 he went back to sea on the destroyer HMS Edinburgh. It was the long separations which would drive the wedge between them – and lead Fergie on her global gallivanting which would earn her the cruel nickname 'Freebie Fergie' from

Above: *Major Ron Ferguson with Sarah. He had his own secrets, such as visiting a London massage parlour for extra services of a sexual nature.*

THE PICTURES WERE PROOF THAT PHILANDERING WAS ALL PART OF THE GAME WITHIN THE MONARCHY

piness too in March 1990 when Princess Eugenie, their second, was born. But Andrew was only able to snatch brief weekends with his family as he was at sea most of the time. The cracks began to show as Fergie became the most knocked royal in living memory in the newspapers. She was Frumpy Fergie when an outfit was deemed inappropriate. She was Fat Fergie when compared with gorgeous Diana, and Freeloading Fergie when off on another jaunt to somewhere exotic. And she was reeling under the strain of a marriage that allowed her and Andrew just 42 days together during the whole of that year.

Insiders to the clan say that he was immersing himself more and more in shipboard life, always feeling let down by the humdrum existence of a day-to-day life on dry land. The ghastly modern mansion they had built at Sunninghill in Berkshire – nicknamed Southyork or the Dallas Palace because of its gauche style – was the scene of many parties, but none of them attended by him. He seemed happy to slump in front of a TV set and watch old war videos whenever he was home. Fergie was beginning to look elsewhere for companionship – and perhaps even love.

NEW ROMANCE

In that same year Fergie went to North Africa with a rich Texan called Steve Wyatt, heir to a Houston oil fortune, and, later, on his private jet to the South of France. In 1992, this holiday came to haunt her when 120 photos of the two together – including one of Wyatt with his arm around Princess Beatrice – were mysteriously found in a London flat and printed in a daily newspaper. For Andrew it was the last straw. He told the Queen in a private audience that he could stand many things, but being a cuckolded husband wasn't one of them. He wanted out of the marriage, saying he realised now that it had been a mistake from the word go.

The Queen sympathised and realised herself just what a disaster the pictures were; it was the proof (which the royals had hidden so successfully for so many years) that philandering was all part of the game within the monarchy. The Queen, however, did her best to try to keep the marriage together – without success.

the press as she swanned from one exotic location to another, seemingly without a care in the world.

In May 1988 Major Ron Ferguson was caught in a classic Sunday newspaper expose as being the frequenter of a London massage parlour which offered considerably more to its clientele than a back rub. The royal family rallied around Major Ron, although Andrew was furious, seeing the incident as a major slur upon his choice of partner in marriage.

The birth of Princess Beatrice, their first daughter, seemed to gloss over the scandal and actually served to bring them closer together for a while. There was more hap-

Both sides called in lawyers and on 19 March a terse statement was issued from Buckingham Palace to the effect that the couple was separating. It made no mention of a divorce – Princess Anne would later be the first offspring of Her Majesty to inflict that upon the royal household.

'In view of the media speculation which the Queen finds especially undesirable during the general election campaign,' the statement said, 'Her Majesty is issuing the following statement. Last week lawyers acting for the Duchess of York initiated discussions about a formal separation for the Duke and Duchess. These discussions are not yet completed and nothing will be said until they are. The Queen hopes that the media will spare the Duke and Duchess of York and their children any intrusion.'

This was a crisis unparalleled within the royal family for years and Fleet Street pursued the story with a vengeance. Soon it transpired that there had been some sort of dirty-tricks campaign against Fergie within the walls of Buckingham Palace itself, with advisers to the Queen laying down misinformation about the Duchess. Despite huffy denials to the contrary at first, Her Majesty's press secretary Charles Anson was later to issue a humble apology to the Duchess in which he admitted making unauthorised remarks after a press briefing.

But there was worse – much worse – for the royal family and the British public to come. In 1992 Fergie took up with a dashing, balding man named Johnny Bryan,

Above: *Fergie cuddles her children Beatrice and Eugenie on a Swiss slope.*

Top: *Happy families – the Duke, Duchess, Beatrice, Eugenie and grandfather Major Ron.*

described as a 'financial adviser'. It did not take the wolverine British press long to dig up the facts on Mr. Bryan – and discover that he was a close friend of, and social gadfly with, one Steve Wyatt, the Texan who had caused such distress to the royal household in the first place. There was an exotic holiday in Thailand and Indonesia while Prince Andrew stuck his square jaw out at home and tried to put a brave face on an increasingly distressing situation.

A CLOSE ADVISER

Royal gossips said that Bryan was indeed advising Fergie on financial matters; mainly on the settlement that she should receive when she pushed the ultimate panic button in Buckingham Palace and pressed for a divorce. But there was surely something unique about his style of 'advising' when the next shock was to hit the establishment like a speeding rocket.

In August 1992, they went away together again, with the children, to a villa in the south of France. A cunning French paparazzi photographer had crawled in the undergrowth, unbeknown to them, to capture on colour film just what a unique advising style it was! There were topless pictures of Fergie. There was Bryan sucking her big toe. There was Bryan massaging suntan oil on her and gently tucking her hair behind the back of her neck. And all of it was done in front of her two children and two male bodyguards. A unique style of money management indeed!

The photographs earned photographer Daniel Angelli a fortune from British tabloids and European magazines, reducing Fergie's already low status to zero. Andrew was humiliated beyond belief, with one newspaper, the *Daily Star*, saying in a leader column: 'This silly strumpet has behaved in a way which would disgrace a council house, let alone a palace.'

In a symbolic gesture, Fergie left Balmoral the morning the pictures were published in her car, a modern day banishment after the photos of her dreadful performance were served up at the royal breakfast table along with the kippers and the kedgeree.

A few months later there was more misery in the House of Ferguson when Major Ron was exposed again by a 26-year-old former stablegirl called Lesley Player who wrote a book about her affair with Major Ron and other assorted royal romps, including Fergie's fling with Steve Wyatt – someone, she claimed, who also bedded her. It was all too much to bear for the embattled royal family.

PRINCESS ANNE

The first divorce, however, came from an unexpected quarter. Princess Anne, who started off as the most unloved royal in the eyes of the public, ended up carving herself out a unique position of affection thanks to her tireless work on behalf of charities, such as Save the Children. Born in August 1950, she grew up with all the privileges of

Below: *Ron Ferguson and Lesley Player – another kiss-and-tell beauty who heaped more embarrassment on the House of Windsor.*

Above: *Princess Anne and Captain Mark Phillips in 1981, before the irreparable rift that grew between them.*

Above Right: *Princess Anne found solace in her work with children around the world.*

the royal household and seemed to be developing into an acerbic-tongued hothead by the time she was a teenager. Like her father the Duke, from whom she seems to have inherited her temper and her inability to suffer fools gladly, Princess Anne hated the royal press corps which followed her every move – and let them know it.

In 1982, when she fell off her horse at the Badminton Horse Trials, she screamed 'naff off' to cameramen seeking to record the inglorious moment for newspaper history. Another time a newspaper man mistakenly called her 'love' while attempting to take her picture and she erupted in fury at him. She was, therefore, hardly the darling of the brood.

She had been married, almost a decade earlier, in 1973, to Captain Mark Phillips. Phillips, a dour, humourless sort, was an army officer known as 'Foggie' to his mess room chums because he was 'thick and wet'. A man from the shires with a love of the countryside, shooting, riding and assorted other pursuits of the tweedy set, Mark seemed a splendid match for Anne, who had had a succession of boyfriends without ever seeming to be serious about any of them.

The couple married on 14 November 1973 at Westminster Abbey with all the pomp and circumstance of state surround-

ing them. It seemed a match made in heaven – and even if Anne was a bit sour-faced sometimes, seemingly pompous and rude on others, the ecstatic thousands who turned out to wish them well on the wedding day seemed to indicate that even the frostiest of the royals was deserving of the fidelity of the masses.

After a couple of years the Queen parted with some of her immense wealth and bought them the £5,000,000 mansion Gatcombe Park in Gloucestershire where royal offspring Peter and Zara would spend their formative years. If people were expecting the Princess Royal to spend her life shooting pheasants and riding in the local hunt they were disappointed. If anything, domestic life disagreed immensely with her.

She found herself bored by the constraints of staying at home and as she turned 30 plunged into work. Her list of public engagements grew, her travels to perilous, dirty places abroad enhanced her public image as a royal who really cared

Above: *The Queen and Princess Anne with royal children Peter and Zara. Of all the Queen's children, Anne is said to be closest to her.*

ANNE WAS A BIT SOUR-FACED SOMETIMES, AND SEEMED POMPOUS AND RUDE ON OTHER OCCASIONS

---

about the ordinary people of the world and her marriage to Mark Phillips seemed merely of secondary importance.

It was in 1984 that the first whispers of marital discord began circulating in places of power. Both were at the Los Angeles Olympics as part of the equestrian team – and they slept in separate accommodation. In society there were reports of bitchiness and pointed exchanges between them on the occasions when they were seen together at balls and dinner parties. But it was to be the extraordinary revelations of a former royal bodyguard which first gave the hint as to how deep the trouble might be between them.

DAMAGING RUMOURS

In 1985 Peter Cross, her former 'minder,' touted round Fleet Street tabloids – for an asking price said to be over £500,000 – the story that he and she had enjoyed a 'special relationship' together. So special, he alleged that she even telephoned him on the night baby Zara was born. He boasted that she was in love with him, but the palace weathered the scandal as Fleet Street exposed him as a man who had enjoyed several affairs during his marriage. Nevertheless, the 'no smoke without fire' school of commentators believed that the damage was done.

By the following year, the marriage was damaged beyond repair but Anne, who is imbued with as much sense of duty as her mother, insisted that they should stay together for the sake of the children and the nation. In 1986, a naval officer who would later steal her heart began working for the Queen as an equerry.

Tall and handsome, Timothy Laurence moved with grace and charm through the palace and court life, liked by everyone, including her Majesty, and her daughter, who was by this time thoroughly miserable with her own lot. A lack of spark on her husband's part, his worries about money and the gradual drift between them since the heady day that they had walked up the aisle at Westminster Abbey together had combined to destroy her love for him and place passions elsewhere.

THE NEW ATTRACTION

It wasn't until 1989 that the world learned of the attraction between Anne and Commander Laurence. A number of personal letters written by him to her – emotional love letters to be exact – had been stolen from her briefcase and posted to *The Sun* newspaper. For once that salacious organ did the decent thing and refused to publish any of their contents and the letters were returned intact to the Princess Royal. But they showed to the public that yet another crisis was about to break over the bows of the ship of state and in less than four months the terse statement came from Buckingham Palace that the couple were to separate, with no plans for divorce.

Anne and Mark remained friends, determined to be civilised about the whole thing. Their love of horses and other pursuits meant they still met at functions, and they never seemed to harbour any animosity towards each other. But in March 1991, there was yet more trouble in store for the royal family. A 40-year-old New Zealand

art teacher named Heather Tonkin named Captain Phillips as the father of her six-year-old child, and launched a paternity suit against him.

Below and Bottom: *Anne with her new husband, Naval Commander Timothy Laurence.*

She said that she had conceived the child on a night of passion at a hotel in Auckland in November 1984 when she was 31 and Captain Phillips 35. She alleged that some £40,000 in maintenance money had been paid over the years – disguised as 'equestrian' fees – but that she was seeking more because of the reputed £1,000,000 he was supposed to be getting from the royal purse for parting with Anne. Eventually the paternity suit was dropped, probably because of an out-of-court settlement reached between the two parties.

On 13 April 1992, Princess Anne became the second royal since Margaret to get divorced. There was a statement from Buckingham Palace as the nation turned its eyes heavenwards, wondering what next to expect in the ongoing royal pantomime. Harold Brooks Baker, editor of *Debretts Peerage*, took the view that divorce among the royal family was no longer a tragedy, saying: 'Because the Princess Royal has served her country so well she will be the first royal to re-marry with her parents' approval. The public will also approve because they respect her so much.'

To save embarrassment for her mother, as head of the Church of England, Princess Anne chose that re-marriage to take place in the Church of Scotland. She married the commander on Saturday 13 December at the modest Crathie parish church near Balmoral, watched by about 30 family and friends. She had, it seems, proved Brooks Baker correct; of all the royals, next to Her Majesty and the Queen mum, she remains the most treasured.

PRINCESS MICHAEL OF KENT

So much for the wayward hormones, wretched marriages and shattered secrets in the House of Windsor. But it was an inherited blemish from the royal they all called

Above: *Princess Pushy, otherwise known as Princess Michael of Kent.*

IN APRIL 1985 IT WAS REVEALED THAT PRINCESS MICHAEL OF KENT'S FATHER HAD BEEN A MEMBER OF HITLER'S DREADED SS

'Princess Pushy' which several years earlier had plunged the House of Windsor into crisis. In April 1985 it was revealed that Princess Michael of Kent's father had been a member of Hitler's dreaded SS!

Baron Gunther von Reibnitz, her aristocratic German father, had joined the ranks of Hitler's cruellest servants – the men who ran the death camps, who massacred innocent prisoners of war and civilians and against whom many thousands of Britons had died.

The Baron, Nazi party member 412855, was not involved in ghastly medical experiments, nor had he any part to play in the evil genocide of the Jews. But he joined the

Left: *The notorious SS, of which Princess Michael's father was a member.*

Below: *Simon Wiesenthal, Nazi hunter, ascertained that her father was involved in the awful SS baby farms.*

Nazi party as a volunteer and was closely involved in the SS 'Lebensborn' programme, the Nazi baby farms where Hitler urged strapping SS men to breed with Nordic maidens in pursuit of his twisted master race. Nazi war criminal hunter Simon Wiesenthal said from his office in Vienna: 'It is evident that he was an early enthusiast – someone who joined the party very early on in the 1920s.'

THE SS CONNECTION

The story broke in tabloid newspapers on the eve of its publication in detailed historical books. It hit hardest among veterans and monarchy fanatics – the idea that an SS man's daughter was in the upper echelons of the House of Windsor! There was a public outcry followed by frantic meetings at Buckingham Palace between the Queen and Princess Michael.

This time there would be no question of banishment or disgrace. The Queen, on the advice of her ministers, agreed that it was a distasteful episode and that no-one could deny the immediate impact it had had upon the royal household. But she confirmed that the sins of the father were not to be visited upon the daughter.

And the following day Princess Michael became more popular than she had in years when she went on TV to speak about the affair. She said: 'Here I am, 40 years old, and I suddenly discover something that is

really quite unpleasant. I shall just simply have to live with it. It was a very, very great blow because I have always hero-worshipped him.' Princess Michael went on to state that she had a document which proved that her father's membership of the Black Guard of Nazism was 'honorary'. She added: 'He never served with the SS, he never wore the uniform.'

Nazi hunter Wiesenthal, himself a death camp survivor who lost some 80 members of his family in the extermination centres, described her claim that he was an honorary member of the SS as 'nonsense'. But he did help to defuse the scandal for the Princess by saying: 'He did not work in a concentration camp. Had he done so I would have been aware of it. However, he added: 'He pledged his ideals to Hitler, and the Hitler ideals and hatreds, very early on.

Above: *Princess Diana, when she was Lady Diana Spencer and on the verge of becoming engaged to Prince Charles.*

Right: *The happy couple upon the announcement of their engagement.*

PRINCESS MICHAEL'S FATHER PLEDGED HIMSELF TO HITLER'S IDEALS AND HATREDS VERY EARLY ON

It doesn't make him whiter than white.' Princess Michael weathered the storm, but she would have to live with the stigma of it for the rest of her days.

CHARLES AND DIANA

No scandal, however, in recent or ancient times, bears comparison with the break-up of the marriage between Prince Charles and Princess Diana, once the supposed epitome of happiness and solidity in British public life. Their marital woes, played out on a public stage, and lapped up in newspapers and magazines around the globe, culminated in a separation and there was soon talk of another royal divorce. How could this seemingly loving couple, who had the whole nation joining in their union with a day off and street parties the length and breadth of the land, somehow break that cardinal rule of the royals – duty above self

Below: *The wedding of Prince Charles and Princess Diana was watched by millions around the world, but the fairy tale later degenerated into a story of sleaze and deceit.*

– and plunge the very existence of the monarchy into doubt?

Rumblings of unhappiness between Charles and Diana had been growing for some time. The dizzy days of 1981, when the couple married and behaved like the besotted creatures they were, had long past. The loving looks that Diana used to throw Charles with those marvellous blue eyes of hers had frozen into icy stares of contempt whenever the duo were photographed together at official functions.

A HUGE DIVIDE

Perhaps Princess Diana should have known what she was marrying into when he proposed to her. Long into their relationship she still had to address him as 'sir,' as protocol demanded, and closer scrutiny of his tastes, in everything from fashion to music to food to friends, would have shown her that there was a huge divide between them. Diana, who, as Lady Diana Spencer, first fell in love with Prince Charles when she was 16, undoubtedly put her doubts to the back of her mind, preferring to bask instead in the splendid realisation that she had bagged one of the most – if not the most – eligible bachelor in the land.

She was 20 when she married the 32-year-old Prince – an age gap that began to tell on the relationship even as the honeymoon began. The couple were aboard the Royal Yacht Brittania, cruising in the Mediterranean, away from the prying eyes of the paparazzi photographers who had made the princess the most photographed face in history.

But it was far from an intimate love-boat for two. Diana realised there and then that 'duty' came above everything and her honeymoon was spent at dinners attended by officials, while every romantic moment seemed to be interrupted by the officers of the yacht who raced around seeking to satisfy their every whim. And when Charles wasn't in the dining room or on the bridge of the vessel, he preferred to be alone, reading tracts on mysticism and the meaning of life, heavyweight tomes which had no place in either the head or the heart of the pop-loving princess.

She bore him sons and heirs, Harry and William, and played the dutiful wife at every function where she was called upon

---

DIANA WAS BASKING IN THE REALISATION THAT SHE HAD BAGGED THE MOST ELIGIBLE BACHELOR IN THE LAND

Below: *Princess Diana with her sons, Princes Harry and William, on the first day of the school term.*

---

to do so. But the character differences soon began to tell upon them. It was noted as early as 1985 that on royal tours abroad they rarely shared the same bedroom.

Some 40 members of staff – loyal servants of Charles when he was a bachelor – were dismissed on Diana's orders in the early years. And in 1986, suffering from stress exacerbated by a slimming disease, Diana collapsed at a trade fair in Vancouver, Canada – only to suffer a stinging rebuke about her lack of dignity from her husband when she came round.

Clearly all was not well with the future King and Queen – but the public had, as yet, no inkling of just how disastrously

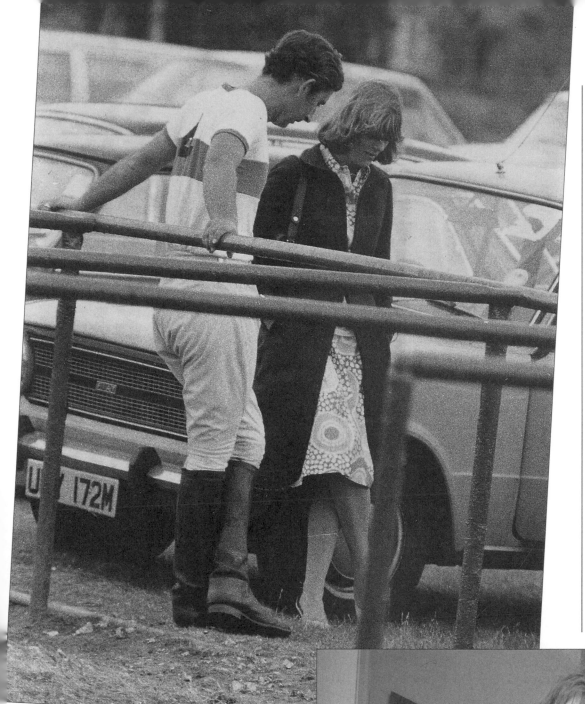

Left: *Prince Charles with Camilla Parker-Bowles, the woman widely reputed to be his mistress.*

Below: *Andrew Morton, a tabloid reporter who turned author and showed the royal marriage to be a sham.*

irreparable the rift between them was growing. Diana took to driving around London late at night, either on her own, or with one of her Sloaney friends from her bachelor girl days. Charles began to holiday alone – in Italy, painting, and in the Kalahari Desert in Botswana, Southern Africa, where he went on a nature trek with his philosopher friend Sir Laurens van der Post.

LARKING AROUND

The press noted that during one particular period they spent just one day together in six weeks. Diana was seen in the company of dashing young army officers. One evening in 1987 she was photographed

Above: *Diana and her sons. She has never hesitated to publicly show her motherly bond with them.*

TEARFULLY, DIANA BEGGED THE PHOTOGRAPHER FOR THE PICTURES, FEARING THEY COULD RUIN HER

'laughing and larking' as she left the home of a friend in Knightsbridge, West London, on the arm of army officer David Waterhouse. Tearfully, Diana begged the photographer for the pictures, fearing they could ruin her. The photos did not appear anywhere, but the story that surrounded their taking did – and it further cemented the rumours which were flying around.

Two years later Diana would be linked to James Gilbey, a car dealing member of the famous gin dynasty. Gilbey frequently invited Diana to his London flat – insisting, once, when she was caught out there that she was the fourth person needed to make up a bridge quartet. He was, however, completely unable to explain to reporters who had watched his residence all night, the absence of any other bridge players! Pretty soon the royal marriage was nothing more than a sham – with Diana finding solace with her own companions while Charles found his with an old friend of his called Camilla Parker-Bowles, a woman who the British public was to know well in the years to come.

Two things finally blew apart the sham marriage of the Princess of Wales and the future King. One was a book released in 1992 by journalist Andrew Morton in which the sad state of affairs was meticulously chronicled – most of it related by people whom the Princess had expressly given permission to talk.

SECRET CONVERSATION

The book chronicled suicide attempts by Diana – cries for help rather than full-blown bids at dying – her eating disorder, her dreadful row with Charles and the massive gulf which had opened up between them as a result. The second was a tape recording, made in 1989, which was buried for a couple of years before surfacing in British and foreign publications. The tape was allegedly of a conversation between Gilbey and the princess, recorded by a sophisticated listening device. More shocking than the eavesdropping was the tone of the telephone chat itself – it was clearly the talk of lovers, reminiscing of times past and arranging future trysts.

It was branded the infamous 'Squidgy' tape, Squidgy apparently being the pet name that Gilbey had given to his princess. The tape was of two conversations, recorded on New Year's Eve 1989 and on 4 January 1990, allegedly made on Gilbey's car phone to Diana at Sandringham. Here are some extracts from the phone calls that were heard around the world:

GILBEY: That's all I want to do darling. I just want to see you and be with you. That's what's going to be such bliss, being back in London.
DIANA: I know.
GILBEY: I mean, it can't be a regular feature, darling, and I understand that, but it would be nice if you are at least next door, within knocking distance.
DIANA: Yes.
GILBEY: What's that noise?

DIANA: The television drowning my conversation.
GILBEY: Can't you turn it down?
DIANA: No.
GILBEY: Why?
DIANA: Because it's covering my conversation.
GILBEY: All right... don't worry... I can tell the feeling is entirely mutual. Uuuummmmm Squidgy, what else? It's just like unwinding now. I am just letting my heartbeat come down again now. I had the most amazing dream about us last night. Not physical, nothing to do with that.
DIANA: That makes a change.
GILBEY: Darling, it's just that we were together an awful lot of time and we were having dinner with some people. It was the most extraordinary dream, very vivid, because I woke up in the morning and remembered all aspects of it. All bits of it. I remembered sort of what you were wearing and what you had said. It was so strange, very strange and very lovely too.
DIANA: I don't want to get pregnant.
GILBEY: It's not going to happen.
DIANA: (A long sigh.)
GILBEY: Don't worry about that, it's not going to happen darling. You won't get pregnant.
DIANA: I watched 'Eastenders' today and one of the main characters had a baby. They thought it was by her husband but it was by another man. Ha ha!
GILBEY: Squidgy... kiss me. Oh God, it's wonderful this feeling, isn't it? This sort of feeling. Don't you love it?
DIANA: I love it.
GILBEY: Umm.
DIANA: I love it.
GILBEY: Isn't it absolutely wonderful? I haven't had it for years. I feel 21 again.
DIANA: Well you're not, you're 33.
Later he says to her: 'Do you know, as we go into 1990, honey, I can't imagine, you know, what it was that brought us together on that night.
DIANA: No, I know.
GILBEY: And let's make full use of it.
DIANA: I know.

Diana goes on to talk about how 'tortured' her life is with Charles, about her weight, about a meeting she is arranging in London with Gilbey and small talk about going on a swimming trip soon with Fergie and their respective children. One of the conversations ends on this note:

DIANA: I'd better, I'd better. All the love in the world, I'll speak to you tomorrow.
GILBEY: All right. If you can't get me in the morning... you're impatient to go now.
DIANA: Well, I just feel guilty because I haven't done my other business.
GILBEY: Just that I have to wait until Tuesday.
DIANA: All right.
GILBEY: I'll buzz off and simply behave. I'll approach the evening with such enormous confidence now.
DIANA: Good.
GILBEY: And you darling, don't let it get you down.
DIANA: I won't, I won't.

Above: *It is all smiles for the princes and Diana on a skiing holiday in Austria, even though the royal marriage teeters on the brink of extinction.*

DIANA TALKS ABOUT HOW 'TORTURED' HER LIFE IS WITH CHARLES, ABOUT HER WEIGHT, AND ABOUT A MEETING SHE IS ARRANGING WITH GILBEY

The effect upon the marriage – coupled with the impact of the book – was electrifying. Now there could be no doubt in the minds of the British public that the end was in sight. But there would be another tragedy in the House of Windsor in this, the *annus horribilis* of Her Majesty, which was to strike before the end of 1992. On 21 November fate itself, rather than the oversexed genes of her offspring, seemed to conspire against the Queen to cap an altogether miserable year.

That night, Windsor Castle, the most celebrated of royal retreats, guardian of the realm's treasures, was consumed by a massive blaze. It was a fire which, if there had been adequate sprinkler systems installed, might have been contained much more quickly. But the castle wasn't built as a hotel or a government office with all necessary fire exits. It was a medieval structure, scene of over 600 years of pomp and circumstance.

In the fire, sparked by a picture restorer or a loose cigarette end – the cause is still

Above: *Her Majesty the Queen – symbol of a monarchy galloping towards oblivion.*

Right: *The devastation of Windsor Castle ended 1992 – a miserable year for the Queen – she described it as her* annus horribilis.

WINDSOR CASTLE, MOST CELEBRATED OF ROYAL RETREATS, GUARDIAN OF THE REALM'S TREASURES, WAS CONSUMED BY A MASSIVE BLAZE

unclear – some of the finest rooms known to British history were destroyed. Gone in the smoke and flames were many paintings, valuable woodcarvings and the magnificent St. George's Hall, scene of 600 years of state banquets. The Brunswick Tower, Chester Tower, Star Chamber and the Queen's private chapel were also severely damaged, at a cost of £60,000,000. It was a burden which the British taxpayer was expected to foot – initially.

PUBLIC ANGER

In the end, to assuage a mounting tide of anger from her subjects – many of them no doubt turned against the idea of paying for a monarchy which behaved so unregally behind the scenes – she broke with centuries of tradition and agreed to pay taxes on her considerable wealth. The restoration of the castle would not come from the public purse after all.

The fire may have destroyed the Queen's home – but it was an announcement in the House of Commons a few weeks later that burned into her heart. Following the disastrous fire, on 9 December in the House of Commons, John Major rose to deliver this statement about the collapse of the royal marriage between Charles and Diana. The House, and the nation, listened in hushed tones as he spoke: 'It is announced from Buckingham Palace that, with regret, the Prince and Princess of Wales have decided to separate.

'Their Royal Highnesses have no plans to divorce and their constitutional positions

Below: The devastation caused by the fire was clear: one of Britain's best-loved landmarks had been irreparably damaged by the blaze.

are unaffected. Their decision has been reached amicably, and they will both continue to participate fully in the upbringing of their children. Their Royal Highnesses will continue to carry out full and separate programmes of public engagements and will, from time to time, attend family occasions and national events together. The Queen and the Duke of Edinburgh, though saddened, understand and sympathise with the difficulties that have led to this decision.

'Her Majesty and His Royal Highness hope that the intrusion into the privacy of the Prince and Princess of Wales may now cease. They believe that a degree of privacy and understanding is essential if their Royal Highnesses are to provide a happy and secure upbringing for their children, while continuing to give a wholehearted commitment to their public duties.'

After the statement the prime minister said: 'The succession to the throne is unaf-

fected. The children of the Prince and Princess retain their position in the line of succession and there is no reason why the Princess of Wales should not be crowned queen in due course. The Prince of Wales' succession as head of the Church of England is also unaffected.'

But it was gross naïvety, or stupidity, on the part of Buckingham Palace and Downing Street to think that the speculation and debate about the future of the monarchy would subside with such a statement. In fact, the debate increased because of the notion, left hanging in the air, that Britain could have a king and queen who never speak to each other!

ROYAL HYPOCRISY

The thought of such gross hypocrisy being presented to the people of Britain set the chattering classes chattering as never before. And at the beginning of 1993 came publication of a second secret taped phone conversation which probably put paid to a King Charles and Queen Diana combination forever – the alleged chat between Charles and Camilla Parker-Bowles.

In a conversation of 1,574 words, Charles tells her that he loves her twice and she responds in a similar fashion 11 times. The conversation, recorded in 1989, two weeks before the Squidgy tape between Diana and James Gilbey, is far more lewd, and seriously damaged the credibility of the man who would be King:

CHARLES: Oh stop! I want to feel my way along you, all over you and up and down you and in and out.
CAMILLA: Oh!
CHARLES: Particularly in and out!
CAMILLA: Oh, that's just what I need at the moment.
CHARLES: Is it?
CAMILLA: I know it would revive me. I can't bear a Sunday night without you.
CHARLES: Oh, God.
CAMILLA: It's like that programme, 'Start the Week'. I can't start the week without you.
CHARLES: I fill up your tank!
CAMILLA: Yes, you do.
CHARLES: Then you can cope.
CAMILLA: Then I'm all right.
CHARLES: What about me? The trouble is

I need you several times a week.
CAMILLA: Mmm, so do I. I need you all the week. All the time.
CHARLES: Oh God, I'll just live inside your trousers, or something. It would be much easier!
CAMILLA: What are you going to turn into, a pair of knickers? Oh, you're going to come back as a pair of knickers.
CHARLES: Or, God forbid, a Tampax! Just my luck.
CAMILLA: You are a complete idiot! Oh, what a wonderful idea!
CHARLES: My luck to be chucked down a lavatory and go on and on forever swirling round the top, never going down.

THE ALLEGED CONVERSATION HAD CHARLES, HEIR TO THE BRITISH THRONE, FANTASISING ABOUT BECOMING A TAMPAX

Opposite Top: *John Major announced the separation of the Waleses (below), but stipulated that Diana could still reign in Buckingham Palace (opposite bottom).*

Above: *The woman reputed to have stolen Prince Charles' heart – Camilla Parker-Bowles.*

Below: *The Queen Mother, a figure of stability amidst unrest, waves to crowds on her 86th birthday, surrounded by the rest of the family.*

I think you ought to give the brain a rest now. Night night.
CHARLES: Night darling. God bless.
CAMILLA: I do love you and I am so proud of you.
CHARLES: I am so proud of you.

There was a time when newspapers would never have dared to print anything quite so scandalous associated with the future monarch. Now is not such an age and the press broke ranks to print the whole, tawdry talk. It was the conversation which has virtually assured an end to there ever being a queen Diana sitting with Charles on the throne – that is assuming that he ever ascends to the title of King of Britain.

Just who made the tapes is still an issue, with many believing that the security services were behind them. But it is a side issue at best. What they reveal are all the petty jealousies, intrigues and scheming that have been part and parcel of the House of Windsor for years. Someone once said that for monarchy to retain its full majesty, it would be best for much of it to remain shrouded in mystery. Now there is no mystery, very little majesty and a very, very uncertain future for the most regal royal household in the world.

CAMILLA: Oh, darling!

Later in the conversation, as they begin saying an extended goodbye which seems to last forever, he says to her: 'Love you too. I don't want to say goodbye.'

CAMILLA: Well done for doing that. You're a clever old thing. An awfully good brain lurking there, isn't there? Oh darling,

ABUSE
OF
TRUST

J. EDGAR HOOVER
FBI Boss

J. Edgar Hoover was the iron-fisted ruler of the FBI for 48 years. They all came to gaze upon him in Washington, laid out in state like a general or a politician, or a chief of police who had served his nation well. Hoover was all these things and more.

When he died in May 1972, J. Edgar Hoover left behind a legacy of strength in the crime-fighting agency, solid principles upon which to battle crooks, killers, con-men, robbers, spies, kidnappers and criminals of every hue. However, as he lay in his open casket in the rotunda of the Capitol in Washington, the secrets of the empire he created were not yet known. He was still, in the public mind, the law and order hero who tamed the criminals of the land he loved, he was perceived as the man who stood for everything that was decent and good and true in the American character.

It was a magnificent charade, for Hoover was most often the worst kind of policeman. Massive prejudices against liberals, blacks, immigrants, communists and other enemies real and imagined led him to run the FBI like some massive personal vendetta, aimed at the heart of the enemies he regarded as corrupting influences upon the nation he loved.

All the time that he promoted christian, family ethics, he was bound in a life-long homosexual relationship with his closest aide that also led him into gay orgies with young boys and bizarre transvestite evenings that he spent clad as a French maid! Hoover bound presidents to his will because of the massive files he kept on them – every peccadillo, every transgression, every item large and small that could be twisted against them. All the while, scrutiny from without upon the inner workings of the labyrinthine bureaucracy he created was barred. It was only after they laid to rest J. Edgar Hoover that the real story of his incredible power came to light.

Hoover loved bureaucracy throughout his life and no wonder – he was born into it. His father and grandfather worked in a government surveying office while his brother was a steamboat inspector on the Mississippi River. Various other relatives worked in government departments too, so there was never any question that in a 'company town' like Washington – the company in question being the federal government – that he would follow suit.

After a relatively unremarkable high school education J. Edgar Hoover landed a job at the Congress Library for four years, sweating away at night school to earn a master's degree in law, which he finally gained in 1917 at the age of 22. He used his qualifications to get a job with the Justice Department, and on 26 July 1917 Hoover crossed the threshold of the department's

MASSIVE PREJUDICES AGAINST LIBERALS, BLACKS, COMMUNISTS... LED HIM TO RUN THE FBI LIKE SOME MASSIVE PERSONAL VENDETTA

Opposite: *J. Edgar Hoover, all-high crimebuster of the USA, father of the FBI, pictured here in his heyday in the 1930s. But he was as corrupt as the bad guys he pursued.*

Below: *The lawman shortly before his death at the age of 77. Only after he was gone did the story of his twisted rule become fully revealed.*

> HE BECAME KNOWN FOR HIS RUTHLESSNESS IN COMMITTING MOST OF THE PEOPLE WHOSE NAMES CROSSED HIS DESK INTO HARSH INTERNMENT

Below: *The wanted poster for John Dillinger, public enemy number one of his day. Fighting such celebrity villains ensured a cult-like status for Hoover.*

headquarters for the career which would shape and influence American justice for the next half-century.

Almost immediately he felt at home. His ordered mind and cloistered upbringing made him rigorously pro-American and fiercely anti-foreigner – a sentiment sweeping the streets at the time because America had just entered the World War One, and spies and bogeymen were being seen at every turn. In the middle of this hysteria, Hoover thrived.

He dealt initially with regulations governing German aliens in a newly created Alien Enemy Bureau and had the power to order individuals detained for the duration of the war if he deemed them a security risk. He became known for his ruthlessness in committing most of the people whose

names crossed his desk into harsh internment – even going against his superiors on several occasions when they felt surveillance or limited movement in sensitive areas, like near docks or power stations, was more appropriate.

In *Secrecy and Power: The Life of J. Edgar Hoover*, author Richard Gid Powers wrote: 'Hoover was vindictive towards those aliens whose actions might be innocuous, but whose files indicated disloyalty. The enemy status of the aliens Hoover supervised had stripped them of the protection of the Constitution, and so he got his first taste of authority under circumstances in which he could disregard the normal constitutional restraints of the power of the state.' In short, he had tasted power and he liked it very, very much.

THE RED YEARS

What followed became known as the 'Red Years', the years when America turned inward again and battened down the hatches against the new bogeymen – the communists who had seized power in Russia. There was, initially, no job for Hoover at the war's end – the problem of immigration and illegal aliens passed back into the hands of the Labour Department. But his skill had not gone unnoticed. When a wave of radical bombings, linked to Soviets and their agents, blew up in 1919 J. Edgar Hoover was appointed to head the Justice Department's fledgling Bureau of Investigation's Radical Division.

With enormous energy and ambition, he threw himself into the job, hunting down enemies with the same zeal with which he had pursued them during the war. His trademark in the bureau became his mania for files. Overwhelming his enemies with intelligence became his main task and he set about doing so with vigour – Powers referred to this vigour in his book as 'near demonic energy'.

Hoover arrested literally thousands upon thousands of communists, alleged communists, radicals and other barrack room socialists as his lust for power was fuelled by a presidency which believed it was being undermined by seditious elements. Often jails were filled to overflowing, with people being held in unsanitary conditions and without food for days, while the over-

worked agents under Hoover's command struggled to process them all. His struggle against the enemies of the state – many of whom couldn't spell 'communist', let alone understand its meaning, is best illustrated by a memorandum he wrote at the end of 1919: 'Civilisation faces its most terrible menace of danger since the barbarian hordes overran western Europe and opened up the dark ages. We have to prevent international collapse!' Hoover at this time also further cemented his own secret links with a most secret society. He became a Freemason, something he remained to his dying day. It was an invaluable contact point to meet the judges, politicians and the men of influence he would later need in his rise to the top. And its very nature satisfied the cosy, secretive world which Hoover so thoroughly enjoyed.

By 1921 he was assistant director of the bureau – in time for a generation of gangsters like Dillinger, and Bonnie and Clyde to cross his path. In 1924, President Herbert Hoover appointed him director of the bureau – a post he would hold for the

Above: *President Hoover – no relation, but a man whose patronage ensured the FBI leader's rise to prominence.*

Above left: *Bonnie and Clyde, perhaps the most famous diabolical duo that Hoover's G-Men ever tracked down and slaughtered.*

Above: The sour-faced Clyde Tolson, appointed acting-director of the bureau upon the death of his boss. For years Tolson was Hoover's constant companion – and most likely his homosexual lover too.

HE LAID DOWN RULES ON SUITS, SHIRTS AND TIES, AND DELVED INTO THE DRINKING AND DATING HABITS OF HIS AGENTS

next 48 years. The two Hoovers – no relation – shared a common vision for the bureau to become a dogged pursuer of all lawbreakers, particularly the more violent kind that were beginning to crop up as the nation trundled at full speed towards the Great Depression.

Hoover insisted that only college graduates could become agents in the bureau and his watchword was secrecy. He laid down regulations on haircuts, suits, shirts and ties, and even delved into the drinking and dating habits of his agents. He was determined to have an army of zealots who were almost as puritan as he was. An incident in 1932 showed how cunning he was when he once tricked an agent into taking a swig of medicinal alcohol – and then fired him on the spot. He was a disciplinarian who demanded personal loyalty more than any other kind. But he was undeniably a brilliant organiser – within three years the bureau had the best fingerprinting techniques in the country, the best trained agents and the most scientific methods for analysing crime scene clues.

In May 1932, Hoover showed the kind of unethical power he could wield if he thought it was to his advantage. A rag-tag

army of pathetic World War One veterans had marched on Washington to demand early payment of a promised bonus to ease their financial plight. Some 17,000 camped out in a tented city near the Capitol, most of whom dispersed, but a hard-core of 2,000 refused to do so. General Douglas MacArthur sent in troops with fixed bayonets and fired tear gas among the ranks of the men. There was national sympathy for the men, so it was left to Hoover to plot ways to discredit them. Instead of recognising that they were desperate individuals, merely seeking to feed their wives and families, he tarred them as communists and radicals, turning over his extensive fingerprint files for the Washington police to pursue the unfortunates caught in the melee. Hoover would only ever pull this kind of stunt throughout his life when he was assured the full support of the presidency, or other authority figures.

VEILED THREATS

Four years before this it is worth noting the friendship that Hoover formed with Clyde Tolson, the special agent who would become his travelling companion, confidante and rumoured homosexual partner for the rest of his life. Eyebrows were raised when, less than a year after they became friends, he was appointed assistant director. They rode to and from work together, ate lunches together, played golf together and went on holiday together.

Inevitably, the stories of homosexuality swirled around the duo like wildfire – and most of them ended up burning Hoover's ears. He made it his business to track down each and every rumour. He used his agents to visit people all over the country if he heard that they had been the source of the rumours. These agents acted like the musclemen of some gangster, visiting people in their homes with a menacing air, telling them to stop in case certain things happened. Hoover's personal effects were destroyed when he died, in accordance with his wishes, and it's believed many photos of Tolson and letters exchanged between the men went up with them. A homosexual union, of course, is nothing these days to bring public approbation. But in his public dealings, Hoover was a vicious homosexual basher, referring to them as 'queers' and 'fairies'. He often pursued people merely because of their sexuality – while denying to the world that side of his character.

After his death the homosexual allegations surfaced with a vengeance, and none documented them more closely than a book published in America in 1993. *Official and Confidential: The Secret Life of J. Edgar Hoover* by British journalist Anthony Summers – a book which branded him 'Gay Edgar Hoover, a cross-dressing old queen whose sexploits included orgies with young boys'. According to Summers, his secret life involved dressing in 'fluffy black skirts', stockings, black wig and high heels. He had romps with teenaged boys, couplings with rich businessmen and trysts with male prostitutes. And he allegedly paid off top mobsters who obtained porno pictures of his sordid life.

One of the sources of the book is Susan Rosenstiel, fourth wife of distilling magnate Lewis Rosenstiel, one of the richest men in the country in the 1940s and 1950s. She tells how the cold, calculating Hoover dressed himself up as a French maid called Mary for sex orgies at New York's posh Plaza Hotel. She said: 'I couldn't believe what I saw. He was dressed in a black outfit with make-up and false eyelashes. It was a very short skirt and he had a garter belt and stockings on. A friend of my husband's introduced him as Mary.' Susan, who left her husband because of his perverted lust for young boys, claims she then saw Hoover have sex with two blonde teenaged boys. At another party a year later – sometime in the late 1950s – he dressed as a 1920s flapper with a feather boa for his illicit sex games. But he was fearful of gangsters Meyer Lansky and Frank Costello – because they had photos of his sexcapades while dressed as 'Mary'.

HEAD-TO-HEAD

While his own private life was his affair, crime was becoming a national obsession in Hoover's America. Soon his bureau was going head-to-head with Al Capone, Machine Gun Kelly, Pretty Boy Floyd and Baby Face Nelson. As the government sought out his agency to tackle the depression-era inspired crime wave, his 'G-Men' became the most famous crimebusters in the nation's history.

While his public profile grew, however, it was the behind-the-scenes covert arm of his organisation which gave him such clout. For he assembled, on President Roosevelt's orders, the machinery of a domestic intelligence agency, the purpose for which was the suppression of any thought, action or organisation that the government – but most often Hoover – disagreed with. It was enormous power to be wielded by one individual, especially one with such rigid ideas as his.

His war on gangsters was always conducted with two aims in mind – successful missions and the glorification of J. Edgar Hoover in every high-profile case. Whether it was Dillinger or Kelly, agents were always told to issue press releases that put the director in command – and often placed his own life in danger.

He even took the glory for the arrest of Bruno Hauptmann in the Lindbergh kidnapping case of 1934 – even though the bureau had done the least of the police work. He had an uncanny sense of the pub-

Above: *Al Capone, the Chicago mobster who turned America's second city into his own crooked fiefdom.*

Right: *President Roosevelt, whose law and order mandate was coupled with a policy for social justice and equality. Hoover reined in the bad guys while Roosevelt tried to put America to work.*

Below: *Meyer Lansky, the Jewish gangster who built Las Vegas, seen here being taken in for police questioning over the slaying of a rival mobster.*

lic thirst for melodrama associated with justice, and was always eager to play to the gallery. It suited his purpose because it detracted nosy reporters and inquisitive citizens from probing deeply into the intelligence section and his burgeoning dossiers.

THE PRIVILEGES

All the while, Hoover lived like a king. The furniture in his home was made by FBI carpenters and the decorations were carried out by FBI handymen. He had not one but seven bulletproof agency cars that had to be kept spick and span at all times. He used agents to place huge bets for him at racetracks across America, while publicly he kept up the charade of being a small-time gambler with wagers of no more than a dollar. He hired a black man to stand in his office all day and do nothing but swat flies. Such were the privileges of high office.

The war years gave way to the Cold War in which Hoover again excelled in targeting the ideological enemies of America – the McCarthy witch-hunts centred against 'un-American' actors, directors and producers in Hollywood. The black hand of Hoover was in many of the prosecutions which were compared to the Salem witch-hunts of the 17th century. But while he was keen to root out the coffee bar radicals and the avowed liberals, he did nothing to confront the real menace facing society – the absolute stranglehold on crime that the Mafia was developing.

Hoover simply refused to believe that crime was organised to such an extent - or so he said. In reality, he left the mob alone because they owned him. Frank Costello, one of the Mafia's biggest potentates, was a friend of his for years. He made sure that the director scored on the mob-owned racetracks around the states – and Hoover was a chronic, almost uncontrollable gambler – while he kept the heat off his boys. In 1990, mob boss Carmine Lombardozzi said: 'The families, all the mob families, made sure that he was looked after when he visited the tracks on the east coast and California. They had an understanding. He would lay off the families, turn a blind eye. It helped that he denied that we existed.'

Conflicting pressures over his homosexuality – posturing as a moral guardian in public, cavorting in gay trysts in private –

made him a victim of mob blackmail. Meyer Lansky in particular learned of his dark secret and used it as a threat to neutralise FBI operation against his own crime syndicate. Hoover, for instance, knew that Lansky ordered the execution of Las Vegas crime kingpin Bugsy Siegel, but he did nothing about it. It is widely believed that Lansky had pictures of Hoover in bed with Tolson, taken through a two-way mirror at a hotel owned by the Mafia.

FEARSOME REPUTATION

By the time John F. Kennedy came to power in the 1960s, Hoover's reputation at the core of government was fearsome. His files were now legendary and judges, politicians and movie stars did their best never to offend him for fear that he would use the information in them against them. Supporters of JFK hoped that he would retire the snooping Hoover and install a younger, less corrupt individual, but Kennedy knew better. For his was one of the biggest files of all. Hoover loathed Kennedy's liberal attitudes, his plans to bring civil rights to the blacks in the impoverished south and to bring segregated black and white children together. Hoover was determined to nail him.

Hoover's file on Kennedy began back at the start of World War Two when Kennedy romanced a 28-year-old beauty called Inga Arvad who was suspected of having Nazi sympathies. Hoover's perverse morality was deeply offended by JFK's sexual trysts with the woman and he copiously gathered every sordid detail, right down to their pillow-talk gleaned by the use of hidden FBI microphones. When he came to power Hoover was outwardly polite to Kennedy, but worked furiously behind the scenes to smear him as much as possible. Hoover ordered his agents to send such material to newspapers, but little of it was printed.

Hoover knew that women were Kennedy's greatest weakness and he sought to exploit it every way he possibly could. The novelist Gore Vidal said: 'I talked to the president about it, and he gave me one of those looks. He loathed Hoover. I didn't know then that Hoover was blackmailing him, nor did I realise how helpless the Kennedys were to do anything about him.' Ben Bradlee, the tough and fearless editor of the *Washington Post*, which was eventually to expose President Nixon and the Watergate scandal, said: 'All the Kennedys were afraid of Hoover. John F. Kennedy was afraid not to re-appoint him.' When Hoover found out about the affair that JFK and his brother had with Hollywood actress Marilyn Monroe, he used it to twist both their arms, continuing his long service without any interruption from either.

Above: *Marilyn Monroe, who dallied with President John F. Kennedy – and his brother Robert – and whose secrets were kept in Hoover's Pandora's Box.*
Above left: *President Kennedy, who despised Hoover and who was despised in return.*

Above: *Robert Kennedy, Attorney General of the USA, believed Hoover to be a force for evil in the nation.*

He remained in office long after both had been assassinated. For 10 more years, until his death, he worked at his files and remained the Big Brother of Washington, forever spying on all whom he found distasteful or unworthy. Hoover died peacefully in his sleep on 1 May 1972 – sending President Nixon and hundreds of government-appointed flunkies scurrying in a search for the files that could bury them all.

However, Hoover ordered the destruction of many of his dossiers, and many others were still classified. But the Pandora's Box of Hoover's remaining files on Hollywood celebrities and America's most powerful men and women caused a sensation when they were opened in the years following his death. They revealed snooping on a scale never before known – prying eyes that delved into the bedrooms and boardrooms of the high and mighty. It was the FBI who knew Rock Hudson was gay long before they told the world and Hoover dubbed him 'Frock Hudson' in secret reports – the irony lost on him, presumably, considering his own secret predilections for women's clothes.

It was Hoover who ordered the probe into Muhammed Ali's background when he refused to fight in Vietnam – and even pulled his school report cards. It was Hoover who branded Hollywood superstar Jane Fonda an 'anarchist' and 'revolutionary' for her stance against the war. And it was Hoover who considered Britain's former king, the Duke of Windsor, a security risk because he was 'too close to Hitler'. Here are details of four of the files released after Hoover's death, which show the massive paranoia which never left him during his reign as America's guardian angel against crime.

Above: *Richard Nixon, a patron of Hoover's, who ensured a hero's funeral for the FBI man when he passed away.*

Right: *Muhammed Ali in action against Floyd Patterson in Las Vegas in 1965. Ali found his way into Hoover's notorious files due to his refusal to fight in Vietnam.*

THE FBI KNEW ROCK HUDSON WAS GAY LONG BEFORE THEY TOLD THE WORLD. HOOVER DUBBED HIM 'FROCK HUDSON'

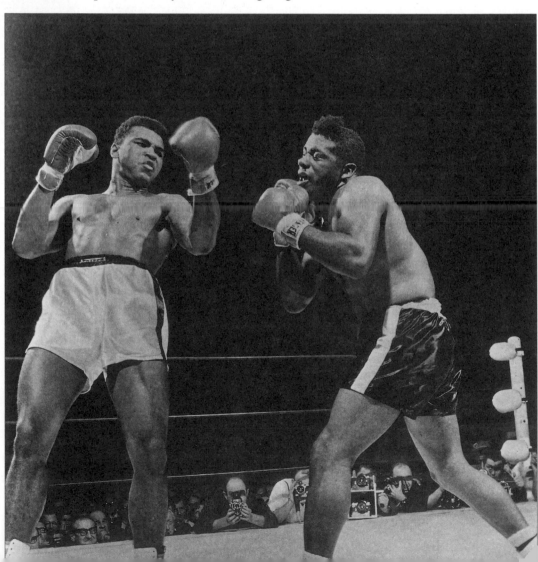

CASE 190 - 29575:
THE PRINCE OF SPIES

Many thought the Duke and Duchess of Windsor's love story was the romance of the century. He was, after all, the man who gave up the throne of England for the woman he loved. But to Hoover he was foppish and weak, a puppet of the Nazis, and a man not to be trusted in case he passed on allied wartime secrets. The file on the couple contains secret letters – one alleging that the marriage between American-born Wallis Simpson and the Duke was arranged by Nazi foreign minister Joachim von Ribbentrop and Hitler to prevent Edward signing a declaration of war against Britain!

Another letter to Hoover's right-hand man Clyde Tolson, written by a high-level agency informant, claimed that the Duchess regularly sent her clothes across the Atlantic for dry cleaning. He believed that secret messages to a Nazi spy inside America were hidden in the clothes. Hoover's case file says: 'Certain would-be state secrets were passed on to Edward, and when it was found out that Ribbentrop actually received the same information the British prime minister was forced to accept that the leakage had been located. We believe it was leaked by the Duchess.'

CASE 94 - 62 63352:
FROCK HUDSON

The FBI knew long before the rest of the world that Hollywood's sexiest leading man was a rampant homosexual. Hoover personally ratted on him to Lyndon Johnson in the White House – calling him a 'sex offender' and pervert. One memo in his file, about an interrogation over orgies with young boys, said: 'In view of his homosexual tendencies the interview will be conducted by two mature special agents.' One piece of paper in his file has names of several prominent Hollywood figures blacked out – these are the men who participated in gay orgies with Hudson. And several of the memorandums marked

Above: *Rock Hudson, the secret gay whose homosexual lifestyle infuriated and fascinated the hypocrite Hoover.*

Left: *The Duke and Duchess of Windsor, who Hoover suspected of being Nazi sympathisers.*

'director's eyes only' were sent to Hoover by a special agent who had as an informant a star actor who was a gay lover of Rock's for six years. Rock was referred to by the informant as 'Frock Hudson' and said that he particularly liked orgies with young boys at 'poolside parties'.

The actor's homosexuality was only revealed towards the end of his life when he was dying from AIDS. Hoover managed to keep his own homosexuality masked, despite rumours for most of his life, until after his death.

Below: *French film director Roger Vadim and his bride Jane Fonda. Hoover's bureau tried to destroy liberals like them because he saw them as a cancer eating into America's soul.*

CASE 876 - 8535: JANE FONDA

Jane Fonda's file was listed under 'Security Matters' – and Hoover branded her 'Anarchist' for her repeated outbursts against the Vietnam War. Hoover paid out hundreds of thousands of dollars to spy on her. Eventually there was a 1,000 page dossier on her in FBI files as her phones were bugged, her mail opened, her garbage rifled through, her friends followed and her associates photographed by spy cameras.

The file reveals that the FBI even tried to frame her with a phoney letter when they couldn't get her on treason charges. In June 1970, Wesley Grapp, chief of the Bureau's Los Angeles office, suggested to Hoover that a letter about Jane's involvement with the violent Black Panther party should be concocted and sent to a columnist on the *Hollywood Variety* paper. The letter to columnist Army Archerd read: 'I saw your article about Jane Fonda and happened to be present for her performance of her Joan of Arc for the Black Panthers Saturday night. I hadn't been confronted with the Panther phenomena before, but we were searched upon entering the auditorium, encouraged to contribute for jailed panther leaders and buy guns for the coming revolution. And led by Jane and one of the Panther chaps in a "we will kill Richard Nixon and any other motherf***er who stands in our way" refrain. I think Jane has gotten in over her head.'

The letter was signed 'Morris' and mailed by Grapp. Archerd ignored it, but it shows the depths that Hoover was willing to allow the FBI to go to when his blood was up. He knew no bounds in discrediting a citizen that he despised.

CASE 100 - 4699910: JOHN LENNON

John Lennon found no friends in the FBI. His drug use, his hippy lifestyle, his 'bad influence' on American youth made him the target of a fierce Hoover witch-hunt. At one place in his two inch-thick file are scrawled the words, in Hoover's handwriting: 'All extremists should be considered dangerous'. The bureau's agents also noted: 'Our source advises that Lennon appears to be radically oriented. However,

he does not give the impression that he is a true revolutionist since he is constantly under the influence of narcotics.' Another memo in the file claimed Lennon was a member of an extreme left-wing political party called the Progressive Labour Party. The memo reads: 'Its objective is the establishment of a militant working class based on Marxist-Leninist and Mao Tse Tung thought.' Yet another said: 'Lennon wanted an open society where free dope, free sex and free rock music abounded.' Hoover hated Lennon and ordered the FBI to work hard to turn up dirt on him in a bid to get him deported from the United States. Hoover requested, in a memo found in the file, that any information on Lennon's drug

use was to be directed immediately to him. He tried to get an obscenity trial underway when Lennon posed with Yoko Ono naked on an album cover. However, a letter to the disappointed FBI chief said that top legal advice was sought and they found no grounds for a lawsuit.

His biographer Anthony Summers added: 'It became clear that Hoover had long abused his office, undermining the basic American freedoms he had claimed to hold dear. Yet 20 years after his death, despite the compelling evidence that he was a force for great evil in the nation's life, Hoover's name still gleams in letters of gold, high on the walls of FBI headquarters in Washington.'

Above: *John Lennon and Yoko Ono were to Hoover what holy water is to a vampire. Hoover remained vengeful to the end against the ex-Beatle after having failed to have Lennon thrown out of the United States.*

PAPA DOC
Voodoo King

Papa Doc's reign of terror and dread over the Haitian people began in 1957 when he was propelled to power. He convinced his people that he was a voodoo 'superman' and created the world's one and only voodoo police, the Ton-Ton Macoute.

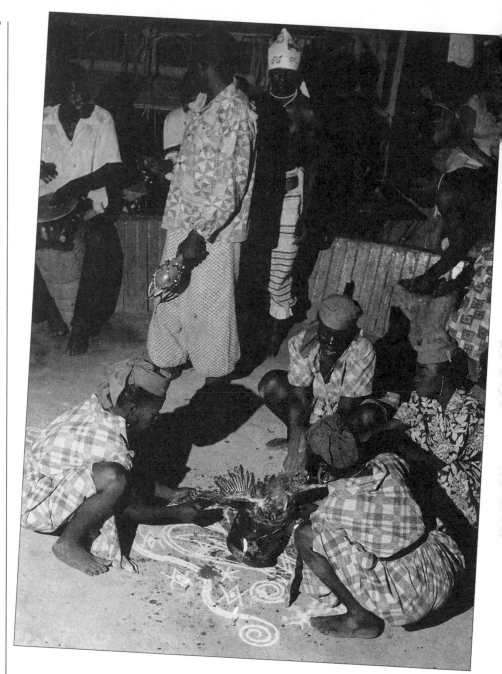

Haiti lies sweltering in the relentless Caribbean sun – an isle of such tropical beauty and promise that it is hard to believe that any evil could possibly lurk beyond the palm-fringed beaches; that there could be anything blacker at its heart than the beans which the dirt-poor natives eat with rice as part of their staple diet. And yet Haiti is a wretched land, its people beaten and brutalised by successive regimes of intolerance and corruption, its leaders wicked to the core. Infants born here have a one in 50 chance of reaching their first birthday, while employment for adults means backbreaking work in the sugar cane fields or serving as a waiter or kitchen hand in one of the few decrepit hotels. Whatever they do, the United Nations lists the median net income as less then £200 per adult per year.

The Haitian people themselves are bright and kind, happy (without much to be happy about) and deeply religious. Religious, that is, until the sun goes down... when they begin to worship spirits of a very different hue to those sanctioned by the Catholic church. There is a common maxim in Haiti that the people worship Jesus Christ on a Sunday – and all the rest of the time devote themselves to voodoo. It is precisely because of their age-old, deep rooted belief in voodoo that they were to be ruled for almost three decades by the Duvalier clan – first 'Papa Doc' Duvalier and then his son 'Baby Doc'. Capitalising on their superstitions, their fears, the ancient dread of the

night and the forest, this evil family were able to live like feudal lords while their countrymen sweated and starved and died.

Like all dictators, Papa Doc knew the value of a security force to keep them in check – to stop any radical ideas from permeating society. Ideas like freedom and truth and justice. Just as Caesar had his Praetorian Guard and Hitler had his SS, so Papa Doc created his own elite force, the Ton-Ton Macoute.

During the reign of the Duvaliers the Ton-Tons were the apocalyptic harbingers of death and misery upon Haiti's sun-kissed shores. Preying on the superstitions inherent in the population, they were

Above: *When the sun goes down on Haiti the locals practise their ancient and dark voodoo rites to the beat of drums and by the embers of glowing coals.*

Opposite: *Dr. Francois Duvalier, otherwise known as Papa Doc, the Voodoo King of Haiti, whose evil reign blighted his superstitious country forever.*

Above: *Port-au-Prince, the capital of Haiti, is a city of quaint colonial architecture.*

Above right: *A stilt walker entertains the city's poor. While his people scraped a living on the streets, Papa Doc resided in a splendid Port-au-Prince palace.*

HUMAN RIGHTS GROUPS PUT THE DEATH TOLL DURING PAPA DOC'S REIGN AT 40,000, WITH ANOTHER 20,000 MURDERS UNDER BABY DOC'S TENURE

regarded as the messengers of Baron Samedei, voodoo's Spirit of Death, at one and the same time the most feared and respected of voodoo gods. The Ton-Tons were paid little – but they took what they wanted in terms of food, money, women – even houses and children. And they killed what they didn't. Human rights groups put the death toll during Papa Doc's reign at 40,000 – another 20,000 murders under Baby Doc's tenure. The voodoo police have left a stain on the island that will never be erased.

To understand how a 20th century people could lead themselves to be cowed by such a brutal force – and to accept their sway over life and death with such equanimity – it is necessary to have a comprehension of the roots of voodoo itself. It originated on the west coast of Africa, at a place called Dahomey, where the slave trade had one of its main centres. The slaves, taken from peaceful villages by men with guns and held under appalling conditions, considered themselves to be captives of evil, yet powerful gods.

Escapism from such vile torments resulted in trance-like states being induced at late night, illicit revels. The sacrifice of animals to the forces of darkness was a crucial part of the ceremonies – the belief that Baron Samedei would leave an individual alone if his appetite was satisfied with other offerings. The religion flourished for three centuries of slave trading but died out across Africa as man's enlightenment gradually spread. But in outposts like Haiti, which the French colonialists flooded with slaves, the secrets of voodoo remained locked in the native heart.

Worshipping the dark side of man's soul, voodoo was, and remains, a potent force. Even now, though a casual tourist to the capital Port-au-Prince may see the outward signs of 20th century civilisation – a marble hotel entrance, an automatic bank machine – he would do well to know that in the hills and the villages, when the sun goes down, the coals are lit, the chickens are slaughtered, and the human zombies walk in celebration of all that is base in man's conscience.

Someone who understood this need for voodoo, who capitalised on it like a natural resource, was Francois Duvalier. Duvalier was a medical student in the 1940s who cared less for the Hippocratic Oath and more for his own ambitions. Educated abroad, he was familiar with all the advances of science and medicine – skills which his sponsors hoped he would put to good use in dealing with the chronic ailments which afflicted the population. But the strain of voodoo ran deep in his veins, too. This doctor-dictator's views on the matter can be be gauged in his own words. In a book written shortly before he attained power, entitled *The Gradual Evolution of Voodoo*, Duvalier said: 'Every country has its own folklore. It is part of its patrimony. It is so in England, in Japan, and in Central Europe. So it is in Haiti. Voodoo is in our blood, it is part of the people.'

He then goes on to extol the virtues of the black religion, saying it is a 'natural and integral part' of the Haitian character. Charles Delwin, a historian who made a study of the Duvalier years, summed him up thus: 'He wore Paris suits and English suits and threw American dollars to the starving, underfed masses at his feet. He conned millions of dollars in foreign aid which he salted away in Switzerland and other investor-friendly nations. He talked

with heads of state and held sway over life and death. And yet the beating of the voodoo drums never left his heart. Even though he used the religion to his evil advantage, there can be no doubt that in him, Baron Samedei and all the other voodoo deities had a true believer.'

A son of one of the few wealthy families on Haiti, Duvalier practised medicine for just a brief time before, in 1946, he became director general of the national public health service. Shortly afterwards he became minister of health and labour and

> 'HE HELD SWAY OVER LIFE AND DEATH. AND YET THE BEATING OF THE VOODOO DRUMS NEVER LEFT HIS HEART'

Above: *Papa Doc, looking disinterested in old age, receiving a foreign emissary at Port-au-Prince airport. The Haitian leader begged for aid from abroad to help his poor land – and spent it on himself and his family.*

Left: *One of the last photos of the old despot before his death. Power passed to his son, who turned out to be as corrupt and murderous as his father.*

in 1950 was forced to flee into the voodoo-infested interior of the country after opposing a military coup led by Paul Magloire.

For six years, probably the most worthy period of his life, Duvalier practised medicine in the country's hinterland while all the time gaining more and more experience of voodoo. It was during this period that he hit on the idea of making himself into a voodoo 'superman'. If he could convince the cowed and ill-educated population – 90 per cent of Haitians are illiterate – that he possessed supernatural powers, endowed by Baron Samedei, then he could rule unchallenged in the manner that he dreamed of. Such was his dream – a dream that he turned into reality in 1957. After a general political amnesty the previous year, Duvalier enlisted the support of army generals, without whom no aspiring dictator could think of becoming boss. They propelled him to power and the terror began.

The natives called him Papa Doc because of his benign appearance and his apparent understanding of 'their ways'. He encouraged the nickname, believing it gave him a paternalistic, human air. He changed the colours of the Haitian flag to red and black – the colours of secret voodoo societies – and unleashed the Ton-Tons on their lethal missions.

Ton-Ton Macoutes is a Creole phrase that literally translates into 'bogeyman'. He formed this elite guard as a bulwark against the kind of military coup that he himself had staged to take power. Dressed in an informal kind of uniform consisting of blue serge pants, blue shirt and red neckerchief, they were heavily armed and given powers far beyond those of normal police officers. The president sanctioned their bloody crusade and their mission was a simple one: to reduce the peasantry to cringing, subservient vassals who believed that Papa Doc had a direct link into the very heart of Baron Samedei.

APPALLING ACTS

They operated much like the Khmer Rouge of Pol Pot's brutal Cambodian regime. Ton-Ton squads would alight on a village, round up men and women into separate groups and then pillage what food and valuables were available for themselves. Women were raped, village elders killed by having their throats slit or their heads bashed in with rocks. Rarely were there wholesale massacres – the entire purpose of the Ton-Ton campaign was for the survivors to see and spread the methods which they employed to scare the living daylights

> DUVALIER PRACTISED MEDICINE IN HAITI'S HINTERLAND... ALL THE TIME GAINING MORE EXPERIENCE OF VOODOO

Right: *Portrait of a tyrant: the tired face of the dictator as the end nears.*

Below: *Ancient voodoo rites in praise of the zombie god Baron Samedei.*

out of their neighbours. And one of the most appalling acts that they lived to tell about was the wholesale plunder of children. In Haitian society a child is a valued commodity, and a man and woman with many children are more exalted than those with few or none.

Many Ton-Tons stole children for themselves, or for friends, or simply for those who paid for them. In Haitian mythology, the Bogeymen of legends traditionally came calling at Christmas time to take away children who did not deserve presents. Duvalier turned this tale into monstrous reality. To this day, the island is covered with people searching for their roots.

ding. Also in the cellars of the palace was a torture chamber where Duvalier was said to delight in the spectacle of his countrymen being branded with red hot pokers or being suspended from their thumbs until they confessed to some true or imaginary crimes that his inquisitors had conjured up.

While his Ton-Tons fleeced the peasants, Papa Doc fleeced the country with astonishing skill and dexterity. He convinced many foreign governments, particularly America, to pour in masses of aid dollars to help his poor, blighted land. Duvalier was a consummate con man whose bespectacled image led many western leaders to think of him as a philanthropic leader, intent only

DUVALIER TURNED THE BOGEYMEN INTO MONSTROUS REALITY. TO THIS DAY, HAITI IS COVERED WITH PEOPLE SEARCHING FOR THEIR TRUE ROOTS

It is estimated that some 600 people were executed in the first year – although no lists were kept. And much worse was to come as Papa Doc's tyranny reached crueller and crueller heights.

Papa Doc relished the dead, praising them in a necrophilic way. Many corpses were brought to the cellars of the presidential palace where he visited them at night with voodoo priests, attempting to conjure up zombies, the 'living dead', to do his bid-

on the best for his poor countrymen. In reality, the aid which arrived in Haiti went nowhere but his own bank accounts. Literally millions was creamed off to satisfy his lust for fine wines, fast cars and high living. In a show of grotesque assurance he took to riding his bullet-proofed limousine through the pot-holed streets of Port-au-Prince, throwing $50 and $100 bills like confetti at the cringing feet of the peasants. Afterwards, when the TV cameras had

Above: *Catholicism is the official religion of Haiti, but it is to the dark and sinister forces of voodoo that the people always turn.*

Above: *Papa Doc Duvalier's son Baby Doc and his fiancée Michelle Bennett on the day their engagement was announced.*

Above: *Baby Doc takes a walk through the troubled streets of Port-au-Prince in February 1986. It was a last-ditch bid to quell the mutinous population, who were rising up against him.*

gone, the Ton-Tons paid a visit to those unfortunate enough to have scooped up the alms from their leader.

When he wasn't imprisoning, torturing or sanctioning wholesale slaughter, Duvalier was a keen practitioner of voodoo himself. He was a supreme believer in its powers and often held dark rites in the palace cellars or in his own study. One story has it that in 1967, while Alec Guinness, Elizabeth Taylor and Richard Burton were in Port-au-Prince filming the Graham Greene novel, *The Comedians*, he became incensed at reports of the film's tone. The screenplay was a scathing attack of life in Haiti under his regime. Rather than appear despotic to the west and expelling them – thereby running the risk of a loss of aid which was feathering his nest nicely – he resorted to the ju-ju doll and the pin. An ex-aide reported many years later that he fashioned wax effigies of the trio, dressed them in glamorous clothes made by a doll manufacturer, and proceeded to stab them! 'His rage was intense,' said the aide. 'He wanted to boot them out but knew he couldn't. He invoked spirits for them to die.'

Voodoo gods who held particular sway for Papa Doc were Ogoun, the warrior spirit who liked fire and the colour red, and Damballah, who supposedly represented wisdom. But as the ancient Greeks and Romans had a whole panoply of Gods, so in voodoo there were others who had to be constantly appeased. A visiting foreign dig-

nitary was dumbstruck at a formal dinner party when Duvalier began lecturing him on the spirits. Papa Doc said: 'You must serve all the spirits otherwise they get jealous. I love all the spirits but I got a special thing for Ogoun and Baron Samedei. I call God and the spirits. I light my candle and I throw the water. Like you brush your teeth everyday, I light a candle every day and throw some water for my God. If I want to make Ogoun happy I buy him a chicken and some Barbancourt rum and some good rice and beans which I put in bowls on the floor. For Damballah, you get a big fish and some white rice. And then you must buy all their favourite drinks. For the spirit Guede you must put a hot pepper in a bottle of gin. It is important to honour them otherwise something will go terribly wrong.'

The foreign dignitary, visiting from France, thought the pilot had told him upon landing that he had to set his watch back one hour. Listening to Duvalier he realised that visitors to Haiti had to set their minds back 500 years!

VOODOO SPELL

The late president John F. Kennedy was a man who got similar voodoo treatment – posthumously. After his death there were disturbing reports coming out of Washington that Papa Doc might not be the benevolent ruler that he cast himself as. Some $500,000,000 of American aid had gone to Haiti – and the advancements in society seemed negligible even to the untrained eye.

Seeking to avert what might have been a complete cut-off of aid, Papa Doc despatched one of his voodoo agents to JFK's grave at Arlington National Cemetery outside Washington to collect the necessary items for a voodoo spell. 'A pinch of earth, a withered flower and a vial of air,' the voodoo priest had told him. With these Papa Doc sat in his office in the crumbling presidential palace and invoked the spirits of the dead. He hoped that the spell would imprison president Kennedy's soul – and thus control US policy in the region. It was yet another example of the lengths to which he was prepared to go to get his own way.

Papa Doc died from natural causes in 1971, with his Ton-Ton Macoute police still terrorising his people and his power base intact. There was hope in the island, and in the countries which had poured in so much aid, that at last there would be a return to decency and civility in the country's internal politics. It was not to be. The reigns of power passed to his son, who rapidly became known as 'Baby Doc' among the cowed Haitians. He kept the voodoo priests satisfied in the villages, paid lip service to the Catholic priests in the towns and ensured that life continued in the same, corrupt fashion.

Baby Doc was, if anything, more corrupt than his father. He bought off the military – without whom he could not have maintained power – and was absent from Haiti for upwards of six months of the year as he went on lavish spending sprees abroad for gems, furs, fine wines, silver, currencies, antiques, artwork and furnishings. But he was a despot living on borrowed time.

The evil work of the Ton-Ton Macoute had spread around the world. Too many foreign journalists had slipped into Haiti to interview the terrified people and several mass burial sites of victims – in the end a staggering tally of 40,000 – had been unearthed. The spell was close to being broken, and when it finally was in 1986, a tidal wave of revenge swept over the sun drenched island. As Baby Doc fled to France – pressured from the United States on the outside and his own military hardliners within – Baron Samedei was once again summoned up. Only this time he was on the side of the people. Hundreds of Ton-Ton men were massacred, butchered with the long sugar-cane machetes usually wielded by the oppressed workers in the plantations. Their homes were burned, and their corpses mutilated in a frenzy of revenge at so many years of suffering.

SHORT-LIVED

Democracy visited Haiti but it didn't stay very long. The government of Jean-Bertrand Aristide was ousted in a coup two years ago by the military hardmen, who continue to rule without a hint of conceding to outside calls for the return of the democratically elected leader.

If anything, the disappearances and torture under the military government exceed the brutalities of the Duvalier clan. The Haitian Constitution promises basic human rights to all who live under it – but the reality of the situation is far different. In April 1992, Joe Sills, spokesman for United Nations Secretary General Boutros Boutros-Ghali said international officials are 'profoundly worried about the number and severity of violations of human rights, consisting of arbitrary detentions, systemat-

Below: *Father Jean-Baptiste Aristide, the only democratically elected leader in Haiti, pictured here saying mass in 1987.*

ic repression and torture inflicted and perpetrated by members of the armed forces and persons aligned with them. The attacks are to restrain, prohibit, and forbid freedom of expression, the right to meet peacefully and demonstrate.' Father Antoine Adrien, who was the head of the Presidential Commission, a group chosen to represent Aristide while he is in exile, said: 'The main target of the repression is the youth and community organisers, those who try to awaken in the people the injustices that are being heaped upon them. The core of the problem is no longer the Ton-Ton Macoute, but the army, for they have taken the law into their own hands.'

And for the people, periodically at least, there is release in voodoo, in the trances, in the chants and the fire-walking. At night the same, age old practices are repeated time and again, the same spirits as those worshipped by their oppressors are summoned up by the wretched people.

Voodoo will probably always remain the one constant bedfellow to poverty in this blighted land.

> BABY DOC WAS, IF ANYTHING, MORE CORRUPT THAN HIS FATHER. HE BOUGHT OFF THE MILITARY AND WENT ON LAVISH SPENDING SPREES

THE JUNTA
Argentine Terror

From 1930 onwards there have been six coups and 21 military governments in Argentina. Humanity ceased to exist in the land of the pampas in the years between 1976 and 1983, reaching its cruel zenith as Leopoldo Galtieri assumed power in 1981.

Leopoldo Galtieri was heir to a sordid and ignoble past in the military's history in his native land of Argentina. The qualities of machismo and strength, inherent in the Argentine male character, were multiplied tenfold in the armed forces – particularly in the officer corps. Galtieri and the other leaders of the Junta – the ruling military caste – believed that civilians were not fit to be governed by other civilians, and people like him were always ready to step into power. From 1930 until the present day there have been no less than six coups and 21 military governments in Argentina. No civilian government managed to last its full term, save that of Juan Peron's first term in office.

When the Falklands War broke upon Argentina in 1982, finally forcing Galtieri and the other military leaders from power, he and his cohorts had overseen the mass murder of their own citizens in the most chilling genocide programme since Hitler's slaughter of the Jews in World War Two.

Given a clinical name, 'The Process of National Reorganisation' was nothing less than the extermination of anyone and everyone who disagreed with the Junta's rule. At first the targets were left-wing terrorists who had wreaked terror in Argentina's countryside. These could, at a stretch, be considered fair game – they had murdered and extorted, tortured and kidnapped in the name of political progress. But as the net was thrown wider and wider, so the victims were increasingly innocent,

LEOPOLDO GALTIERI WAS HEIR TO A SORDID AND IGNOBLE PAST IN THE MILITARY'S HISTORY IN HIS NATIVE LAND OF ARGENTINA

Opposite: *General Galtieri takes a parade salute in Buenos Aires before the Falklands War decimated his forces – and led to the downfall of his rotten regime, under which many of his countrymen had been murdered and tortured.*

Below: *Lami Dozo, Galtieri and Admiral Anaya – the warlords of Argentina stand trial for the dirty war they waged against dissidents in their own country.*

*Above: **Buenos Aires, 'The Paris of South America', was the nerve centre for the generals and the hub of all their power.***

SYMPATHIES WITH ANYONE BUT THE GENERALS WAS PUNISHABLE BY DEATH. THOUGHT CRIME WAS A CAPITAL OFFENCE

including coffee bar radicals, student protestors, left- wing journalists and authors, sociologists, preachers and doctors. Soon the jails were full – and the killings began.

Galtieri, the leader of the army, assumed power in Argentina in 1981. He was the head of a corrupt junta of three. The other lynchpins of this triumvirate of evil were General Lami Dozo of the air force and Admiral Jorge Anaya of the Navy. All knew about the Process of National Reorganisation, launched in 1976 by General Jorge Videla, whose tanks rolled onto the streets on 23 March 1976 to overthrow the massively inefficient government of Isabelita Peron.

Videla, having seized the radio and TV stations, put it to his people like this: 'Since all constitutional mechanisms have been exhausted, and since the impossibility of recovery through normal processes has been irrefutably demonstrated, the armed forces must put an end to this situation which has burdened the nation. This government will be imbued with a profound national spirit, and will respond only to the most sacred interests of the nation and its inhabitants.' There was a tone of harshness

and determination in his voice which made the people of Argentina embrace rather than shrink from military government. Under Isabelita, inflation was a staggering 800 per cent in the first quarter of the year. Strikes were rife, unemployment was rising, and civil disturbances were increasing in number. But by far the biggest problem, as Videla and his generals saw it, were the left-wing rebels called the Montoneros and the ERP, the Ejercito Revolucionario del Pueblo, the People's Revolutionary Army. They had plunged much of the country into crisis as, much like the IRA attempts against Westminster today, they tried to bring about political change with the bullet and the bomb.

Lawlessness and terror rode alongside the gauchos on the plains of Argentina. They surfaced in the streets of South America's jewel, Buenos Aries, and were prevalent all the way down to Tierra del Fuego at the very bottom of the continent. To combat it, Videla and his generals drew up a secret agenda. They were going to declare war on the terrorists in the same fashion that the terrorist had declared war on society. It would be a war without rules, unhindered by such sentimentalities as a Geneva Convention. The targets for this war were the citizens of their own nation.

DIRTY WAR

Videla's dirty war was riddled with Orwellian thinking; not only were the terrorists to be targeted, but also anyone who had ever vaguely held an opinion or read a book that ran contrary to conservative Argentine political thought. Sympathies with anyone other than the generals became a crime punishable by death. Thought crime, the transgression of Winston Smith in *1984*, was now a capital offence in the new Argentina.

The strategy for this grand clash of ideas – the warriors of the right versus the heretics of Marxism – was laid out at a secret meeting between Videla and his generals a year before he came to power. In August 1975, he summoned army officers of the rank of Brigadier or above and let them in on what he proposed for the dissenters in the country. Galtieri, who was later to govern, was one of those present who unequivocally endorsed the blueprint for the Process of National Reorganisation. Two months later, at the seaport of Montevideo in Uruguay, Videla made a speech to army officers of that nation in which he alluded to the decay of society in his own country. 'In order to guarantee the security of the state,' he said, referring to Argentina, 'all the necessary people will die.' His aim, and that of the military leaders who supported him, was to smash terror with terror.

By 1976 the army which was about to oversee mass murder was a different body of men from the generations that had preceded it. Over 600 officers had attended a course, begun in the administration of John F. Kennedy, at the US Army School of the Americas in Panama.

Intended by the western powers as a showcase academy for democracy – how to defeat guerillas and other subversive elements while still sustaining the support of the people – it was an academy that specialised in torture and murder. JFK was a president who came to power at the height of the Cold War. Communism was seen as a threat that could destroy the American way, if not the world. It was not a time for sentimentality – communists and their agents had to be eliminated in every way possible. It was a curriculum that the Argentine 'students' who went there found to their liking in every way.

DIRTY WARFARE

John Simpson and Jana Bennett, two journalists who chronicled the Argentine tragedy in their book *The Disappeared and the Mothers of the Plaza* wrote: 'Argentina's military command took up the opportunities offered with particular enthusiasm. The 600 officers underwent training which lasted for up to 40 weeks, concentrating on the techniques of irregular warfare and counter-intelligence. The methods and theory of torture were an important feature of the course, and students were reportedly hardened to the idea by being tortured themselves, usually by being hung up by the arms for several hours at a time.

'By the time of the coup in 1976, therefore, a very different kind of officer corps had been built up in Argentina: men who

COMMUNISM WAS SEEN AS A GREAT THREAT THAT COULD DESTROY THE AMERICAN WAY, IF NOT THE WHOLE WORLD

Below: *President Jorge Videla, centre, leads Argentina's military top dogs on a parade during National Day – 25 May. Videla instigated the dirty war against his 'internal enemies'.*

had been trained, not to emulate the officers and gentlemen of Europe who had once provided the role models for the Argentine armed forces, but to see themselves as being in the front line of a particularly dirty form of warfare. They had the techniques and they had the ideas.'

THE MURDER MACHINE

The terror machine operated under the cloak of night and fog. People simply disappeared. They were snatched from street corners by 'patotas', the armed squads of arresting officers who cruised the streets of cities and towns looking for victims. Green government-issue Ford Falcon cars became the symbol of terror, every bit as intimidating to the unfortunates who were taken away as Madame Guillotine had been to

her victims in the terror of the French Revolution. Nominally, the murder machine was directed by the Ministry of the Interior, where a master list of those who vanished was said to be kept. But in reality, the kidnapping and killing was something of a gigantic, grotesque free-for-all among all branches of the security apparatus. The navy had its death squads. So did the air force and the army and the National Gendarmerie. So did the police.

And then there were government agencies such as the National Oil Agency getting in on the act. All vied in the crazy lottery to snatch innocent people and take them away to their deaths.

One result of this disorganisation pleased the generals immensely. Although relatives who came looking for their loved ones were met with stony silence at barracks and at police stations, the chaos meant that often the authorities consulted genuinely did not know what the searcher was talking about. It meant secrecy – and to the secrecy obsessed military men, embarked on their crusade against the devil, it was a blessing.

The patotas usually came cruising for their victims at dawn or dusk, when potential witnesses were either scurrying home or scurrying out. The targets were arrested at gunpoint, usually handcuffed, and dumped in the boot of the car. Then they were driven away – most of them never to be seen again. They were taken to places like the Navy Mechanics School on the outskirts of Buenos Aries. A name rich with suggestions of science and engineering, it was nothing of the sort. It was a human abattoir where people were stripped, beaten, tortured and killed as part of the mosaic which made up the total picture of the 'Process of National Reorganisation'.

At this 'school', tutored one of the worst criminals in modern Argentine history. Alfredo Astiz was a handsome naval lieutenant of wealthy parents who drank deeply from the poisoned chalice offered by Videla. He believed him when he said that the enemies of Argentina were within its own frontiers. With the zeal of a Spanish Inquisition cardinal upon him, he was instrumental in the founding and operation of ESMA, the Navy Mechanics School.

The Navy Mechanics School was one of the last places that thousands of victims of 'The Process' saw on this earth. Prisoners were brought in, subjected to the most horrific beatings and torturing imaginable, and then taken out for execution; very few people made it back to their families and their loved ones. The centre was run by the Navy, but the enemy within, captured from street corners, cinemas and even coffee bars, were brought there by operatives of all the competing services.

PEOPLE SIMPLY DISAPPEARED. THEY WERE SNATCHED FROM THE STREETS BY 'PATOTAS', THE ARMED SQUADS

Below: *Dagmar Hagelin, the beautiful Swedish innocent who became a victim of the terror sweeping Argentina.*

PRISONERS WERE BROUGHT IN AND SUBJECTED TO THE MOST HORRIFIC BEATINGS AND TORTURING IMAGINABLE

THE TIP OF THE ICEBERG

What happened to 27-year-old nursery school teacher Isabel Gamba de Negrotti was typical. Pregnant, she was seized at gunpoint by the patotas and taken away in a green Ford Falcon car and dumped in The Navy Mechanics School. Accused of being a leftist sympathiser, she was one of the rare few who was handled by Astiz and his men and survived to tell the tale. She said: 'They took me to another room after arrival where they kicked me and punched me in the head. Then they undressed me and beat me on the legs, buttocks and shoulders with something made of rubber. This lasted a long time. I fell down several times and they made me stand by supporting myself on a table. They carried on beating me.

'While all this was going on they talked to me, insulted me, and asked me about people I didn't know and things I didn't understand. I pleaded with them to leave me alone, otherwise I would lose my baby. I hadn't the strength to speak, the pain was so bad. They started to give me electric shocks on my breasts, the side of my body and under my arms. They kept questioning me. They gave me electric shocks in the vagina and put a pillow over my mouth to stop me screaming. Someone called 'The Colonel' came and said they were going to increase the voltage until I talked, but I didn't know what they wanted to talk to me about. They kept throwing water over my body and applying electric shocks all over. Two days later I miscarried.'

The widespread extent to which enemies real and imagined were seen in Argentine society by officers of the junta is illustrated by this comment by Fifth Army Corps Commander General Adel Vilas after several months into 'the process'; 'Up to now only the tip of the iceberg has been affected by our war against subversion... it is necessary to destroy the sources which feed, form and indoctrinate the subversive delinquent, and the source is the universities and secondary schools themselves.' The junta was going after the children.

The students and the trade unionists, the journalists and the teachers were swept up in the vortex of terror. No pattern existed among the various security branches seeking out fresh prey. People who were caught yelled out their name and address over and over to passers-by before they were bundled into the Ford Falcons on what turned

'I PLEADED WITH THEM TO LEAVE ME ALONE, OTHERWISE I WOULD LOSE MY BABY. I HADN'T THE STRENGTH TO SPEAK'

Below: *Alfredo Astiz, the most notorious torturer and killer, arrives at court to answer for his crimes.*

FOR THE GENERALS AND THE TORTURERS, LIFE WAS SWEET

Below: *A mother beside the moving images of the terror – the faces of the missing children who were snatched and killed by security squads because they were deemed a danger to the state.*

out most often to be a one-way journey into hell. The kidnapped became 'los desaparecidos' – 'the disappeared'.

Often the military disposed of the bodies from their grim harvest by the 'NN' flights – standing for no name – when people who were both alive and dead were kicked out of helicopters flying above rivers. Almost 5,000 of the 15,000 people killed under 'The Process' were believed to have met their deaths this way. Others were buried in mass graves on the pampas or in remote corners of country churchyards. They were buried without sacrament or ceremony, lost forever to the faceless torturers.

Jacobo Timerman, a Jewish newspaper editor who was deemed sympathetic to the enemies of the state, was also imprisoned and tortured by Astiz, but was one of the fortunate ones; he survived to re-enter society and shame the military men with a classic account of his suffering in the book *Prisoner Without a Name, Cell Without a Number*. Describing the simplicity of the torture, he wrote: 'When electric shocks are applied all that a man feels is that they're ripping his flesh apart. And he howls.

Afterwards, he doesn't feel the blows. Nor does he feel them the next day, when there's no electricity, but only blows. The man spends days confined in a cell without windows, without light, either seated or lying down. The man spends a month without being allowed to wash himself, transported on the floor of an automobile to various places of interrogation, fed badly, smelling bad. The man is left enclosed in a small cell for 48 hours, his eyes blindfolded, his hand tied behind him, hearing no voice, seeing no sign of life, having to perform his bodily functions upon himself. And there is not much more. Objectively, nothing more.'

LIVED LIKE KINGS

For the generals and the torturers, however, life was sweet. Videla and his generals lived like kings. In the Casa Rosada, the Pink Palace in Buenos Aries that was the traditional home of the nation's ruler, Videla wallowed in fine wine, silk bedsheets and the finest gourmet cooking money could buy. His generals creamed off

¡YA! RESPUESTA A NUESTRO RECLAMO
APARICION CON VIDA
FAMILIARES

stolen property from the disappeared, while the torturers and the kidnappers traded and bartered in the most sinister trade of áll – children. Thousands were taken, palmed off to families that had none for money, or kept by the inquisitors themselves. To this day, the search for children of the disappeared ones goes on unabated in Argentina.

CHILLING DOSSIERS

Such wholesale vanishing acts could not, of course, remain secret for very long. Soon human rights groups like Amnesty International were compiling chilling dossiers of the missing, together with reports of the few, the very few, who made it back, on what conditions were like in the numerous hell-hole jails. And governments of the west did not have to rely on the reports of outside agencies like Amnesty. Allen 'Tex' Harris was the first secretary at the U.S. Embassy in Buenos Aries, entrusted with the task by his superiors in Washington of monitoring human rights abuses in Argentina. Tex Harris chronicled no less than 15,000 cases which he for-

warded to the Carter administration. Harris saw the systematic round-ups for what they truly were – a systematic civil war with one side doing all the killing and the other side doing all the dying. He said: 'They killed some real terrorists early on in shoot-outs, sure enough. And they captured some too. But the great majority of the ones they captured were just wine-and-coffee subversives – kids who sat around in cafés talking about socialist ideals and how the country should be changed.

'There was a guy from army intelligence who told me in person that the real tragedy of the operations was that half the people they killed were innocent even by their own criteria. But it was easier to kill them because it was less risky than going through the legal procedures. It was easier to just handcuff them to a lamppost and shoot them.'

But governments had their own agendas while Argentina was carrying out its own. The thinking in Washington was that a right-wing regime was infinitely preferable to a left-wing one. The CIA had actively dictated the policy of America in neigh-

Above: *The mothers of the Plaza De Mayo shamed the government with their worldwide press coverage. In the end it was these dignified, brave mothers, who had lost their loved ones, who helped bring about the collapse of the Junta.*

THOUSANDS OF CHILDREN WERE TAKEN, SOLD TO CHILDLESS FAMILIES OR KEPT BY THE INQUISITORS

Galtieri, who had been present at the meeting six years earlier in which the methods of terror had been agreed, indicated that he intended to keep waging the dirty war when he told the population: 'We do not just want a country, but a great country; not just a nation, but a great nation.'

NOBLE WARRIORS

Such dreams were evaporating faster than the morning mist which rose off the River Plate. Inflation was again rampant, international hackles were bristling over the tales of torture and murder and Galtieri's own people, specifically grandmothers and mothers, had begun ramming home the consequences of the government's murderous policies in daily demonstrations outside the Casa Rosada.

This latter group, the Mothers of the Plaza de Mayo, were among the most noble warriors of all in the battle to bring civility back to Argentina. Twice weekly they stepped on to the plaza, bearing names and photographs of the sons, husbands, brothers, daughters and loved ones lost to the madness that had gripped their country. At first the police tried intimidation, then dogs, then water cannon. Finally, they gave up on their attempts to arrest the women. It was harder, Galtieri reasoned, to justify to the world why 80-year-old women were being locked up as security risks than it was to persuade his military underlings that they were doing no harm.

By November 1981, as Galtieri lived life high on the hog, the storm tide of what Galtieri and his kind had unleashed was beginning to break. In their pursuit of enemies real and imagined the military had paid no heed to the massive problems which had beset the Argentine economy.

So ruthless were they in their pursuit of wrong-thinking students and left-wingers, they overlooked the fundamentals of government, particularly with regard to the economy. Strikes were becoming commonplace, inflation was rampant, employment was down and the general discord over the disappeared was weaving itself into a threadwork of general resentment against the ruling junta. Galtieri saw his way out of internal strife in an age-old fashion – by turning the focus of his people upon bogeymen from abroad.

Top: *The warrior sons of Argentina, pictured here in the Falklands getting the official news from home just weeks before they surrendered in droves to superior British forces.*

Above: *Ill-equipped, illtrained and ill-led, the soldiers of Argentina in defeat. Their rout on the battlefield hastened the demise of the generals back home.*

bouring Chile, engineering the coup which deposed democratically elected president Allende, and thereby unleashing a dictatorial terror which claimed thousands of innocent lives. Britain, for her part, played a cool role, never publicly condemning that which was obviously corrupt and rotten until it suited the nation to do so at the outset of the Falklands War.

Such was the Argentina which Leopoldo Galtieri and his cohorts in the junta inherited when he came to power. His reign was to be the last throw of the dice for the military men who had wreaked such havoc and such shame on the country. Videla retired, but none of the wickedness or evil which he practised went into retirement with him.

A GROTESQUE FARCE

The Falkland Islands – or, to the Argentine, Las Malvinas – became the focus of his ambitions. Galtieri believed that if he whipped up enough nationalistic fervour he could re-take the islands from British possession, ease the country's economic woes and carry on the dirty war against his own people unhindered. His military misadventure has long gone down in the annals of warfare as a grotesque farce which cost over 2,000 young conscripts their lives. Britain's massive military response to it has been questioned, but there can be no doubt that the decision of Mrs. Thatcher to resist the invasion, and regain the islands as a crown possession, signalled not just an end to the junta but also an end to the war waged against Argentina's own people.

Now the murder gangs, cruising in their Green Ford Falcons, could no longer manoeuvre on the streets, choked as they were with demonstrators calling for the blood of the junta. Years of repression burst upon the military leaders like a broken dam and within weeks of the sight of the Union Jack fluttering again over the rooftops of Port Stanley, the junta was consigned to the dustbin of history.

It was in December 1983, the year following defeat, that Raul Alfonsin came to power as a democratically elected leader. Only then did the full horrifying details of what Videla and Galtieri had overseen come to light. Gravesites across the country were opened up, the mass burial grounds for casualties of a war fought without rules or mercy. And the guilty men never paid for their crimes. Although the junta was indicted to stand trial, in the end they were pardoned. Only a few torturers, the bottom rung on the ladder of responsibility, ever came to court.

Even now, in this volatile land, the effects of this dirty war are still reverberating. Some 9,000 people simply disappeared as the military attempted to carve out its brave new world. Still the search goes on for the missing babies, the stolen children, the lost fathers and mothers, brothers and sons, cousins and daughters. And still the Mothers of the Plaza de Mayo continue their woeful vigil, eager to remind the new rulers – and the world – what can happen when a nation surrenders its will to military demagogues with no compassion or concern for democracy.

Above: *Abandoned jeeps and trucks of the invading Argentine forces litter the dockside in Port Stanley. The grand military adventure for the Junta had evaporated into total defeat.*

Above: *Margaret Thatcher, shortly before the final victory of the campaign she engineered from Downing Street.*

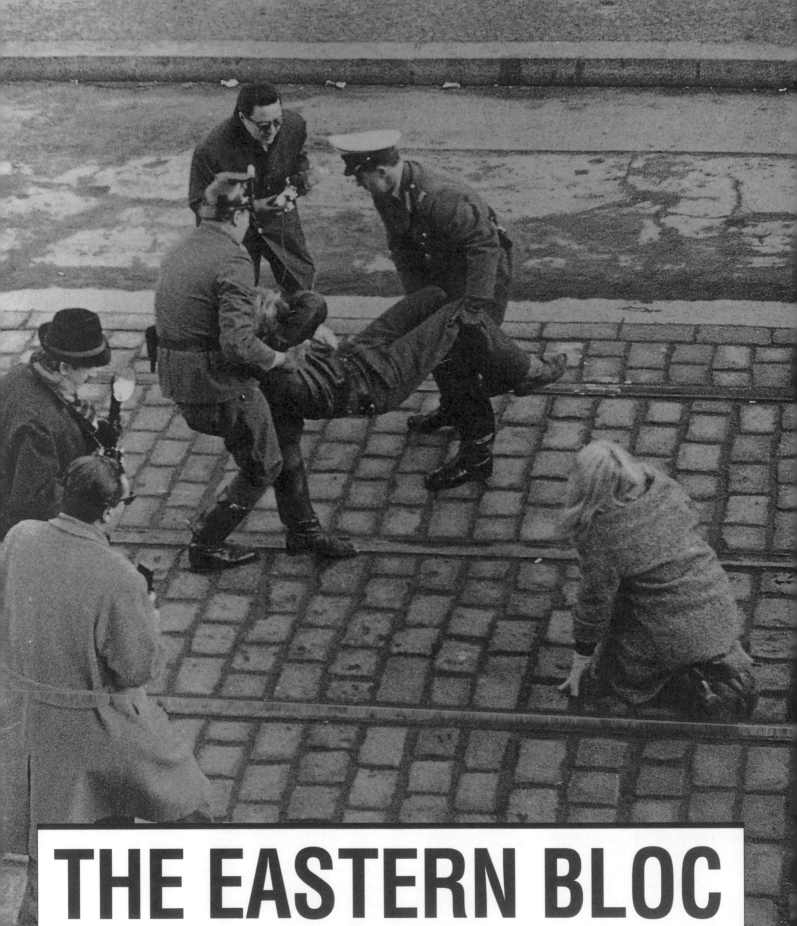

THE EASTERN BLOC
The Wall Falls

After Mikhail Gorbachev set the Soviet Union on the path to reform, it was merely a matter of time before the dictators in East Germany, Czechoslovakia, Hungary, Poland, Romania and Bulgaria were toppled and the Iron Curtain was fully opened.

The Berlin Wall was the grimmest of man's works – an edifice that not only stood as a physical barrier between peoples, but also a psychological one. On the west lived those under capitalism; on the other side, the dwellers under communism. Although it was the communists who built the wall, both camps nurtured suspicions and hatreds of each other behind it. For the generations born after World War Two, it seemed as if the world had always been split into such ideological zones, sheltering behind concrete topped with wire and ringed by minefields and machine gun posts. But The Wall was a legacy of that war, an artificial blockade where none existed before, erected by communist zealots to keep their people in and, allegedly, the warmongers of capitalism out.

In November 1989, the maxim that it is impossible to suppress an idea whose time has come was played out on TV screens around the world. Amazing scenes were being relayed from Berlin – of youngsters, old men, women, children – standing and singing atop the most hated symbol of Cold War mistrust ever erected. Some were hacking at the concrete with picks and sledgehammers, while still others sprayed the solemn faced border guards of East

Above: *That grimmest of human works, the Berlin Wall, and its wire, seen in all its hideousness in 1966.*

Opposite: *The price of freedom – East German border guards carry away the corpse of a young man who failed to make it over the wall.*

Left: *When the wall finally tumbled, East Germans scaled the barrier that had divided Berlin for so long.*

ALTHOUGH IT WAS THE COMMUNISTS WHO BUILT THE WALL, BOTH CAMPS NURTURED HATREDS OF EACH OTHER BEHIND IT

THE DDR WAS THE SHOW-CASE FOR THE SOVIET UNION, THE EPITOME OF WHAT A WORKERS' PARADISE COULD BE LIKE

Bottom right: *Walther Ulbricht, the first ruler of East Germany, waving flowers to the crowd after returning from a visit to his puppetmasters in Moscow.*

Below: *Erich Honecker, the fervent communist who succeeded Ulbricht – the man who initiated the wall's guards shoot-to-kill orders.*

Germany with cheap champagne. It was the end of the Cold War – and it had come not with a bang, but with the biggest street party in history.

After Mikhail Gorbachev set the Soviet Union on the path to reform, and loosened the shackles on the satellite states of eastern Europe which the old regimes had watched over with puppet leaders dancing to Moscow's tune, it was merely a matter of time before the crumbling dictators in East Germany, Czechoslovakia, Hungary, Poland, Romania and Bulgaria came tumbling down. But no-one expected it to happen quite so suddenly – not the people of the west, and certainly not the despots themselves. Tumble they did, and with a rapidity and a determination that put communism into a deep grave, never to be resurrected again in the lands taken by Stalin in 1945 as spoils of war.

When the Iron Curtain was fully opened it was to reveal a succession of states that had been ruled by self-serving tyrants, many of whom had lived in the lap of luxury while their virtually enslaved people toiled, building the great socialist society that forever remained a dream. Stories of bread queues, of shortages, of the poor quality of goods in the eastern bloc, had long permeated through to the west. But the lifestyle enjoyed by the rulers had never undergone such scrutiny – usually because of the veil of secrecy that the leaders drew around themselves. And to keep their subjects as uncomplaining chattels of this great society, they employed every device known to them in the catalogue of the security services. East Germany and Romania were the two states which contained the hardest of the hardline regimes – examples of what can happen when an unwitting populace lets itself be governed by self-serving tyrants.

A WORKERS' PARADISE

Erich Honecker, totalitarian head of the German Democratic Republic, was the man who ruled the most sinister state of all. He attained absolute power in 1971 from Walther Ulbricht who had fashioned the East Germany workers' state in the image of Stalin. But in the long years of service to the regime he had performed many tasks, most importantly those deemed matters of security. Erich Honecker's lasting memorial to the world would be the Berlin Wall.

The DDR was the showcase for the Soviet Union, the epitome of what a workers' paradise could be like. The factories were efficient (by Soviet bloc standards), there was enough food to eat, the state industries always exceeded economic plans and the citizens of this Utopia excelled

themselves at world events like the Olympic Games. Only the Soviet Union's athletes scooped more medals than those won by her natives.

But to keep in check this nation, carved artificially from the Germany of the west, Honecker wielded terror as an instrument of state policy. His dreaded Stasi secret police built up the most extensive informer network of any nation on earth. It amounted to husbands telling Stasi bosses about their wives, bosses informing on employees – and vice versa – and children informing on their parents. Criticism of the state was not permissible at any level. Even the merest whisper of admiration for some aspect of Germany's glorious past – be it Frederick the Great or Bismarck – was enough to get a person thrown in jail.

Honecker had been jailed under a totalitarian regime before – that of the Nazis. But while he despised the experience, he was later to emulate their methods. Like the Hitler Youth, he turned the Free German Youth, or FDJ movement, into a brainwashed socialist mind police. Children were given rewards by the state if they reported on conversations deemed anti-government. They were taught from an early age that party leaders and not parents were the ones deemed truly worthy of their love. And the children were taken away and placed in state orphanages if the government found out that their parents were 'subversive'.

Honecker's long road to power began back in the 1950s when he became chief henchman to Ulbricht. In 1961, he suggested, and was given the task of, building the wall around Berlin which made the western sector of the city an island of capitalism in an ocean of communism. It was a panic measure aimed at stopping the haemorrhaging of workers from this workers' paradise. Cynically, he portrayed it as something else, an 'anti-fascist' barrier aimed at stopping what he claimed were western forces intent on invading the east. The building of the wall was the greatest physical barrier to detente between east and west, an obscene symbol of mistrust and cruelty. But in the eyes of his Soviet sponsors, Honecker's star rose rapidly – not least because it was he who suggested to Ulbricht that those who tried to cross it should be shot.

KGB TRAINING

Throughout the 1960s Honecker refined the police state to a high art. His Stasi thugs were trained by the KGB in Moscow in torture and surveillance, while border guards were promised extra money and liquor if they shot would-be escapers. In 1968, when the Prague Spring occurred and the Czech people rose in a show of doomed defiance, Honecker was first to send in Peoples' Army troops in support of the Soviet steamroller which crushed the fledgling freedom movement.

CHILDREN WERE GIVEN REWARDS BY THE STATE IF THEY REPORTED ON CONVERSATIONS DEEMED TO BE ANTI-GOVERNMENT

Bottom left: *Josef Stalin, bloody ruler of the Soviet Union, whose forces gained an empire in the east in their advance on Berlin during the closing stages of World War II.*

Below: *The Brandenburg Gate, symbol of Imperial Prussian glory, sat in the eastern sector of the divided city, with the flag of the German Democratic Republic flying from its lofty heights.*

THE FUTURE OF HIS SOCIALIST PARADISE WAS DECIDED ON THE STREETS BY HIS PEOPLE, NOT IN THE HALLWAYS OF POWER

Below: *Erich Honecker, unbowed in defeat, gives the clenched fist salute to diehard communist supporters as he appears in court on manslaughter and embezzlement charges after the fall of the wall. The charges were later dropped and he fled to exile in Chile.*

By the 1980s, it was only Honecker and his henchmen in the politburo who were living the high life in palaces and country estates. The economy had deteriorated so badly by then that whole sections of his country were literally in ruins. Visitors through Checkpoint Charlie in Berlin could come to the east and gaze upon serviceable, if drab, buildings. But the merest distance away revealed an infrastructure shattered by Honecker's centrally planned economy. The factories were death traps, the roads built by Hitler's slaves were now potholed ruins, the fine architectural wonders of places like Dresden and Erfurt had been allowed to sink into decay. And over everything hung the pervasive fear of the Stasi, of the knock on the door at midnight.

Honecker was an old, hard-line communist, his jaw set forever against the 'bourgeoisie running dogs' of capitalism whom he despised. He truly believed that the west would collapse, and gave arms, equipment and sanctuary to terrorists who operated throughout the late 1970s and early 1980s in west Germany. Most notorious of these were the Baader-Meinhoff murderers who were allowed to hide in his nation after murdering innocents in the west on his specific orders.

But stagnation in the economy, a whiff of freedom in the air (thanks to Gorbachev) and a sense of change had combined to make the population restless. By 1989, Stalin had been dead for two decades and the sense of his empire had long receded. East Germans were fed up with living behind barbed wire and concrete, especially as the positive images of life in the west – fully stocked supermarkets, flashy cars, big houses – were beamed into their living rooms by powerful TV transmitters. In the summer of 1989, Comrade Falin from Moscow was despatched by Gorbachev to warn Honecker that all was not well beneath the surface of their model state. KGB intelligence had gleaned vast data of a riptide of discontent about to break over the East German politburo unless Gorbachev-style reforms were instigated. Honecker scoffed at the reports and assured the puppetmasters that he was still in firm control.

RIPTIDE OF DISCONTENT

The nation, however, was bleeding citizens, even with the Berlin Wall in place. In 1989 alone, some 350,000 – many of them youngsters with fathers who were bigwig government officials – made it to the west via visa offices in other eastern bloc countries. Intellectuals, poets, artists, architects – many were let go by Honecker, believing as he did that it was workers who made up a state, not dreamers. In the end, the future of his socialist paradise was decided on the streets by his repressed people, not in the hallways of power. With the stream of refugees from the east reaching catastrophic proportions, Honecker and his cohorts were ready to deploy desperate methods. Honecker had already praised the Tiananmen Square massacre in China earlier that year and was prepared to pull off another one in his own country if things did not quieten down.

Leipzig became the Tiananmen of Germany. Every Monday evening after church services in the Nikolai Kirche, there were anti-government demonstrations. It started with a few hundred and by October there were hundreds of thousands. The demonstrations spread all over the country and in October 1989 half a million people

marched in Berlin. Stasi thugs tried to break up the marches and provoke the people into violence, but there were too many for them. Honecker gave the orders to open fire. They were not obeyed and the anti-fascist fighter who turned into a communist dictator knew, at 77, that his vision of a socialist Utopia was at an end. Honecker resigned on 17 October and the Berlin wall fell on 9 November in the greatest display of spontaneous human joy that Germany had ever witnessed.

Freedom revealed the extent of the police state workings in East Germany on a hitherto unimagined scale. Stasi informants were so widespread that whole families were split asunder because of the traitors in their own midst. Files stretching twenty feet high on individuals deemed untrustworthy filled huge warehouses in Berlin and other major cities. It was clear that Honecker was a man who believed deeply in spying on his neighbour. Freedom also showed the extent of the decay of East German industry and the pollution in the countryside – much of it caused by Soviet troops camped on her territory since the end of the war. It was an ecological nightmare.

Honecker, suffering from cancer, fled to Chile, from where he later returned under guard to stand trial for ordering the execution of people who died trying to cross his grotesque wall. The trial ended in confusion and acrimony, the state deciding it was no longer productive to prosecute an old tyrant for crimes in a state that no longer existed. 'His punishment,' wrote American author James Nelson, 'is that humankind which he professed to love has damned him for the abominable state he presided over. A thousand years will pass and the stain of Nazism will not be erased upon Germany. It will take a further thousand for the stain of his wall to be fully bleached out.'

CEAUSESCU'S PLAYGROUND

Nowhere over the rotting carcass of the eastern bloc was the stench of corruption stronger, the cries of the persecuted louder, than in the shattered, pitiful country of Romania. Nicolae Ceausescu, with his hard-faced, petty minded and deadly wife Elena, ruled this land of gypsies, songs and wine as if it were their own personal playground. Ceausescu was a coarse peasant

with a peasant's low cunning; he understood nothing of kindness, nothing of grace or understanding in his rule which lasted nearly three decades.

Instead he ran Romania into the ground, making it a place where a Big Brother secret police called the Securitate ruled by fear, where babies were snatched by the torturers and bartered, where AIDS was a condition denied in the face of its existence – leading to thousands of orphans trapped in stinking hospitals and tended by just a few nurses. They were the babies who never cried – because no-one came to tend them or love them or care for them when they did. Nicolae and his Marie Antoinette lived like robber barons over this blighted land, building for themselves ever more

Above: The banality of evil – smiling like peasants on a country walk, the evil Ceausescus of Romania were responsible for state terror and wholesale misery on an immense scale.

THE WALL FELL ON **9** NOVEMBER TO THE GREATEST DISPLAY OF HUMAN JOY THAT GERMANY HAD WITNESSED

---

grandiose, vulgar palaces and country retreats while the beautiful Romany villages that dotted his nation were bulldozed and the peasants who had lived in them for a thousand years were herded into new communal living spaces made of poured concrete and prefabricated steel.

Ceausescu was a hard-line Stalinist, one of the last in the patchwork quilt of Soviet satellite states who believed irreversibly in the autocratic rule as practised by his idol Josef Stalin. Romania was practically a hermetically-sealed state where few westerners ever saw outside Bucharest, never glimpsing the torture chambers of the Securitate or the deprivations in the provincial towns where children as old as 14 had never eaten an orange or a banana.

Ceausescu's country exported oil and grain, and in theory there should have been enough to make Romania as wealthy as East Germany or Czechoslovakia. But everything was squandered on his grandiose public works schemes, such as palaces, hunting lodges and shooting retreats. When he went on boar hunts his Securitate men had to herd the beasts directly into his line of fire – otherwise they would be executed.

Ceausescu's wife, a debauched nymphomaniac who insisted on massive subservience from her husband's politburo hacks, was kept satisfied by endless studs press-ganged in from the farms surrounding the capital to give her an afternoon of pleasure. Everything was leeched from the people for them, who didn't even have the solace of religion to turn to, as all places of worship were closed down, the churches turned into liquor warehouses or cow sheds. No wonder that he had a unique nickname in the land which encompasses the province of Transylvania: 'Dracula'.

It was the children who suffered most in his topsy-turvy socialist paradise. Hospital conditions were monstrously primitive and there was little money in the state medicine coffers for drugs, bedding, light, heat or even personnel in the nation's infirmaries. It was only after his nation fell that the true extent of what had gone on in Romania in the 'years of darkness' became horrifyingly clear.

TIDE OF CHANGE

Such hypocrisy and corruption was doomed to die – it was only the length of the expiration period of the corpse which caused so much misery and death for the Romanian people. But Ceausescu, who called himself 'Father of the Nation', could not hold back the tide of change that was washing over the eastern European nations. At Christmastime 1989, as dissent and dissatisfaction began to sweep over his blighted land, he believed he could play the Kremlin-style hardman one more time to assuage the feelings of his angry people. But fear, the one thing he held over them for all the years he was in power, was no longer an effective tool.

In the city of Timisoara 12,000 men, women and children were murdered in battles with the security police and army units loyal to the tyrant. It was the biggest display of defiance that Ceausescu had ever encountered in his refusal to bend to demands for social and economic reforms. But Ceausescu could not stifle the growing resentment aimed at him, nor keep news of the disaster that was befalling his dictatorship from reaching the west. Satellite TV news pictures showed the mass graves in Timisoara, the torture chambers where Securitate thugs splashed the walls with the blood of their victims, the pieces of smashed skulls and torn clothing, still singed from electrocution marks. In Bucharest, the clock was ticking fast.

In his comic opera palace, the folly still under construction in the centre of the city – costs for which were borne by the peasantry who had neither heat nor light nor hope in their countryside hovels – Ceausescu believed he could play the elder statesman one more time and placate the mob one week before Christmas. His lackeys in the state TV service were there to record the 'Father of the Nation' speaking wisely to the workers, asking for calmer heads to prevail. But this time it was the workers who forgot the script, not Ceausescu, who was used to rambling on

WHEN HE WENT ON BOAR HUNTS, HIS SECURITATE MEN HAD TO HERD THE BEASTS INTO HIS LINE OF FIRE, OR BE EXECUTED

Below: *A keen hunter, President Ceausescu is seen here shouldering a rifle on his 60th birthday. Just over a decade later, he would find himself on the wrong end of several rifles – facing a firing squad.*

for hours in his monotone voice without interruption. Suddenly there were shouts of 'anti-Christ', 'child murderer', 'butcher', 'kill him' careering up in a banshee howl of hate from the protestors outside. Ceausescu realised then that he had stared into the abyss – and the abyss was staring back at him.

BATTLE ON THE STREETS

In the next frenzied hours Ceausescu tried to order his army units to open fire on the protestors. They refused and the chief of the armed forces was executed. Only the Securitate – the Gestapo-style thugs who were rewarded for their fidelity over the years with food, western liquor and perfumes, silk scarves, stereos and TV sets – stayed loyal. Meandering through the maze of secret tunnels the paranoid Ceausescu had built under the capital – built for just such a day as this – they took to the streets to begin liquidating the protestors. But this time it was their turn to die – the victims of the rebelling army soldiers who were determined to join with the masses in overthrowing Ceausescu for good.

For several days the world held its breath as the forces of good and evil battled it out on the streets of Bucharest, but it was a one-sided fight. The Securitate were no match for tanks and trained soldiers. One by one they were flushed out. The fortunate ones were held pending a trial – the majori-

ty were summarily executed for crimes against the Romanian people. There was not a peep out of world watchdog groups; there was a sense that justice was a long time in coming to these thugs. As the fighting died down, the polarisation of Romanian society was seen in all its hideousness. The apartment of Ceausescu's daughter Zola-Elena was opened for the TV cameras and the booty of years of pillage put on display. There were gems, paintings from the nation's galleries that had been stripped and given to her by her father as 'gifts'. There was prime meat shipped from Vienna for her two poodles – when most meat fed to Romanians was pickled, rotten or simply not available in state-run stores. There was cash, leather sofas, perfumes, fine wines – all the accoutrements of splendid living that had been bought at the expense of the suffering of the people.

Above: *Happy days for the despot, as he addresses a 1967 stage-managed rally in the capital.*

Top: *The appalling Stalinesque folly that Ceausescu built in Bucharest as his personal palace. Such extravagances hastened his end.*

THERE WAS PRIME MEAT SHIPPED FROM VIENNA FOR HER TWO POODLES, WHEN MOST MEAT FED TO ROMANIANS WAS ROTTEN

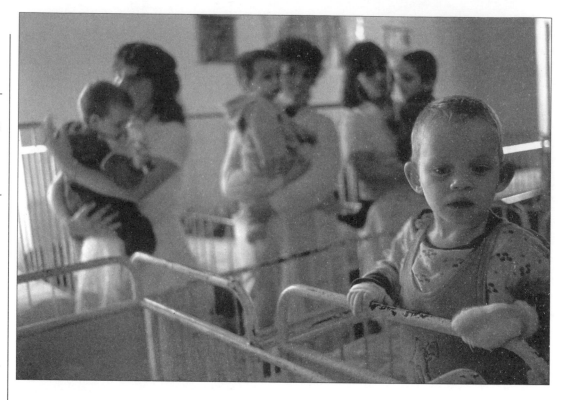

SOME 100,000 BABIES
WERE FOUND LANGUISHING
IN FILTH AND NEGLECT,
MANY OF THEM INFECTED
WITH THE AIDS VIRUS

Right: *The babies whose plight touched the world – the orphans of Romania, who were crowded into institutions across the country after having been stolen from parents who opposed the state.*

Below: *The pathetic Ceausescus at their trial, shortly before their execution by firing squad.*

At the opposite end of the spectrum were the orphanages – mausoleums of suffering where AIDS babies lived and died in their thousands. Some 100,000 of them were found languishing in filth and neglect. Many of the babies were infected with the AIDS virus, contracted from the contaminated national blood supply; others were simply dumped there when their parents were executed because of their opposition to the regime. Many of the children who were over five years old were hopelessly brain damaged – the result of abuse during their formative years. There could be little sympathy for a fallen leader if he had allowed this to go on in the land which he considered 'progressive'.

Within hours of the street battles in Bucharest and other cities subsiding, the capture of the Ceausescus became the main goal of the provisional government called the National Salvation Front. Rumours abounded that they had been airlifted out of the capital, flown into Iran and the welcoming arms of the Ayatollah, who was the last foreign dignitary whom 'Dracula' visited before the storm broke upon him. But in the end they were stopped at a road block, cowering, frightened, but in no way humbled – certainly not she, who regarded herself as the mother of all Romania. She was soon to be stripped of her notions.

CHRISTMAS TRIAL

Tearful and terrified the Ceausescus were given a secret trial on Christmas day, which was videotaped for posterity. At one stage in it the 70-year-old tyrant complained that it was too brief; later a spokesman for the new government said that his comment was ironic, as it was carried out exactly in accordance with the judicial reforms he had instigated to summarily despatch critics of his regime without too much fuss.

The trial was nothing more than a study in hate and pity; the pitiful Ceausescus and

EXÉCUTION

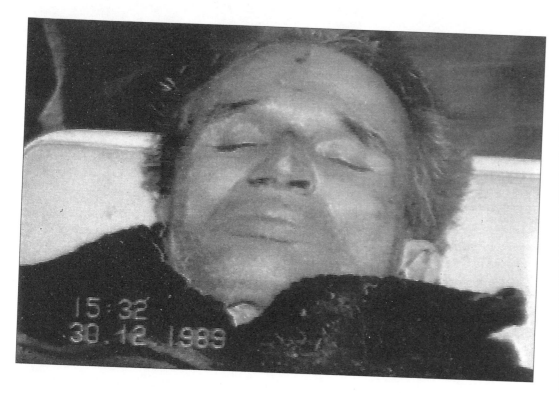

15:32
30.12.1989

Left: *Ceausescu as his countrymen wanted to see him for years – dead.*

the people who hated them. 'I gave my entire life for the people!' cries out Elena at one point. 'Our people. I was a mother to you!' It was pointed out to her, firmly but politely, that mothers did not kill the children of other mothers.

The Ceausescus were told succinctly just what they had done to their country by a gravelly-voiced army prosecutor: 'There are today more than 64,000 dead in all cities. You have forced poverty on to people. Learned people, true scientists, have left the country to escape from you... you have used violence during the 25 years in power. Violence was done by starving the people, denying them heating and electricity, and especially grave was the violence against the spirit of the people. Innocent children were run over by tanks. You dressed Securitate officers in army uniforms in order to turn the people against the army. You ordered oxygen tubes in hospitals to be disconnected. You ordered explosives to be planted in storages where blood plasma was kept... what possessed you to reduce the people to the state they are in? Not even the peasants had enough wheat and had to come to Bucharest to buy bread. Why did the people have to starve? You destroyed the Romanian people and their economy. Such things are unheard of in the civilised world.'

There were outbursts periodically from Elena, but the outcome was inevitable and

just. Death by firing squad. Outside the 200 soldiers there argued bitterly – not because they were upset at the proceedings, but because each and every one wanted to be part of the detail assigned to shoot the butchers. In the end just three men were chosen. The unrepentant pair were led into a courtyard and shot dead with bursts of gunfire. They looked like a pair of confused pensioners, but their actions over the years had told of more cunning than that.

They were buried in unmarked graves as the bells in the churches which they had shut pealed across the nation. No prayers were said for them – and certainly no tears shed for them.

Below: *A pious peasant woman lights a candle on Ceausescu's makeshift grave.*

US SCANDALS
The White House

Over the years, US politics has been dogged by political scandal. From Watergate to Nannygate, and from Travelgate to Irangate, Presidential administrations have been rocked by political intrigue and sex scandals that have shocked the world.

In the early morning hours of Saturday, 17 June 1972, police in Washington DC responded to an emergency call from security guards at the Watergate hotel and office complex that a burglary was in progress. When the officers arrived on the scene, they conducted an office-by-office search. They found five men, hiding in a vacant office. Much to their amazement, the burglars looked more like businessmen than thieves. In fact, they were all wearing suits!

The arresting officers could not have known, not even in their wildest dreams, that they had just laid the first stone in what would become the veritable cathedral of lies, corruption and misconduct we now know as the Watergate Scandal – the explosive outrage that would unfold over the next two years and lead to the most serious peacetime threat to American democracy and the downfall of President Richard Nixon.

The climate that allowed such a scandal to fester began when 56-year-old Nixon, the 37th President of the United States, took America's highest political office in 1968. He was obsessed with secrecy, and had a morbid distrust of anyone he feared could one day challenge his almost-dictatorial rule. Political opponents were smeared, unauthorised telephone-taps were ordered, and illegal campaign funds were amassed.

Indeed, well before Watergate, the Nixon Administration wallowed in a web of deceit and blatant lies, though the details did not surface until years later, when the full extent of that burglary at the

TO THEIR AMAZEMENT, THE BURGLARS LOOKED MORE LIKE BUSINESSMEN THAN THIEVES. IN FACT, THEY WERE WEARING SUITS!

Opposite: *President Richard Nixon used the powers of the Oval Office to subvert and corrupt the American political system. He remains the only American president to ever resign his post.*

Below: *The Watergate complex in downtown Washington DC became synonymous with scandal.*

Right: *Senior Nixon adviser John Ehrlichman played a key role in the Watergate break-in and the subsequent cover-up. He was later sentenced to prison for his part in the scandal.*

Above: *G. Gordon Liddy was an intelligence professional who helped plan and execute the break-in. He, too, later paid for his crimes with a jail sentence.*

NIXON'S LEGAL LACKIES QUIETLY CLAIMED THE PRESIDENT COULD WIRETAP ANYONE, WITH OR WITHOUT COURT APPROVAL

Democratic National Committee headquarters became known. But in 1969, for example, Nixon's legal lackies quietly claimed the President could wiretap anyone with or without court approval! Then, a year later, Nixon approved the use of America's intelligence network to undermine opponents at home, a clear violation of the law.

Nixon's growing paranoia manifested itself in the form of the aptly-named 'plumbers unit', a group of specially-selected intelligence professionals, whose job was to plug all leaks from the Administration as well as investigate certain 'security' problems. The group, which was to lie at the centre of the Watergate scandal, was set up in 1971, when the so-called Pentagon Papers were leaked to the New York Times. Even though the documents contained no negative information about the Nixon White House – they detailed the secret history of the Kennedy and Johnson administrations' policies in Vietnam – the distrusting president somehow believed the leak was a scheme to undermine his rule.

The plumbers, which included senior adviser John Ehrlichman, Gordon Liddy and Howard Hunt, also helped to draw up the notorious 'Priority List' of 20 of the President's 'political enemies' for John Dean, the chief counsel to Nixon. Heading the list was Senator Edward Kennedy, the heir to the famous political family and a man Nixon was clearly fearful of. But the unit did more than try to discredit the president's enemies. On one occasion – concerning the well-informed newspaper columnist Jack Anderson – there were actually discussions held on his possible murder.

SECOND-RATE BURGLARY AT WATERGATE

Moreover, the plumbers dreamed up ways of infiltrating anti-Vietnam War organisations, as well as plotting acts of sabotage against the Democratic Party. Indeed, the second-rate burglary at Watergate was but a drop in a cesspool of illegal and villainous acts of a wide-ranging conspiracy that included all the president's men as well as the entire US intelligence community.

But the incident at Watergate started a chain reaction of lies and cover-up which become so widespread that two Attorney-Generals, most of the senior White House staff and Vice President Spiro Agnew were all toppled. And as the probe spread higher and higher up the political chain, it became increasingly clear that Nixon, who did not know of the actual break-in, had orchestrated the entire cover-up using the far-reaching powers of the presidency.

As the investigation closed in on him, it also became apparent that Nixon had lied on numerous occasions to the American people and the Congress about the incident, and during one national TV speech, actually felt compelled to say: 'I am not a crook'. Yet the discovery of a high-tech taping system inside the Oval Office, which Nixon had had installed many months earlier, proved behind a shadow of a doubt that he was, in fact, a crook. When some of the tapes were made public, there were growing calls for his resignation. When he refused to even consider the possibility, the Congress moved to impeach him for obstruction of justice, abuse of presidential power and his steadfast refusal to comply with subpoenas issued by the legislative body.

SCATHINGLY ATTACKED

The impeachment proceedings were a biting indictment of Nixon the man and Nixon the president. In part, it accused him of acting 'in a manner contrary to his trust as President and subversive of constitutional government, to the great prejudice of the cause of law and order and to the manifest injury of the people of the United States... such conduct warrants impeachment and trial, and removal from office'.

Never before in the history of the American republic had a President been so scathingly attacked by his colleagues in government. But Nixon's problems weren't

with the Congress alone. His popularity ratings plummeted to record lows as his part in the cover-up became increasingly apparent. Yet the president refused to yield. He was a veteran of political scrapes and almost miraculous comebacks, and he sincerely believed he would again come back from the political grave. 'I have no intention whatever of ever walking away from the job that the American people elected me to do', he said as the clamour for his removal grew even louder.

Yet even this wily old politician could not stop the juggernaut that Watergate had become. The existence of the taping system, disclosed by a former aide in July 1973, made it inevitable that Nixon had better co-operate or be impeached. Still, Nixon delayed and stalled, claiming the tapes were covered under 'executive privilege', an indeterminate term that theoretically protected the confidentiality of all his communications with aides.

Left: *White House Counsel John Dean. He had an 'enemies' list drawn up for the Nixon Administration.*

Below: *President Nixon being sworn in for his second term in the Oval Office. Within 18 months, he would be forced from office, a bitter and broken man.*

Above: *Nixon, with his family, bids farewell to supporters inside the White House.* **Below:** *The* New York Times *the following day.*

summaries of the tapes. Archibald Cox, a special prosecutor who had been appointed by the Justice Department to co-ordinate the various Watergate investigations, was not satisfied, and demanded the complete, unedited tapes.

It was his last demand, because on 20 October, Nixon dismissed him in what has become known as the infamous 'Saturday Night Massacre'. Three more months went by, and still the President refused to yield, but it was obvious to everyone – even to his closest aides – that Nixon was fighting a losing battle. By late February, as the wall of silence surrounding the president began to crack, a host of his former associates pleaded guilty to a wide variety of criminal wrongdoing. Further, eight corporations also admitted their guilt in making illegal campaign contributions to his re-election committee.

Other inquiries also uncovered some disturbing facts, including the revelation that there were some serious flaws in Nixon's tax returns, which forced him to pay more than £250,000 in back taxes. It was further learned that he had used millions of pounds of government money to improve his homes in Florida and California – writing off the lavish refurbishing as security measures needed to protect him.

Months of legal wrangling followed, but eventually even Nixon realised he had no choice. He had to comply with the Congressional order. But 'Tricky Dicky' had one last ruse. He would only hand over

A VIRTUAL PRISONER

Not a week went by without some damning new evidence against him. By June, with the entire nation calling for his removal, Nixon was a virtual prisoner inside the White House, and was rarely seen outside his well guarded white walls. The end was drawing inexorably closer and closer, and the following month proved to be the final nail in his political coffin. Senior aide John Ehrlichman and other White House 'plumbers' were found guilty of conspiracy, and just 12 days later the Supreme Court ruled unanimously that Nixon had to turn over 64 missing tapes – which not only revealed his key role in the cover-up, but also exposed him as a foul-mouthed, malicious man who routinely abused the trust of his people for personal glory.

On 5 August, he was ordered to turn over another three tapes, which proved it was he who had organised the scheme to have the Federal Bureau of Investigation

stop its probe of the Watergate break-in for 'political' as well as 'national security' reasons. Four days later, even Nixon came to realise the end had arrived. Knowing he was certain to be impeached by an openly-hostile Congress, he finally resigned in an emotional address to the nation he had so blatantly betrayed. He retreated to his home in California a bitter, disgraced man.

Richard Nixon was also totally physically and mentally drained. Within a few months, while recuperating in hospital after emergency surgery for blood clots, he admitted: 'I could see no reason to live. It seemed that I had had nothing left to fight for except my own life. I am convinced now that but for the support of my family and the thoughts and prayers of countless people I have never met and would never have a chance to thank, I would not have made it. I was a physical wreck; I was emotionally drained; I was mentally burned out. I could see no reason to live, no cause to fight for.'

Nixon eventually recovered, but he was still the target of government special prosecutors in the wake of the Watergate scandal and he faced dozens of lawsuits which cost more than £1 million defending. In the years since, however, he has successfully restored much of his tarnished image.

In effect, his renaissance began less than a month after his disgraceful exit from Washington, when his hand-picked successor, Gerald Ford, pardoned him of all crim-inal doings while in office. And today, he is considered by many to be an expert on foreign policy, and has written eight political books in the past 14 years. But Watergate still haunts him, and even he admits that he will live with the burden of his actions 'every day of the life that is left to me'.

'Looking back on what is still in my mind a complex and confusing mass of events, decisions, pressures and personalities, one thing I can see clearly now is that I was wrong in not acting more decisively and more forthrightly in dealing with Watergate, particularly when it reached the stage of judicial proceedings and grew from a political scandal into a national tragedy,' he recalled. 'I long ago accepted overall responsibility for the Watergate affair. What's more, I have paid, and am still paying, the price for it. I know that many fair-minded people believe that my motivation and actions in the Watergate affair were intentionally self-serving and illegal. I now understand how my own mistakes and misjudgments have contributed to that belief.'

IRAN-CONTRA AFFAIR

If the Watergate scandal was the gravest crisis to ever hit peace-time America, then the mire of lies, distortions and scams implicit in the Iran-Contra affair of the Reagan years was not far behind in its abuse of presidential power.

Above: *Nixon confers with his hand-picked replacement, Vice President Gerald Ford. Less than a month after Nixon had resigned, President Ford pardoned him of all criminal doings.*

HE FINALLY RESIGNED IN AN EMOTIONAL ADDRESS AND RETREATED TO HIS HOME A BITTER AND DISGRACED MAN

TODAY, HE IS CONSIDERED BY MANY TO BE AN EXPERT ON FOREIGN POLICY AND HAS WRITTEN EIGHT BOOKS IN THE PAST 14 YEARS

Above: *Colonel Oliver North faces a congressional grilling over his part in the Iran-Contra Affair.*

Top: *President Ronald Reagan appears before Congress to explain his part in the Affair.*

friendly to Ayatollah Khomeini's Tehran. Critics, however, said the shipment was a straight arms-for-hostages deal – a flagrant violation of Reagan's own policy decision not to deal with terrorists.

Moreover, the money that was collected for the arms was then secretly funnelled through a murky link of back channels to the Contra rebels fighting the Marxist regime of Nicaragua – an illegal act since the 1

Congress had earlier outlawed any aid for the rebel force with the passing of the Boland Amendment.

The scheme was organised by a cadre of Reagan's closest advisers – including CIA director William Casey, former National Security Adviser Robert McFarlane, current NSA Admiral John Poindexter, and the fanatical Marine Lt. Col. Oliver North – who knew they could not continue to help the Contras through official channels.

The deal was brokered through a series of clandestine meetings in Paris and Tehran, in which American operatives reportedly gave gifts of a bible and a cake to their Iranian colleagues as they talked of arms shipments.

THE VIETNAM VETERAN

North, who would gain widespread notoriety during the much-watched televised hearings into the affair which began in 1987, was at the heart of the plan. A decorated Vietnam veteran, who organised the daring capture of the hijackers of the ocean liner Achille Lauro, North joined the National Security Agency in 1981, and quickly asserted his power and knack for getting the job done. He became so powerful, that by the time the Iran-Contra scam was at its zenith, he was reportedly ordering around generals and ambassadors as he grabbed for more and more power. It has never been proven beyond doubt, however, what North's actual role was. Was he a Reagan's appointed 'can-do' man, or was he a proverbial 'loose cannon'? He was almost assuredly a little of both.

When the scandal finally broke, in November, 1986, North and Poindexter were fired by Reagan, who claimed he knew nothing of the Contra diversion. Yet during the Congressional hearings, North said he believed he was working on the orders of the President. It was never

Indeed, in hindsight, many historians and critics believe the Iran-Contra affair was an even more serious episode than Watergate, because it was the brainchild of a shadowy elite group that sought to run America's foreign policy in flagrant disregard for the diplomats, the Congress and the law. Only Ronald Reagan's personal popularity, say observers, kept the affair from exploding into another Watergate.

The events that led Reagan's darkest hour and the Iran-Contra affair began in May, 1986, when American operatives sent a secret plane-load of weapons to Iran. Reagan claimed the arms shipment was to open a channel to Iranian 'moderates', who might help with the release of US hostages being held in Lebanon by Muslim terrorists

proven, but most observers agree that Reagan had to know..

Although the hearings proved dramatic television and shed much light on the conspiracy and cover-up, the real criminal case against the perpetrators was handed over to Judge Lawrence Walsh, who was hired as a special prosecutor. For the past seven years, Walsh and his band of crack lawyers, have waged a £25 million war against those who sought to circumvent the Congress and the Constitution, and yet he has been continually stymied by politics, secrecy and flagrant disregard for the letter of the law.

He successfully prosecuted both North and Poindexter, yet both convictions were later overturned on appeal. He got former President Reagan on the stand, only to hear the one time chief executive say 'I don't remember' more than 100 times. He believed that Reagan 'deliberately defied the (law)... in a deliberate defiance of Congress' – a violation of presidential power that he said should have prompted Congress to consider impeachment.

Then, President Bush, whose own role in the scandal has never been satisfactorily explained, destroyed years of hard work when, soon after his 1992 election defeat to Governor Bill Clinton, he handed a Christmas eve pardon to former Secretary of Defence Caspar Weinberger and five other convicted officials, including McFarlane and Elliott Abrams, a former top official in the Reagan State Department. His Christmas present, which came less than four weeks before he was to leave the White House, killed the possibility that there would be any further significant indictments in the case.

THE FINAL ANALYSIS

Walsh was furious, and publicly implied that Bush was simply protecting his own involvement. 'President Bush has failed to produce to investigators his own highly relevant, contemporaneous notes (about the scandal) despite repeated requests,' the special prosecutor thundered. 'In light of President Bush's own misconduct, we are gravely concerned about his decision to pardon others who lied to Congress and obstructed an official investigation.'

Walsh, who was scheduled to write his final report on the scandal in late 1993, said

the account will tell of things he knows, but could not prove. In the final analysis, that sums up the entire Iran-Contra affair and the ensuing cover-up. Much is known, but little can be proved. Unfortunately for Walsh and the American people, there were no 'smoking guns' to link the White House to the conspiracy like the Nixon tapes had done a dozen years earlier in the Watergate scandal.

AFFAIRS OF THE HEART

While the Iran-Contra affair took up much of the nation's attention throughout 1987, there was one other major political scandal which did knock it off the front pages of the newspapers for several weeks. But unlike Iran-Contra, this affair had nothing to do with guns and money. It was, quite literally, an affair of the heart.

It was May, and Colorado senator Gary Hart was the firm favourite to win the Democrat Party's nomination for the presidency and square off against George Bush in the campaign for the White House. For months after announcing his candidacy, however, there were rumours that the 50-year-old Hart, a Kennedyesque-type figure beloved by liberals and conservationists, had been having extramarital affairs, despite his long union with his wife, Lee.

Nothing was ever proven, however, and the polls showed that most of his supporters remained loyal. But the constant media barrage about the rumours dogged his bid

Below: *Senator Gary Hart saw his presidential hopes nosedive when it was learned he had been keeping company with a beautiful blonde model. Handsome Hart soon faded from the public spotlight.*

Above: *Sexy Donna Rice, the leggy bombshell at the centre of the Hart fiasco.*

A FRIEND OF THE SENATOR'S REMEMBERED THAT HART AT TIMES 'SORT OF THOUGHT HE WANTED TO BE WARREN BEATTY'

for the nomination and, in what can only be described as an amazing example of self-assurance, he literally challenged the media to tail his every move to prove he was not having an affair. 'If anyone wants to put a tail on me, go ahead,' he said defiantly. 'They'd be very bored.' As it turned out, they weren't.

Following an anonymous tip, a team of reporters from the *Miami Herald* newspaper staked out the Senator's home in Washington, and found that Hart had spent the weekend with a 29-year-old aspiring actress called Donna Rice. When the story hit the streets, Hart angrily denied the account, and both he and the leggy blonde denied any sexual relations. He claimed they were merely friends who had met some months earlier at a New Year's Eve party in swinging Aspen.

Indeed, Hart and his wife, Lee, did meet Rice at a party that year at the vacation home of pop star Don Henley, who had dated the sexy stunner several times, as had Prince Albert of Monaco. There were several other celebrities present at the party, which was in keeping with Hart's tendency to gravitate to the glitz and glitter of the show business world. In fact, some of the early rumours about his extramarital conduct stemmed from his longtime friendship with Warren Beatty, Hollywood's most notorious lady-killer until his recent marriage. A friend of the Senator's during those days remembered that Hart at times 'sort of thought he wanted to be Warren Beatty'.

A few days after the incident at his Washington home, Hart was forced to confess that the 'meeting' at his townhouse wasn't the first time he and Donna had been together while the Senator's wife, Lee, was not around. He admitted he and another middle-aged man had taken an overnight boat trip from Miami to a nearby Caribbean playground with Rice and another young beauty. Amazingly, the name of the yacht was the 'Monkey Business'.

UNFOLDING SCANDAL

Both Hart and Rice insisted the only reason they and their friends stayed overnight on the island was that the customs office was closed. But it was soon learned that the 'Monkey Business' had cleared Bahamian customs on arriving, shortly before dusk. And according to Bahamian authorities, American pleasure boats are not required to clear customs upon departure. Later, their insistence that the trip was totally innocent would be unmasked when photos of the young actress sitting on Hart's lap surfaced.

As the week unfolded, Hart found himself at the centre of the biggest political sex scandal since the incident at Chappaquiddick, involving a young Senator Ted Kennedy in 1969. Inevitably, his campaign contributions dwindled, even though he brazenly continued to deny any sexual relationship with Rice, and many supporters fled his candidacy. Even a brave announcement from his wife, Lee, couldn't stop the blood-letting. 'If it doesn't bother me, I don't think it ought to bother anyone else,' she said stoically. 'If he says nothing happened, nothing happened.'

Because of his womanising reputation, nervous aides carried out a death watch, waiting for yet more bombshell disclosures. They didn't have to wait long. A few days later, a reporter from the *Washington Post* told one of the Senator's aides that the newspaper had firm evidence of a recent extramarital liaison involving the senator and yet another woman. It was the final nail in Hart's coffin.

Faced with this new evidence, Hart flew home to Colorado from a campaign stop in New Hampshire, and called a press conference to announce his decision to leave the presidential race. Yet even as he was making his announcement, he seemed remarkably unrepentant. He did allow that he had 'made some mistakes', but added they were not 'bad mistakes'. However, he refused to answer questions as to whether he had committed adultery or not. 'I do not have to answer that question,' he repeatedly replied.

However, Hart did not deny that his relationship with Rice and their unchaperoned meetings were politically fatal errors of judgment. Once again, the vague 'character issue' that had haunted his 1984 presidential campaign – Hart could never satisfactorily explain why he had changed his name, age, official biography and his signature – had resurfaced.

For the next seven months, Hart licked his wounds at his home in Colorado. Then, in December, he made the incredible decision to return to the fray! He brazenly sought to blame the news media for the entire scandal, lambasting them for focusing on personal matters rather than substantive issues. At the press conference to announce his renewed candidacy, he said he would 'let the people decide'.

His chances were doomed from the start. Many voters still distrusted him and influential financial backers stayed away in droves. However, he battled on in primary after primary until the inevitable came in March, 1988, when even he finally admitted defeat and realised his life-long dream of running the White House was over.

A CAMPAIGN IN TURMOIL

Ironically, four years later, then-Governor Bill Clinton faced a similar firestorm. But unlike the ill-fated Hart, Clinton survived his brush with notoriety and went on to win

the White House against incumbent George Bush in a big victory in the 1992 election.

No one, probably not even Clinton himself, really gave him a chance at winning nine months earlier when the name Gennifer Flowers was on the lips of every American. Her emergence from obscurity threw his campaign into turmoil with her startling claims of a torrid, 12-year affair. Flowers, a beautiful blonde singer who bore a striking resemblance to Donna Hart, claimed she even had evidence of Clinton's adulterous double-life, secretly taping phone conversations with him, including one in which she is told to 'just say "no"' if reporters ever ask her if she has been having an affair with Clinton.

Although it was not verified completely, reporters who heard the remarkable tapes agreed the male voice sounded much like the Arkansas governor. Flowers said she had decided to come forward when she heard Clinton deny allegations of their affair, which were first levelled by a dis-

Top: *Governor Bill Clinton gives the victory sign during the 1992 presidential race.*

Above: *Gennifer Flowers, who claimed to have tapes of romantic phone conversations between her and Clinton.*

Above: *Gennifer Flowers sold her story to an American magazine, and claimed that Governor Clinton was lying to the country when he denied the affair.*

SHE SAID IN AN INTERVIEW THAT CLINTON'S ASSERTIONS THAT THEY WERE 'JUST FRIENDS' WAS 'A TOTAL LIE'

---

gruntled Arkansas state government worker, Larry Nichols, several months earlier.

The sultry nightclub singer said in a paid magazine interview that Clinton's assertions that they were 'just friends' was 'a total lie. I was Bill Clinton's lover for 12 years and for the past two years I have been lying to the press to protect him. The truth is I loved him. Now he tells me to deny it. Well, I'm sick and tired of the all deceit and I'm sick and tired of all the lies.'

Flowers said she felt 'disgusted' at Clinton's appearance on a nationally-televised news conference in which he denied all suggestions of an affair. 'I saw a side of Bill I'd never seen before,' she said. 'He is absolutely lying. I would have liked to think that he would have had the guts to say "Yes. I had an affair with this woman but it's over."'

She said there had been 'enormous pressure' on her since the rumours of Clinton's infidelity spread, and that in order to 'protect myself, I began to tape my conversations (with the Governor). I wanted a record. I made the recordings because every time a reporter confronted me, I felt vulnerable. Ninety per cent of me wanted to

believe that he would stand by me – but 10 per cent of me said that maybe my feelings wouldn't be as important to him as wanting to be President of the United States.'

As his campaign aides fretted in private as the campaign went into a tail spin, Clinton continued to steadfastly deny the claims, and berated Flowers for 'obviously taking money to change her story'. He said Flowers – a state employee who previously worked as a club singer and television reporter – had called him and asked, 'What am I supposed to do' about press inquiries. 'I said, "Just tell the truth,"' he explained. '"Tell them it didn't happen." I told her to deny it because it didn't happen.'

ON THE OFFENSIVE

However, the battle-weary governor conceded that he didn't know if he could disprove the allegations, and instead said he would rely on the American people to make their own judgements. Together with his wife, Hillary, he went on the offensive, taking his claim of total innocence directly to the people through TV and press interviews. Hillary, who admitted she and her husband had had problems like those similar to any other married couple, stood by her man, saying: 'My husband and I have been very straightforward in telling the American people from the very beginning, we have a strong and committed relationship. Like every couple that I know who have been married 16 years we've had our ups and downs.

'I don't know what to do about that, other than say it's (claims of the affair) not true and trust the American people to make the calculation themselves. Whatever anyone would say or imply about our relationship won't affect the way we feel about each other and won't affect our commitment to each other. And it won't affect this campaign.'

Amazingly, Hillary Clinton proved correct. Despite the constant media barrage, the polls indicated that people did, in fact, believe her husband. Slowly, as the questions gradually subsided, he regained lost ground, and within a month was back enjoying his front-runner status as the Democratic Party's likely nominee to face President Bush in the November election. Clinton had done what Hart couldn't... he had staved off rumours and claims about his sexual infidelity, and gone on to capture the biggest prize in the political world.

Yet while the Flowers furore was soon behind him and played no role in his head-to-head confrontation with George Bush, there were other scandals looming on the horizon even before he took the oath of office to become America's 42nd President, and people were already starting to question his suitability to sit in the Oval Office.

Clinton's first post-election chaos stemmed from the co-called Nannygate fiasco, in which not one, but two of his choices for the important cabinet position of Attorney General – the highest law enforcement office in the nation – had to withdraw from consideration for breaking the law!

NANNYGATE AFFAIRS

Prior to his inauguration in late January, 1993, Clinton had nominated Zoe Baird as his choice for the first woman to ever hold down the Attorney General's spot. Anyone considered for a cabinet level position – and most certainly as the nation's 'top cop' – is routinely the subject of an FBI background investigation to ensure there are no potentially embarrassing skeletons in the closet.

During the probe, Baird, a £300,000-a-year corporate attorney for a major insurance company, told agents and Clinton aides that she and her husband, a Yale law

> HE HAD STAVED OFF RUMOURS AND GONE ON TO CAPTURE THE BIGGEST PRIZE IN THE POLITICAL WORLD

Below: *Despite the controversy surrounding her husband's fidelity, future First Lady Hillary Clinton doggedly stood by her man.*

Above: President Clinton's first choice for Attorney General, Zoe Baird. Within days of his announcement, Baird was forced to withdraw her nomination after it was revealed she had hired illegal immigrants to care for her children.

CONGRESS WAS OUTRAGED THAT SOMEONE AS WEALTHY AS BAIRD WOULD FAIL TO PAY THE REQUISITE TAXES

AT FIRST GLANCE, WOOD SEEMED AN IMPECCABLE CHOICE. A LEARNED, WELL-READ JUDGE, SHE COMMANDED RESPECT

professor, had hired an illegal immigrant to care for their child. For some reason, Clinton and his top advisers didn't think the admission too serious.

Then, just before the inauguration, it was revealed that not only did she hire an undocumented Peruvian couple for £300 a week, but she failed to pay the necessary social security and unemployment insurance taxes required by law for all employers. Suddenly, chaos reigned. Congress was outraged, and ordinary men and women aghast that someone as wealthy as Baird would fail to pay the requisite taxes. And they were a little more than miffed at Clinton, who had promised to hold his cabinet officers up to the highest ethical standards.

Yet the President insisted the nomination process continue, so Baird was compelled to duly front the Senate Judiciary Committee which oversees all major appointments within the Justice Department. While the White House continued to play down the error as a technicality, Senator Alan Simpson quite rightly pointed it that Baird had violated a key feature of the Immigration Reform and Control Act of 1986. That law was designed to deter illegal immigrants from streaming across America's borders, and sought to dissuade people from hiring non-documented workers.

Baird compounded her perception problems when she tried to excuse her actions by saying it was her husband who had han-

dled the matter and that their lawyer had misinformed them! It was a flimsy excuse, given that she and her husband were among America's top legal eagles.

The Judiciary Committee, spurred on by an angry public, lambasted Baird, and grew increasingly reluctant to confirm her as Attorney General. Mercifully, an embarrassed President Clinton withdrew her nomination, realising that she didn't have a hope of being confirmed.

But the wolves were already baying for blood, and Republicans fuelled the notion that Clinton was simply not ready to lead the nation. His bumbling handling of the Baird nomination was positive proof, they said. Yet even the gloating Republicans couldn't believe what happened next.

Determined to have a woman as Attorney General – an alleged promise he had made to First Lady Hillary – Clinton then nominated Judge Kimba Wood, who had been the justice who sentenced Wall Street cheat Michael Milken for insider trading. At first glance, Wood seemed an impeccable choice. A learned, well-read judge, she commanded the respect of both lawyers and police officers. But no sooner was her name put forward, than it was learned that she, too, had hired an illegal nanny! Exit Judge Wood!

Finally, Clinton nominated a third woman, Janet Reno, to the position... but there were no more chapters in the Nannygate. Reno, who was confirmed, wasn't married!

TRAVELGATE AFFAIR

It wasn't long afterwards that the Clinton Administration was rocked by yet another scandal – the affair known as 'Travelgate' – in which seven workers in the White House Travel Office were fired at the behest of Clinton's cousin and a Hollywood friend.

The bizarre episode erupted on 19 May 1993, when the seven workers, who handle travel arrangements for the White House, were unceremoniously fired because of what officials described as financial 'mismanagement', and the top job inside the office was given to the well-connected Catherine Cornelius, a 25-year-old distant cousin of the President and girlfriend of a top White House spokesman, John Eller.

She had been pushing for some time to become the new head of the travel section, and Clinton's showbusiness buddy, TV producer Harry Thomason, who created shows like 'Designing Women' and 'Evening Shade', had explored the possibility of bidding for the lucrative White House aeroplane charter business, which handles flights for reporters as well as Administration aides.

After the dramatic firings, however, it became known that Clinton's wife, Hillary, had also played a role in Travelgate – and was given more information about it than even her husband – when she raised the question of 'problems in the travel office' with both White House Chief of Staff Mark McLarty and White House counsel Vince Foster (who later committed suicide, though for reasons unrelated to this affair), one of her former law partners, a full six days before the 19 May firings.

INTERNAL MEMO

Mrs Clinton's press secretary said the First Lady heard about the travel office problems 'from talk circulating in the White House' and 'Thomason may have mentioned it to her in passing'. Following her inquiries, she was sent a memo on 17 May that proposed dismissing the travel officers and putting Cornelius in charge. The memo, written by a presidential aide, was never seen by the President.

Meanwhile, Cornelius began eavesdropping on the staff's conversations, photocopied documents and took home White House records. Her unsubstantiated claims that the workers were living 'beyond the means of government employees' – a smear that was leaked to the press – served to reinforce the decision to fire them. Also, her boyfriend, Eller, took a special interest in trying to get the travel staffers fired.

Reeling from accusations of patronage and a shoddy investigation, the White House ordered a full probe into the affair. That report acknowledged that the White House made several errors in judgment, including pressing the FBI to investigate the travel office. It also raised new questions about whether White House aides told the truth, particularly when they said the firings were just a routine by-product of Vice President Gore's review of govern-

ment. In fact, the 17 May memo that Mrs Clinton saw, states that an 'emergency review' was launched after staffers 'were urged by Harry Thomason and Catherine Cornelius' to do so.

But more alarmingly, it also raised questions about the way friendships and old business ties led to the dismissal of seven people at the urging of the President's cousin and an old friend. Incredibly, the four White House aides, including Cornelius and Eller, were only reprimanded for their role in the plot. As for the seven unfortunates who lost their jobs, five were promised new federal employment, while the other two retired.

On the surface, Travelgate might seem like a relatively small and minor scandal, but coming as it did on the heels of the Nannygate furore – both less than four months into Clinton's term of office – it heightened many Americans' perception that the country was like a ship adrift at sea and that its new President might be totally out of his depth as the leader of the world's only superpower.

REELING FROM ACCUSATIONS OF PATRONAGE, THE WHITE HOUSE ORDERED A FULL PROBE INTO THE AFFAIR

Below: *First Lady Hillary Clinton had her own problems soon after moving into the White House. Her role in the so-called Travelgate scandal has never been fully explained.*

SECRET LIAISONS
Sex and Scandals

The British relish a sex scandal, a naughty indiscretion that is usually committed by the high, mighty and sanctimonious. No single place can have provided more ingredients for scandal than the House of Commons, the mother of all Parliaments.

The House of Commons has been the source of so many sex scandals over the years, it may as well be renamed 'the father of all scandal'. Here the rulers of the nation have lied, cheated on their wives, fiddled, diddled and skedaddled with the loot. Not all are bad, of course; but because so much propriety is expected from elected public servants, it is not surprising that when the unmeritorious few are caught, the rest find themselves somewhat tarred with the scandal.

Sex has usually been the name of the scandal game in the House of Commons and none caused quite so much excitement as the personal disaster which befell Lord Lambton. All the ingredients for a juicy, titillating episode guaranteed to feed the Sunday newspaper headlines for weeks were there. Lambton was a high-flying, dashing Tory MP and parliamentary under-secretary of state for defence when he became embroiled in a call-girl ring that catered for successful, powerful individuals like himself. It was only when his paramour Norma Levy became embroiled in an argument with her pimping husband Colin that the game was up for Lambton and the career of a good man destroyed.

Lord Anthony Lambton came from a distinguished political family and was destined for great things in the Conservative party ranks. Like others who fell before and after him, the prospect of actually jangling the keys to number ten were once a possibility. But as Sir Winston Churchill once said: 'Prostitutes and politics do not go well together, although recent events have shown them to be closely allied.'

So it was the case with Lambton, who sought extra spice in his life with a hooker called Norma. It might have been the case that his political career could have survived had he been a Commons backwoodsman, someone who sat on the sidelines of national policy without actually shaping it. But in his role at the Air Ministry he had access to

much secret material, classified intelligence on every aspect of Britain's aerial defences. This was material that Iron Curtain nations would have sorely liked to get their hands on. Although he would later be determined by a special inquiry never to have been a security risk, it was nevertheless the possibility of what 'might have been' that helped to put an end to his blossoming public life.

In the society world he moved in, in London at the start of the 1970s, Lambton

LAMBTON HAD ACCESS TO CLASSIFIED INTELLIGENCE ON EVERY ASPECT OF BRITAIN'S AERIAL DEFENCES

Above: *Norma Levy, the hooker who forced the resignation of Lord Lambton, promotes her book about their dangerous liaisons.*

Opposite: *Lord Lambton, the man at the centre of the call-girl scandal that almost toppled a government.*

Above: *Colin Levy, husband of Norma, pictured being arrested by Spanish police. It was his plot to get money from newspapers after he found out the identity of his wife's famous and respected client.*

ASPIRING MEMBERS OF THIS VICE CARTEL WERE GIVEN THE TELEPHONE NUMBER OF A MADAM WHO CONTROLLED THE GIRLS

gained access to a high-class prostitution ring. It had no contact telephone numbers listed under 'escorts' in the newspapers or mens' magazines, nor were there direct numbers of the girls for the clients to phone. Instead, by word of mouth, aspiring members of this vice cartel were given the telephone number of a madam who controlled the girls and she in turn arranged the trysts. It was to Lambton's ultimate disgrace that he met Norma Levy, whose husband Colin, 28 – a jobless taxi-driver with a criminal record and a propensity for heavy drinking – was to become the main instigator of his downfall. Early in 1973, his only source of income was living off the earnings of his 26-year-old wife who worked as a call girl, indulging the sexual whims of a number of wealthy clients.

WEALTHY CLIENTS

Lambton's liaisons at Norma's flat in Maida Vale, London, were discreet and risk-free, with Colin Levy never meeting the distinguished government servant. Lambton went there as 'Mr. Lucas' and enjoyed sex sessions with both Norma and another girl called Kim – and on occasion smoked cannabis. He enjoyed sex with them and Norma was well paid: there was never a hint that he wanted to discuss the finer points of British military security with her in the bedroom.

She in turn regarded him as a gentlemanly client who was never any trouble. But it was Colin who, knowing all about his wife's activities, suggested to her that they could make some more money by selling compromising pictures of Lambton to the newspapers. He learned his identity through a slip-up committed by Lambton himself. One day he did not have the requisite £50 for a sex session and so he wrote a cheque – signing his name Anthony Claud Frederick Lambton. He had signed his own political death warrant. Colin Levy, who was always on the lookout for new and easy get-rich-quick schemes, decided to try his hand at a new one.

GET-RICH-QUICK

Boring a hole in a wardrobe in 1973, he took several pictures of Lambton cavorting on the bed with his wife and another woman. Levy was wise enough to know that blackmail ranked high in the criminal calendar of serious offences. But he reasoned that one of the more lurid Sunday newspapers might be willing to pay a small fortune for the photos. But when these photos failed to turn out satisfactorily, he went to the *News of the World* newspaper and demanded £30,000 for the story.

The newspaper, which had been compiling its own dossier on Lambton due to police information that they were closing in on a high-scale prostitution ring in London, assigned a professional photographer to go with Levy to his secret hiding place to take some photographs. The newspaper also tape-recorded the goings-on in the room. The tape-recordings included a conversation which touched on drugs and Lambton's admission that he had once smoked cannabis with Norma.

The *News of the World*, realising the sensitive nature of what they were dealing with, declined to publish and handed the material back to Levy who took it to the *Sunday People*. The *News of the World* did not need to part with £30,000, as much of the information was already in their hands long before Colin Levy came calling. The *People* eventually handed this sensational dossier to the police, but Levy still did not get any money. Eventually he showed the whole lot to the German magazine *Stern*, which was not under the jurisdiction of the Draconian libel laws in England. *Stern* didn't pay Levy a penny either, but it published all his allegations and Scotland Yard was intensely interested.

On 21 May 1973, Norma and Colin fled to Spain as the heat was turned up – and Lord Lambton was interviewed at New Scotland Yard where he admitted that he had been to bed with Norma. He had thrown his career away with the admission.

Left: *Lord Lambton looking confident – in the days before the scandal broke.*

It was also abundantly clear that – although no blackmail had been committed – Lambton was clearly open to it. His career was shattered within days, the press hounded him and his family, and Norma Levy became the most sought-after femme fatale since Mata Hari.

In a statement that was released shortly after his resignation, Lord Lambton said: 'This is the sordid story. There has been no security risk and no blackmail and never at any time have I spoken of my late job. All that has happened is that some sneak pimp has seen an opportunity of making money by the sale of the story and secret photos to papers at home and abroad. My own feelings may be imagined but I have no excuses whatsoever to make. I behaved with credulous stupidity.' It was only when the Security Commission report was published at the end of 1973 that it became clear how Norma was opposed to betraying Lambton, but eventually did so after she had a fierce argument with her husband.

The Security Commission reported: 'Her action is inconsistent with any attempt to blackmail him. Colin Levy, however, thought that he could make money out of Lord Lambton's involvement with his wife – to which he had always been a willing party – not by blackmail, but by selling the story to the press.'

THE RULING

The commission reported that it was 'entirely satisfied' that no classified information was ever passed by Lord Lambton. But it added: 'When, however, we turn to what might have happened if he had continued in the same course of conduct we consider that a potential risk to security would have been involved such as would have compelled us to recommend that Lord Lambton should be denied further access to classified information.'

In reference to his puffing on a cannabis cigarette the commission ruled: 'We are advised that this is a soft drug which produces changes in mood and perception and gives a feeling of irresponsibility. Hallucinations, too, may be caused. Recorded evidence existed of a conversation which suggested, whether correctly or not, his involvement with other drugs as well, together with photographic evidence of sexual practices which deviated from the normal. This evidence was in the hands of criminals and up for sale. Lord Lambton was wide open to blackmail. We are, however, wholly convinced that he would never have yielded to any pressure to betray his country's secrets by fear of disclosure for what he had done, even if it had involved more serious criminal offences than those which the recorded conversation suggest.'

Even though his patriotism emerged unscathed, Lambton was, nevertheless, ruined in public life. He was fined in court for possession of cannabis and amphetamines, found at his home after his confession to Scotland Yard. He eventually went into exile with his wife to a farmhouse in Northern Italy. Colin Levy ended up in a Spanish jail after trying to run Norma over. She divorced him, moved to America and eventually wound up serving time on prostitution charges. Everybody involved seemed to be losers.

Many believed it was an unfair punishment for Lambton, including his biographer Sir John Colville, who wrote in his book *Those Lambtons*: 'Those who take prostitutes to bed do not, with their head on the pillow, discuss guided weapons and electronic devices. The answer is hypocrisy – as Somerset Maugham once said: "Hypocrisy is the tribute vice pays to virtue."' In the next scandal, low cunning, self preservation and a determination to look after number one at all costs were the motive for one of the greatest scandals to ever rock parliament.

THE HIGH-FLIER

John Stonehouse was truly a man who had it all. He was handsome, he was a successful politician, he had made a great deal of money in his life, he was appointed to a cabinet post – he even had a mistress who never infringed on his 'other' life with his family, but was merely there for him when he wanted her. But it all went terribly, terribly wrong for this golden boy of the Labour party, the high-flier who nurtured ambitions himself for the keys to No. 10 Downing Street. Somewhere along the way his financial life collapsed and to escape the shame, the scandal and the sheer burdens of a life that was increasingly weighing him down, he hatched a tragi-comic plot to fake his own death. It was the most extraordinary vanishing act Britain had ever seen.

The roots in his fake ending lie in his beginnings; he was born at Southampton on 28 July 1925, his father a trade union secretary, his mother a former mayor of the town. At the age of 16, imbued by his family's working class traditions, he joined the Labour Party, worked in the probation service until 1944 and then joined the Royal Air Force for his national service as an education officer. After the war, he took a degree at the London School of Economics, determined to enter public life with as many qualifications as he could muster. In 1957, he was returned as the Member of Parliament for Labour for Wednesbury in the West Midlands.

Below: *John Stonehouse, the MP who faked his death to begin a new life in Australia with his mistress, returns to face the music in London.*

After a stint abroad in Uganda with his wife Barbara he returned to Britain to ride the fast track of post-war politics. Gifted with a facile charm and easy-going manner, he was picked out by Harold Wilson for great things. He served in the Ministry of Aviation and at the Colonial Office before becoming, in 1968, the Postmaster-General. He was popular in some quarters, but not with the mandarins of the civil service who truly run all government departments. There were several embarrassing blunders while Stonehouse was at the ministry: an attempt to reorganise the capital's telephone directories which ended in abject failure; the introduction of a two-tier postal system (widely regarded on both sides of parliament as a disaster); and his failure in 1970 after he misled the cabinet about a telegraphist's strike. It was the latter blunder which led to him being dropped from his governmental post.

A HAREBRAINED SCHEME

Commerce, which up until that time he had been dabbling in on the side, then became a full-time occupation. He began setting up a series of companies, many of them balanced on a knife edge of security, which he believed would make him his fortune. On the surface everything seemed to be as it had always been with him – but things were going badly wrong by 1974.

The companies were being kept afloat by a complex series of borrowings – one to another to another to another – in an ever decreasing circle. Stonehouse did have some money put to one side – £100,000 of it, equivalent to roughly three times that by today's rate of exchange – but that was salted away abroad, safe from the prying eyes of the taxman. There was no such safety net to save him from creditors at home who were soon to begin circling like sharks.

Perhaps it was the shame of betraying such humble but worthy parents that led Stonehouse to concoct the most amazingly harebrained scheme that the House of Commons ever witnessed. Stonehouse knew that his financial misfortune could not happen without massive press publicity because of his public life. By 1974, Stonehouse was being investigated by the Department of Trade and his companies were in the red to the tune of £800,000.

The money-go-round tactics would no longer work. He needed an escape.

It is at this point that his loving mistress, Sheila Buckley, who worked for him at the House of Commons, came into the picture. She relished the idea of a new life with him, but realised that with his reputation, his wife and his two children, it was an impossible dream. He revealed to her an amazing plot that he had in his head, one that parodied the popular TV series 'The Rise and Fall of Reginald Perrin'. In the TV series Perrin, played by Leonard Rossiter, decides to stage his own death by leaving his clothes on a beach, allowing those who find them to fall into the trap of believing he had tragically drowned at sea.

Above: *Sheila Buckley, the 29-year-old former secretary to Stonehouse who became his lover and co-conspirator in the plot where he would vanish.*

GIFTED WITH A FACILE CHARM AND EASY-GOING MANNERS, STONEHOUSE WAS PICKED BY WILSON FOR GREAT THINGS

Stonehouse took his idea one step further with some elaborate planning beforehand. He then told Sheila Buckley his plans and the procedure for his faked demise was put into effect.

Under the guise of being a caring and concerned MP, Stonehouse visited two widows in his constituency to share condolences with the loss of their husbands, Donald Mildoon and Joseph Markham. By obtaining from the unsuspecting women the full particulars of their deceased spouses, he was able to then get passports in the two names with his photograph in each. It was the plot used by the assassin in the book *The Day of the Jackal* by Frederick Forsyth – a peculiarity of the British passport issuing office being that they do not check applications to see if the person requesting a passport has, in fact, died.

VANISHING ACT

Stonehouse decided that Markham was the identity he preferred. He changed much of his money in the secret overseas accounts into the account under his new name and finalised plans. He also opened accounts in the name of Mildoon. In all, Stonehouse, at the time of his vanishing act, had 27 accounts, most of them in New South Wales, Australia, where he intended to settle with Sheila Buckley. The idea was to make it seem as if he had drowned while on a swim. He told his wife he was going to America on business and flew to Miami on 19 November 1974. He made sure that the concierge, the barman and the front desk workers at his hotel in the seaside city knew he was off to the beach.

In front of the Fontainbleu Hotel he dumped a pile of clothes... and disappeared.By the time news reached Britain that the former minister was presumed drowned in a bathing accident, 'Joseph Markham' had already arrived in Hawaii on the first leg of his elaborate scheme. Stonehouse later admitted that this was the most challenging part of his plot; he prayed that no-one would recognise him as, after all, he had occupied a high station in British public life for some years before the whole rotten structure of his business affairs collapsed around him.

At the end of November he was in Melbourne and wandering around quite

> IN FRONT OF THE FONTAINBLEU HOTEL HE DUMPED A PILE OF CLOTHES... AND DISAPPEARED

Below: *Cecil Parkinson, highest of the Thatcherite high-fliers, lost it all over his affair with Sara Keays.*

> HE SORELY TESTED THE PATIENCE OF TRIAL JUDGE MR JUSTICE EVELEIGH WHO DID NOT SHARE HIS VIEW OF HIMSELF

freely while the salutations to him were still being read in the House of Commons. He had, to all intents and purposes, gotten away with murder – his own. He kept in touch with Sheila by telephone and began plotting arrangements for her to join him. But the double life was to be short lived.

A bank clerk's suspicions were aroused over the transferral of a large amount of money from New Zealand in the name of Mildoon to a Markham account in Melbourne. Police were called in and the man named Markham was put under surveillance. Lawmen believed initially that they had caught Lord Lucan, the fugitive British peer wanted back in England for the murder of his nanny. He had vanished from a heinous crime and there were regular sightings. Scotland Yard wired photos of Lucan, and pictures of Stonehouse, for good measure. He was under police surveillance for some time until a sharp-eyed detective gained entry to the bungalow he had rented and saw a book of matches lying on a table with the words Fontainbleu Hotel on the cover. They had found Stonehouse, the man who went for a swim and never returned.

Stonehouse was sensationally placed under arrest on Christmas Eve 1974 amid an explosion of publicity. He was brought back to England where his trial on fraud charges exposed him for the cynical cheat he was. He told the court that he had suffered a mental breakdown, that he assumed the new identities to escape the 'cant and humbug' of life in Britain. He sorely tested the patience of trial judge Mr. Justice Eveleigh who did not share his view of himself; the trapped idealist fleeing from the burdens of a society that he no longer wished to live in. The judge told him shortly before he sentenced him to seven years in jail: 'You did not simply decide to disappear because you were oppressed by business burdens. You decided to do so in comfort, and it is clear to me that self-interest has been well to the fore. You aimed to get rich quickly. You falsely accused other people of cant, hypocrisy and humbug when you must have known all the time that your defence was an embodiment of all three.'

CONFIDENCE TRICKSTER

Stonehouse, who once nurtured ambitions for the highest office in the land, was reduced to a number in Her Majesty's prison system. As he began his jail term a Department of Trade inquiry into his failed business interests branded him 'a sophisticated and skilful confidence trickster.' In the end, Stonehouse resigned his Privy Councillorship, and without waiting to be expelled from the Commons, resigned from there too. He served four years in jail, being released on parole in 1979. Upon his release from jail, he concerned himself for a while with good works in welfare projects in the East End of London, but later became a mediocre novelist. He settled in Totton, near Southampton, never fully coming to terms with the great con trick that he perpetrated on his nation, his family and, ultimately, himself.

He died, finally and irreversibly for real, in 1988 at the age of 62 following a massive heart attack. The ever-faithful Sheila was at his side with a eulogy for him. She said: 'He was a fabulous man and a very gentle person. He was a one-off – I never met a man like him before and I know I won't again.' Lord Molloy, one of his closest colleagues in Westminster, who was for a time his parliamentary private secretary, said: 'I could not understand why a person who had such ability and such great pride in his country should have gotten into this terrible mess.'

THE GOLDEN BOY

Cecil Parkinson never staged his own death, but like John Stonehouse, he was once poised on the threshold of greatness in politics. A Tory party golden boy, he was the right-hand man of Margaret Thatcher on her crusade to change the face and nature of British society forever. As Secretary for Trade and Industry, he had a key position to boost the productivity of the nation in the wonder-years of the 1980s, while at the same time trying to promote better, less restrictive working practices throughout many overmanned and underworked industries. But as much as he was successful in his work, he was also seen by many as the acceptable, tolerant face of Thatcherism. It was an image that Mrs. Thatcher valued and there is little doubt that he could have one day become her successor to the highest office in the land.

But Cecil Parkinson lost his bid for glory due to his affair with Sara Keays, his secretary in Parliament who went on to have his child. And the end of the affair – and his career – was played out in the full glare of publicity; publicity which could only lead to his resignation. The handsome and debonair Parkinson – son of a Lancashire railwayman – was to hold another cabinet position once a suitable period of time had elapsed between the height of the crisis and

HE DIED FOR REAL IN 1988, FOLLOWING A MASSIVE HEART ATTACK. THE EVER-FAITHFUL SHEILA WAS AT HIS SIDE

Below: *Sara Keays and baby Flora, the love child who cost Cecil Parkinson his government post and, almost, his career.*

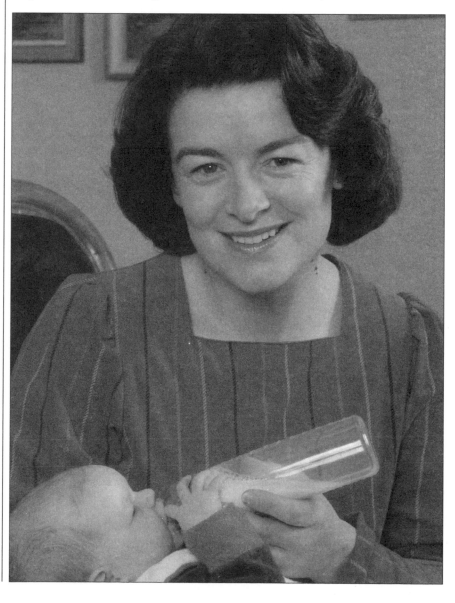

his leaving, but he would never attain the heights of greatness to which he had once aspired.

Educated at the Royal Lancaster grammar school, and Emmanuel College, Cambridge, where he obtained degrees in law and English, Mr. Parkinson was the epitome of Mrs. Thatcher's self-made-man. He qualified as a chartered accountant and a youthful flirtation with the Labour Party was forgotten as he forged ahead in his career. It was his marriage to Ann Jarvis, the daughter of a wealthy builder in Harpenden, which gave him the entrée to the Tory social circle of the Home Counties and eventually a job with a large city firm of accountants.

He entered Parliament in 1970 as the Tory member for Enfield West, and by the time he was appointed trade minister in 1979 his construction and building inter-

---

CECIL PARKINSON WOULD NEVER ATTAIN THE HEIGHTS OF GREATNESS TO WHICH HE HAD ONCE ASPIRED

Above: *Mrs Thatcher. She was a staunch supporter of Cecil Parkinson, crediting him with victory in her election campaign. She could not save him, however, after Sara Keays' bombshell letter to the* Times.

ests, acquired with the knowledge he gleaned while working in the City, were worth close to £750,000. Life was good to Cecil Parkinson – and getting better. Mrs. Thatcher, the new, dynamic leader of the Conservatives, who saw herself as a Joan of Arc figure embarking on a quest to change Britain and the attitudes of its people, plucked him from the junior ministerial ranks and made him chairman of the party in 1981. As such, he did a brilliant job, reorganising the party at grass-roots level so that it functioned with more efficiency

in every way. A reward for this was the task of masterminding the Tory election campaign of 1983 – another mammoth job, which he performed with consummate skill. But while he was busy organising the faithful, a terrible domestic scandal in his life was threatening to explode at any minute. It would eventually detonate on polling day itself.

Rumours of the affair had been whispered for many months in the halls of power in 1983. Sara, the 46-year-old daughter of an army colonel, had been his mistress for 10 years and they agreed that it was love on both sides. In 1979, when he was Minister for Trade, he had actually proposed to her – and she had accepted. But they agreed that everything was to be subjugated to his political career which he could not afford to jeopardise. It was the price they were both willing to pay, and the affair continued in snatched moments alone and secret assignations.

THE SLOW FUSE

In 1980, the affair briefly cooled when Sarah went to Brussels to work in a European Parliament post while Parkinson became the chief political ally and close friend of Mrs. Thatcher. They were not apart for long, however, and the affair resumed upon her return to London. By the time polling day came around on 9 June 1983, Sara Keays was carrying the child of the man she loved. Later she would claim that when she told him, two months earlier, he was mortified and wanted to end the affair there and then – but said that on polling day he had changed his mind again, and pledged that he would marry her.

The slow, simmering fuse of his own destruction had been set that day, but the explosion didn't come until October. As rumours continued to swirl, the satirical magazine *Private Eye* printed a story that Miss Keays was pregnant. Fleet Street tabloids smelled blood and soon were circling like sharks. There was one incident in which Miss Keays was pursued in a crazy car chase across London by reporters eager for knowledge about the identity of the father. Parkinson, a shrewd, adept politician, knew that he was being pushed into a corner from which there could be no escape. On 5 October that year, he issued a short, curt statement via his solicitor which was the only comment he ever made about the affair. It said: 'To bring to an end to the rumour concerning Miss Sara Keays and myself, and to prevent further harassment of Miss Keays and her family, I wish, with her consent, to make the following statement: I have had a relationship with Miss Keays over a number of years. She is expecting a child to be born in January, of whom I am the father. I am of course making financial provision for both mother and child. During our relationship I told Miss Keays of my wish to marry her. Despite my having given Miss Keays that assurance, my wife, who has been a source of great strength, and I decided to stay together and to keep our family together. I regret deeply the distress I have caused to Miss Keays, to her family and my own family.'

An earthquake rippled through British society the next day as Fleet Street pursued every angle of the story with all the tenacity of pit bulls and all the tact of a bull in a china shop. But Downing Street was adamant: the question of his resignation did not come into it. Mrs. Thatcher counted loyalty among her ministers as one of their greatest qualities and she liked to show it in return. But Parkinson had, in fact, just one long week in politics left to him.

PACT OF SILENCE

Cecil and Sara agreed to a pact of silence. However, Cecil committed a massive faux-pas on the Panorama TV programme which banished him into the political wilderness. He referred to Sara as 'the other person'. Sara, who had given him the best years of her life, who was bearing his child, who loved him and who had wanted to marry him, felt there and then that she had been cruelly used. She then drafted a long statement to the *Times* which appeared on Friday 10 October. The ten-point letter stressed the dithering that Parkinson had shown over whether or not to marry her, his broken promises and plans to leave his own wife. She ended the statement saying: 'Press comment, government pronouncements and the continued speculation about this matter have put me in an impossible position. I feel that I have both a public duty and a duty to my family to put the record straight.'

Parkinson was at the the Imperial Hotel in Blackpool for the annual gathering of the Tory faithful at the conference when he heard the news. Sara Keays' statement had pushed him over the edge and he resigned his position after a three-minute conference with Mrs. Thatcher. On New Year's Eve, Sara Keays gave birth to an 8lb 3oz daughter she called Flora – a child for whom Cecil Parkinson wished 'peace, privacy and a happy life'. Parkinson was driven away from the Imperial Hotel in disgrace – the shattered dreams of a loyal courtier reeling through his mind. He had joined the ranks of the 'what might have been' brigade.

A DOUBLE LIFE

There is little doubt that Harvey Proctor, the Member for Basildon and Billericay in Essex, would ever have attained the keys to No. 10, but he was an industrious MP with a great penchant for self-publicity.

PARKINSON WAS DRIVEN AWAY FROM THE IMPERIAL HOTEL IN DISGRACE

Below: *Harvey Proctor, the upright MP for Billericay, Essex, walks to court where he would answer charges of gross indecency against young boys. The scandal finished him.*

Newspapermen call MPs like Mr. Proctor 'rent-a-quote' – they can always be relied upon for a quotable opinion on any subject, from capital punishment to the state of grain supplies in third world nations. How ironic, then, that the man who liked to live his life in a blaze of publicity should find himself consumed in the flames of it when his odd little ways are exposed to the public in a London courtroom!

Proctor was a confirmed bachelor who was on the right wing of the party. He was blonde, good looking and a snappy dresser who, at 40, was considered quite eligible, after almost a decade as an MP in the area, by the local ladies. Yet ladies were not what Proctor was interested in. He led, like so many other notable worthies who sit in the House of Commons, a double life.

PRIVATE AFFAIRS

Max Peters, a 21-year-old youth, told a newspaper that he was approached by a friend of Proctor's as he rode the escalator up a London underground station. 'He said he had a friend called Keith who wanted to see me,' said Peters. 'At his flat this man said that he would play headmaster and I would be the pupil who had done something wrong. He said I must call him sir at all times and must not under any circumstances answer back. !

'He took me into a bedroom and told me to put on a pair of white shorts. Then he went into the living room which he called his office and said that I was to come in. I went into the "office" and from that moment on he was a completely different person. He asked me what I had done wrong. I told him that I skipped prep and he said I had to be punished. He made me do some exercises on the floor and I saw him playing with himself. He made me lean over a big armchair in the corner and told me that I must not struggle or call out and then he gave me six slaps with a cane. It was so painful, I was sure I would be marked. His friend told me he had severely marked other boys.

'He asked me if I had learned my lesson and I had to say "Yes, sir". He asked me if I would do it again and I had to say "No, sir". He said that if I stayed the night he would give me £30. I stayed the night and he tried to have sex with me but I refused.

> 'AT HIS FLAT THIS MAN SAID THAT HE WOULD PLAY HEADMASTER AND I WOULD BE THE PUPIL...'

Below: *David Mellor, Heritage Secretary, went the way of all weak flesh in the House of Commons, beginning an illicit affair with an actress that would produce his political downfall.*

When I went there I was told by his friend that he was a journalist, but then I was told he was an MP. It wouldn't have taken me long to guess – he had books of Enoch Powell all over the place and he watched the Fulham by-election on TV. I wish I had never gone to see him in the first place.'

Barry Haddon, a pimp who served time in jail for indecently assaulting a young boy, was an informant for the *Sunday People* newspaper who led a probe into Proctor's world of vice. *People* investigators trawled through the seedy underbelly of life in the capital, visiting rent-boy hangouts, sado-masochist bars and pubs and clubs frequented by Proctor in his other life.

The police arrested Proctor, as a vice probe, accelerated by rumours and the newspaper stories, highlighted his extra-curricular activities. At Bow Street Magistrates Court in London on 20 May 1987, he was fined £1,450 on charges of

gross indecency with rent boys. A week earlier Proctor had resigned his seat as an MP. His career in tatters, friends in parliament and elsewhere rallied round to invest in an exclusive shirt-shop that he opened up. It was promptly dubbed 'Shirtlifters' by one Sunday newspaper!

'THE MINISTER FOR FUN'

In recent years, connoisseurs of scandal were beginning to think that the House of Commons was getting respectable – there seemed little devilment to make the headlines. But in 1992, a nice little scandal broke which was to cost a government minister his job and send the public into paroxysms of pleasure as all the tawdry details of the dangerous liaison were splashed across the front pages of newspapers. The minister in question was David Mellor, a bespectacled – some would say self-satisfied – Heritage Secretary, or as he was more popularly known, the 'Minister for Fun'. Mellor was a devout Tory and a man who took his career seriously. But it was destroyed over his fling with a sometime actress named Antonia de Sancha.

The high-flying cabinet minister first saw the lithesome 30-year-old Antonia in a posh London restaurant and he suddenly lost all interest in the food on his plate. It was two days before the general election in 1992 – the one all the pundits believed the Tories would lose – and the diners at Le Gourmet restaurant in Chelsea were in a somewhat subdued mood. But Mellor, 43, suddenly found his spirits soaring when a mutual friend introduced him to Antonia – and from that initial introduction he was a man possessed. Torn between his family, his duties and his lust, he discovered that lust conquered all and soon they were bedmates and the game of deceit began.

At his apartment in Three Kings Yard, Davies Street, he made love to her four times on their first night together. Their sex sessions were interspersed with expensive Cristal champagne and smoked salmon. 'David has very fine tastes,' the hot-blooded Antonia was later to say. 'And he knows how to satisfy a woman.' But it was the beginning of a relationship that would turn his political ambitions to dust. Antonia, whose film credits up to then were limited to playing a one-legged prostitute in a soft

TORN BETWEEN HIS FAMILY, HIS DUTIES AND HIS LUST, HE DISCOVERED THAT LUST CONQUERED ALL

porn film, would end up as part of his downfall; but Antonia would not shoulder the blame entirely. There would soon be another woman on the scene, dragged out into the public eye because of his romps with Antonia.

THE STORY BREAKS

A newspaper was soon on the scene of the story and, like so many such embarrassing situations before, it broke over him during eggs and bacon one Sunday morning in September. All the sordid details were there – the liaison, the names, the dates and even snippets of their conversation together. Mellor considered resigning there and then, but he was a close friend of Prime Minister John Major and, after consultation with him, he decided to tough it out and stay. After all, there had been no possibility of him revealing state secrets, she was not a prostitute and blackmail was never on the agenda. He figured that he had just been the victim of bad luck. With his wife standing behind him, he took the view that it must be Downing Street that decides who shall serve in government, not the various tabloid editors of British newspapers.

The minister may have felt, smugly, that he had saved his career and could weather all sorts of lurid newspaper articles –

Above: *Prime Minister John Major fought to save Mellor as he writhed and squirmed in the full glare of press attention.*

Right: *Shortly before the end, and surrounded by a sea of cameras, Mellor tries to tough it out.*

ALL THE SORDID DETAILS WERE THERE: THE LIAISONS, THE NAMES, THE DATES AND EVEN SNIPPETS OF THEIR CONVERSATIONS

including one by Antonia in *The Sun* in which she claimed that he liked to have sex with her while he was dressed in a Chelsea football strip! But another timebomb was ticking away that would explode. In 1990, as Saddam Hussein's legions were rolling over the border from Iraq to occupy Kuwait, Mr. Mellor, his wife Judith and their children had gone on holiday to Marbella with Mona Bauwens, whose father was the finance chief for the Palestine Liberation Organisation, one of the premier terrorist networks in the world. The story broke at a time when 4,000 Britons were in Iraq, possibly about to become hostages of Saddam Hussein – who, incidentally was receiving support in his foreign adventure from the PLO.

Mona Bauwens felt she had been defamed and took the *Sunday People* newspaper to court. But it was revealed in her testimony that she paid for the Mellors and their children to go on holiday. It was swiftly established that Mr. Mellor had *not*

declared this gift in the register of interests in the House of Commons. She also told the court how he was a regular visitor for tea and coffee at her flat. The case ended in deadlock in the High Court – but it was curtains for Mellor. It was revealed later that he accepted two other free holidays from Arabic hosts – one from Mona's cousin Zaki Nusseibeh and the other from his boss, Sheikh Zayed of Abu Dhabi. His political support began to evaporate.

On 24 September, he wrote a letter to John Major in which he stated the case for his resignation. 'I am privileged to count you as a dear friend. I do not want to be seen as a liability to you.' Joanna Horaim Ashbourn, who disclosed intimate details of the affair due to her friendship with Antonia, said: 'As a Minister of Fun he certainly provided a lot of entertainment for the nation.' Mr. Mellor exited the stage of public life, left to ponder forever about a certain meeting in a certain restaurant that had led him to this.

Above: *Judith Mellor, left, holds hands with Mona Bauwens as they leave the High Court after hearing evidence in Bauwens' libel case against the* **People** *newspaper.*

SHE ALSO TOLD THE COURT HOW HE WAS A REGULAR VISITOR FOR TEA AND COFFEE AT HER FLAT…

THE MIDDLE EAST
Reigns Of Terror

The Middle East has been the bane of successive governments of the west as the tyrants of states such as Iraq and Libya sponsor terrorism, harbour murderers and nurture Islamic fundamentalism – an apparent threat to the world order.

Nations of the Middle East are struggling to find a place in the community of nations. However, they are ruled by despots with the power of medieval warlords; and the people of these countries find themselves beaten, tortured and terrified into submission, their will bent to the will of the monsters who rule them. There are at least three regimes that the west would love to see topple – and heading the list is Iraq, the regime of Saddam Hussein.

THE GROTESQUE PHOENIX

Saddam Hussein, the strongman of Iraq seems to many people to be almost invincible. He provoked a war of aggression against Kuwait, intimidated, imprisoned, tortured and slaughtered its inhabitants and then went to war against the most fearsome technological warfare force ever deployed in the region. After sacrificing 100,000 of his soldiers in futile combat – and seeing the destruction of the infrastructure of his country in mammoth bombing raids – Saddam Hussein seemed doomed. However, like some grotesque phoenix, he rose from the ashes of his defeat to impose yet more terror, more suffering and more blind obedience in his *1984* world, where the picture of himself as Big Brother glares down at the frightened citizenry from every building in Iraq.

Saddam Hussein was born to dirt-poor parents in Auja, near Tikrit, in April 1937. A member of the Sunni tribe, his father died before he was born and an uncle took on the duties of raising him. After an uneventful childhood, Saddam moved to Baghdad at the age of 18 for further schooling. Exposure to the metropolis broadened his outlook and hardened him into an opponent of the corrupt premier Quasim. He joined the Baath party when he was 20 years old, and two years later was part of the team that tried unsuccessfully to assassinate the president in October 1959. It was an act that showed the very core of Hussein – that he believed violence was the answer to any and all problems. It was to become his deep and abiding personal philosophy.

The Baath party took power in 1963 and Hussein returned from exile in Egypt. He married the schoolteacher daughter of his maternal uncle and, like Hitler in another age, believed he had a destiny for his country that only he could fulfil. With other conspirators he attempted a coup against the military regime of Abdul Arif, but he was thrown into jail when it failed. He escaped in 1966 and soon after gained control of the Baath party. He was 31 when it came back to power in 1968.

Soon he was on the Revolutionary Command Council, the all-powerful clique which ruled Iraq with an iron fist. He had risen through the ranks of the 22-member

---

THE PEOPLE OF THESE COUNTRIES FIND THEMSELVES BEATEN, TORTURED AND TERRIFIED INTO SUBMISSION

Opposite: *Saddam Hussein, desert strongman and cruellest of a cruel breed, a tyrant who has used every diabolical weapon in his arsenal to keep power.*

Below: *Saddam Hussein exhorts his troops to greater heights of self-sacrifice during the Iran-Iraq war.*

body with wily cunning, allying himself with those who wielded power over the military and secret police, distancing himself from those with more liberal views. In late July 1979, in a classic Stalinist move, he announced that he had discovered a plot against the state. Five RCC members – all close Saddam allies – formed a kangaroo court which ordered the execution of 68 military and civilian enemies. The terror had begun even before he had assumed full power over the state.

The executions consolidated his hold over the council and he was now recognised as Iraq's ruler. In moves designed to win popular support, he raised the salaries of the military, the police and the judiciary, while at the same time allocating massive public funds for statues – of himself. Soon Baghdad would become one giant shrine to Saddam Hussein. His picture hanging from apartment buildings, his arms holding scimitar swords crossing a giant highway on the entrance to the city, his face in every office – this was the brave new world that Saddam brought to Iraq. And the bedrock for it was terror.

Saddam Hussein stood – and still stands – at the apex of three power centres in Iraq: the party, the military machine and the secret services, including the police which included whole cadres of torturers. When war came with Iran in 1980 – a slogging match which in the end would claim close to a million Iraqi lives after a decade of futile battles which accomplished nothing – Saddam's secret police reached the zenith of their power.

Saddam's state-controlled media painted a picture of him as a warlord lying somewhere between Joan of Arc and Mother Theresa; always strong, but always with the needs of his society at heart. It was a grand lie. His dungeons and jails were full with political prisoners, many of them subjected to medieval-style tortures, such as the placing of just-boiled eggs under the armpits of prisoners; floggings, thumb screws and the rack. But it was nothing compared to what he meted out to people called the Kurds within his borders.

WAR AGAINST THE KURDS

In 1988, before his power was stunted, if not altogether broken by the west, Saddam unleashed some of his doomsday chemical weapon arsenal against innocent Kurds as part of his blueprint for their destruction. In contravention of every world treaty and convention, he loosed the silent killers which decimated several Kurdish villages, destroying over 4,000 people. The genie he let out of the bottle was so terrible that he had rarely dared to use it against his arch-enemy Iran during the futile war. But the Kurds were without a land and without a voice. Only afterwards, thanks to courageous western newsmen and the eyewitness reports of relief workers, did the full horror of what Saddam did to innocent civilians become wretchedly and tragically clear.

His chemical weapons programme was one of the most advanced in the world. The old U.S.S.R and America had long curbed production of chemical warfare, proscribed as it was under United Nations rulings and Geneva Conventions. But Saddam, deprived as he was of nuclear power, saw the potential to bring a weighty advantage to his side in the desert with massive stockpiles of cheap but lethal gas.

The technology needed for his gas programme was provided by the western nations that would one day be arrayed against him. During the Gulf War, the Iraqi dictator enjoyed the patronage and dollars of the west. It was a classic case of 'the enemy of my enemy is my friend'. As long

Below: *The silent dead – Kurdish victims of one of Saddam Hussein's lethal poison gas attacks which wiped out whole towns. Saddam stopped at nothing to achieve his ends.*

as Saddam Hussein was keeping the forces of Islamic fundamentalism on the opposite bank of the Euphrates River, the west was happy to keep him supplied with the means for mass destruction. Western companies salved their consciences by saying that much of the hardware necessary for the production of chemical warfare was specified for fertiliser factories within Iraq – it is but a small step from producing fertilisers to poison gas.

CHEMICAL WARFARE

Sefika Ali is now 24, her pretty face wrinkled like that of a much older woman. It is the result of cyanide gas burns which happened when her village was wiped out in a gas attack launched from the air. She fled to Turkey with her husband and three children – they, the lucky ones. Left behind were an estimated 2,000 neighbours, dead in the streets. .

Sefika Ali reported: 'I was cooking breakfast for my family when I heard the sound of aircraft. I heard bombs whistling and the next thing I knew was that there was something wrong with my eyes. I started to vomit almost immediately. I knew what was happening. We had heard what had happened at Halabja. My family suffered the same effects. We all drank a lot of milk and then we ran. We ran to get as far away as we could. We know that not many made it out.'

It was not only the Kurds who faced the wrath of this sadist. His secret police, the Mukhbarat, collated the most comprehensive index system on any people outside of the KGB files of the old Soviet Union. Even when people fled abroad as dissidents it was common policy for the secret police to hunt them down and kill them – or murder or imprison family members left back home.

Shiite Muslims, as opposed to the Sunni tribe which Saddam descended from, make up 55 per cent of the population of Iraq, yet to Saddam Hussein they are lower than dirt – citizens with no rights who deserve extermination. 'No More Shiites After Today' was painted on the bodies of tanks when they were ordered to ransack of the holy Shiite town of Najaf.

This city, a shrine to 1,000 years of Shiite culture, was sacked on Saddam's direct orders. Children who would not tell where

their parents were hidden were doused with petrol and set ablaze. Columns of refugees who fled Saddam's soldiers were machine gunned from the air by helicopter gunships. Fathers were forced to look on while their wives and daughters were raped by the loyal soldiers of Saddam. The libraries were burned, the mosques torched and all the priests were hanged from the lampposts and disembowelled, their corpses left to rot in the boiling sun.

The West had made its pact with the devil, much as it had with the torturers of Argentine during the 'Dirty War' of the 1970s and early 1980s when thousands of innocents died during the campaign to rid the country of real and imagined communist enemies. As long as Saddam was battling the mullahs of Iran they were the good guys, and a multitude of weapons and money was showered on the country. But the West reaped what it had sown in 1990 when Saddam's thirst to be the one strong-

Below: *The Ayatollah Khomeini, spiritual leader of the Iranian revolution and sworn enemy of Iraq.*

Right: *Saddam's forces were no match for the elite troops of the allied coalition. Seen here are British troops, about to inflict a resounding defeat upon him.*

Below: *Downed British pilot John Peters, who was beaten by his captors and displayed on Iraqi TV like a prize.*

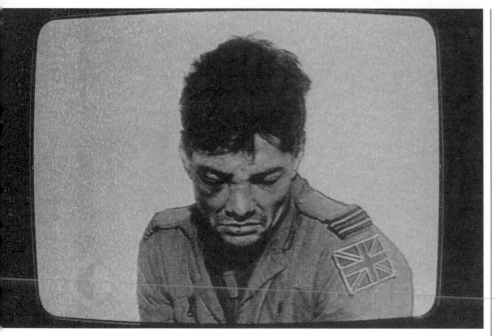

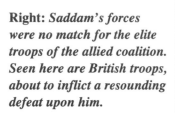

HE WAS DETERMINED TO
FIGHT THE COALITION
FORCES TO THE DEATH

man of the region led him to attempt to invade Kuwait, strip the nation of its sovereignty and declare it a province of Iraq.

THE REGIONAL STRONGMAN

America led a coalition determined to drive Saddam from Kuwait while destroying the bulk of his military power – the muscle that the West had supplied during the years it was happy for Saddam to be the regional strongman. What the West could not afford was his brand of megalomania threatening Nazi-style blitzkriegs in a region where most of the world's oil supplies lay.

Hussein's macho personality could afford no compromises, no backdown from his stance. He was determined to fight the coalition forces to the death, and send the warrior sons of the west home in body bags. History proved him wrong, of course, and the occupation, war and defeat reduced his nation to pre-industrial revolution levels of destruction.

What it did not accomplish, however, was the removal of Saddam Hussein. Each day he remains in power his strength grows. He travels around at night from palace to palace, field camp to field camp, to avoid assassination, while placing his own family members in positions of power as he decimates the military caste with purges that periodically remove potential rivals or assassins. Sooner or later, analysts fear, the West will once again have to reckon with him.

LIBYAN HARDMAN

The same can be said of the man who runs Libya – Colonel Muammar Ghaddafi, truly the main fly in the ointment of the civilised world. Like Hussein, Ghaddafi runs his state as a permanent hosanna to himself. He is the great one, the all powerful one, the mighty one, the merciful one, the just one. He dispenses his wisdom in a quirky manual called the Green Book – a variation on the theme of Mao's Little Red Book – and brooks no dissent, no political opposi-

of King Idris in 1952 when the state gained its independence from the United Nations. During this time Ghaddafi, who was absorbing both fundamental Islamism and socialism, was graduating from college with a degree in history before entering the military as an officer.

Commissioned in 1965, Ghaddafi rose through the ranks of captain within only four years and began formulating his warped theories about the West, the world, and Libya's rightful place in it. As the head of a secret committee of army officers dedicated to the violent overthrow of the state, he made his move against the Idris monarchy in 1969 and proclaimed a Revolutionary Ruling Council, with himself as the chairman. Now it was time for him to unleash his power.

NETWORK OF INFORMERS

Ghaddafi began fashioning his state as an orthodox Islamic state that blended nationalism, revolutionary fervour and harshness in equal measures. In 1970, he booted out all western military bases from his strategically-placed country and nationalised all Italian and Jewish businesses, confiscating for himself the fortunes of people who had lived and worked in the country for a lifetime. It was his first, and by no means least, act of spite that he would show towards Jews and their spiritual home, Israel.

He set up an intricate network of informers, urging schoolchildren to inform against their parents if they heard them uttering anti-revolutionary or pro-western statements. And for those that did, there was a special welcome awaiting them in the dungeons and torture chambers of Tripoli and Benghazi. All political opposition was stifled; there were periodic purges against hardline military men that he perceived as a threat and a militia was formed as his own praetorian guard. Ghaddafi took to dressing like a bedouin chief of old, resplendent in flowing silks with a curved dagger at his side, like some extra in a Lawrence of Arabia movie. But this was no movie – and his next phase of terror was no joke.

Ghaddafi, soaked in resentment at colonialism and what it had done, vowed to export terror to the West. It started with hit squads that he despatched to places like London where, in 1980, three men who had

tion and no thought-crimes against his policies. For years he turned his country into one gigantic training camp in which the guerillas of the world – from the IRA to the PLO – honed their murderous skills. And it is the hands of two of his trusted advisers which were seen in perhaps the most diabolical terrorist act of all time – the destruction of Pan Am Flight 103 over Lockerbie in Scotland in 1988, which resulted in the deaths of 273 people.

This hardman of the oil-rich desert state of Libya is no defender of democracy. Like many in the region, he came to power through an armed coup and has ruled by fear and threats ever since. Ghaddafi was born in 1938 when Libya was part of Italian dictator Benito Mussolini's empire – the empire in which he hoped to bind vassal states to Rome in a throwback to the city's glory days under the Caesars. After the war, which saw Libya as the scene of some of the most bitter fighting of the North African campaign, Libya was ruled by the victorious allies until the installation

Above: *Colonel Ghaddafi, mad dog of the desert, sponsor of global terrorism and the most despised statesman in the world.*

LIKE MANY IN THE REGION, HE CAME TO POWER THROUGH AN ARMED COUP AND HAS RULED BY FEAR AND THREATS EVER SINCE

Bottom right: *WPC Yvonne Fletcher, cut down in the prime of her life by a burst of machine gun fire from within the Libyan Embassy in London.*

Below: *The scene outside the embassy as the police laid siege to the fanatics within.*

criticised his regime were executed. Two years prior to that he had forged links with the provisional IRA in Ulster, agreeing to become a quartermaster for them with Soviet-bought arms and explosives. He hated the British, as the world's supreme colonists of old, and described himself as a brother in the 'fraternal struggle with my brothers, the Irish' to rid Northern Ireland of British rule.

In 1983, five bombs exploded in a Saturday of mayhem across Central London, planted by Libyan fanatics under their leader's orders, and aimed at Arabs who were deemed decadent in the belly of his arch-nemesis. Twenty three people were injured, three of them seriously and Commander Bill Hucklesby of Scotland Yard's anti-terrorist squad pointed the finger firmly at Libya.

While his arm of vengeance and revenge stretched around the world, the desert sands of Libya were becoming packed with fanatics of every kind. Cells of the Red Brigade in Italy, the IRA in Ulster, the PLO from Israel, the Baader Meinhof gang from Germany and the Red Army from Japan were all being trained, equipped and indoctrinated. It was a bizarre paradox that while they were being taught 20th century guerilla warfare in his Islamic chiefdom, the 'Mad Colonel', as the West had taken to calling him, had instituted strict Islamic rule in his own backyard, re-instating Koranic punishments of stoning for unfaithful women, and the chopping off of hands for thieves. So much for the self-styled 'progressive' leader of Libya!

HAIL OF GUNFIRE

It was in 1984, in London again, that the world came to see the colonel in all his fanaticism. In April that year, outside the Libyan embassy in the capital – the self-styled 'Libyan People's Bureau' – demonstrators protesting at the lack of political freedom in Libya suddenly found themselves in a hail of gunfire, coming from within the bureau.

As the bullets flew, one claimed the life of a 25-year-old engaged policewoman named Yvonne Fletcher – martyred by a madman 3,000 miles away who ordered his 'diplomats' to take up arms against any and all detractors of his regime wherever they may be. It was a startling example of the bizarre, berserk lengths he was prepared to go to to forge his brave, new world.

The ensuing siege of the Libyan People's Bureau lasted for nearly two weeks, and when it was finally over Ghaddafi found he had managed to get away with murder. The staff of the bureau, including those that had opened up with automatic weapons, filed away in a line of shame and were flown back to Libya with their full diplomatic privileges intact. To this day, policewoman Yvonne Fletcher's tragic death has gone unavenged.

around the world, now found it was pay-back time as the bombs rained down upon him. Only the fact that he was choosing to stay that night in a bedouin tent saved his life. Tragically, his four-year-old daughter died in the raid; she was an unintentional victim – but then so many hundreds killed by terrorists since it became a boom indus-try in the early 1970s were innocents too. The West hoped that Ghaddafi had learned a tough lesson.

The raid seemed to have achieved its purpose. Ghaddafi stopped supplying the IRA and expelled many PLO guerillas from his territory. For several years there was lit-tle noise from the man who tried to bring about world changes with the bullet and the bomb. But then in December 1988 came the ultimate terrorist atrocity. Pan Am Flight 103, en-route from Heathrow, London, to JFK airport in New York, exploded in the night sky over Lockerbie, Scotland. A global manhunt was launched for those responsible for 273 deaths. It soon transpired that the plane was targeted in retaliation for the downing of an Iranian airliner earlier in the year by the USS Vincennes as she patrolled the waters of the Persian Gulf. The downing of the Iranian jet was a grotesque mistake, but fanatics demanded revenge – hence the slaughter of Pan Am 103.

To this day, the men that the West deem responsible for the massacre are at liberty – aides of Ghaddafi who are still shielded inside his secret police state. The victims of Flight 103, like the policewoman gunned down in London, have still to be avenged. Ghaddafi may have been stunted by the West's action – but he shows no signs of being down for the count, despite interna-tional sanctions against him that make life more difficult for his wretched citizens each day.

CUNNING COLOSSUS

There is one other ruler who remains as slippery as a snake, as untrustworthy as the other two combined, and that is the cold, calculating, cruel Hafiz Assad of Syria, a regional strongman whose power base is perhaps even more solid than those of his Arab compatriots. More bloodthirsty, more cruel, he bestrides the area like a cunning colossus, ever ready and eager to plot his

The world was now under no illusions about what sort of dangerous animal it faced with the desert dictator, but it was in a terrible quandary about how to tackle him – to blunt his assault on civilised behaviour and teach him the kind of lesson that he would both respect… and never forget. That lesson came in 1986, the result of two world leaders with very firm ideas about how the world should conduct itself.

Margaret Thatcher and Ronald Reagan knew that Ghaddafi – isolated though he may have become diplomatically – was still very much in charge and still sponsor-ing terrorism on a massive scale. America was particularly incensed that year because Ghaddafi's terrorists blew up a disco in West Berlin, which injured American ser-vicemen. Reagan gained permission from Mrs. Thatcher to fly U.S. warplanes from Britain to his desert kingdom for a military strike. One April night, as he dined in a tent near to his palace, the night sky over Tripoli echoed with the scream of the jet engines as the aircraft soared in for the mission of revenge. Ghaddafi did not know what hit him. The merchant of death, who had exported so much misery and death

Above: *Ronald Reagan, President of the United States, who delivered a stunning blow against Ghaddafi with an airstrike that struck at the heart of Tripoli.*

THE NIGHT SKY OVER TRIPOLI ECHOED WITH THE SCREAM OF THE JET ENGINES

Above: *Hafez al-Assad, President of Syria and a major player in the global game of terrorism.*

THE BLOOD OF
THOUSANDS OF INNOCENTS
IS ON HIS HANDS – AND HE
KNOWS IT

pendence from the French. He became active in the party's illegal activities, but he stayed out of the clutches of the gendarmes and cheered with the rest of his countrymen when the French finally pulled out in 1946.

In 1952, after graduating from school, he enrolled in the country's military academy where he trained as a fighter pilot. Three years later he was named the best pilot in the country – but politics, not aviation, were his main interest. However, within the ranks of the military he found allies among fellow officers in his vision of a Baathist state which ruled the region. He and three others formed themselves into a secret military committee seeking to overthrow the pro-western government which had been in power since the French departed.

Assad was exiled to Egypt in 1959, due to his covert workings against the government, returning in 1961. Two years later he and his fellow officers played an important role in a coup that overthrew the government and installed the Baath party to power. After assuming various governmental posts, he obtained absolute power in 1970 in another coup and set about turning himself into a god-like figure for his people.

SECRET POLICE

Assad soon began assembling the machinery of terror and repression in the form of the moukhbarat, an omnipresent secret police, which has murdered literally thousands from the day he took over. At the same time he became a big brother of the state, with his picture plastered literally everywhere. The cult of personality he encouraged led the Middle East *Insight* paper to say: 'In no other country in recent memory, not Mao's China, nor Tito's Yugoslavia, has the intensity of the personality cult reached such extremes. Assad's image, speaking, smiling, listening, benevolent or stern, solemn or reflective, is everywhere. Sometimes there are half a dozen pictures of him in a row. His face envelops telegraph poles and trucks, churches and mosques. His is the visage a Syrian sees when he opens his newspaper.'

His great hero was Saladin, the legendary moslem leader of the 12th century and the late Nasser of Egypt. Both were sworn enemies of the Jews; a race for whom Assad has nothing but contempt. He

next chess moves against his own people and his enemies alike. The blood of thousands of innocents is on his hands – and Assad knows it.

Assad was born in October 1930, a Shiite moslem minority in the majority Sunni moslem country. Like many Arabs, Assad grew up fanatically nationalist and despised the French colonial rule over his country. But he was educated in one of their schools, making him a rarity among his countrymen. Education fired his ambitions and his energies; by the time he was 14 he was a member of the Baath Party, the socialist Arab party seeking national inde-

saw his destiny as the emperor of a pan-Arab state, with Damascus at its centre – it is a goal he cherishes to this day. The Arab defeats by Israel in the wars of 1948, 1956 and 1967 left him bitter, hurting his pride as both an Arab and a soldier. He has made it a lifelong pursuit to regain the Golan heights, seized by Israel in 1967, but so far has been unsuccessful. To rub salt into the wounds of Israel's grief over the Holocaust, he openly gives sanctuary to many Nazi killers. The worst of these is Alois Brunner, designer of the mobile gas chamber in which hundreds of thousands of Jews were murdered. He lives openly in Damascus, a feted guest of the government, which has denied countless attempts to have him extradited. Instead, Assad upped his state pension and increased his guard on him.

What he has become is a master of global terrorism. Assad employs terrorism as a tool of government – assassinations, sabotage, guerilla warfare, intimidation – all of which he sees as entirely justified. His country was opened up to the guerillas of the Palestine Liberation Organisation and numerous other factions to establish training and supply camps. Abu Nidal, one of the worst terrorists with the blood of hundreds of innocents on his hand, found a welcome in Damascus.

As well as sponsoring these groups, his moukhbarat refined their own special 'methods' for dealing with internal dissidents. In 1975, a dissident told Amnesty International of some of the devices that Assad's torturers have at their disposal: 'A Russian tool for ripping out finger nails, pincers and scissors for plucking flesh, and an apparatus they call the black slave on which they force the torture victim to sit. When switched on a very hot and sharp metal skewer enters the anus, burning its way until it reaches the intestines, only to be returned then re-inserted.'

POLITICAL ASSASSINATIONS

His agents prowled sovereign foreign nations abroad to assassinate opponents of the regime. In July 1980, Sala al-Din al-Bitar, one of his main enemies, was assassinated in Paris by Syrian gunmen. In March 1981, the wife of another critic was shot by mistake in West Germany. The political assassinations continued through-

out the Middle East and Europe. CIA director William Casey said in a report in 1986: 'Syria uses terrorism as an instrument of foreign policy. Officials, embassies, diplomatic pouches, communication channels and territory are safe havens for planning, directing, and executing bombing, assassination, kidnapping and other terrorist operations.' Four years before this report was published, Assad committed one of the worst atrocities in history – against his very own people.

Assad assembled a massive army force near the town of Hama in 1982, a stronghold of Islamic fundamentalists who were opposed to him. Twelve thousand of them, under the command of Assad's bloodthirsty brother Rifat, began a series of house-to-house searches in which people were tortured or murdered and their possessions stolen or destroyed. The populace rebelled and for ten days the city was in the hands of his enemies. Then Assad hit back with

THEY BEGAN A SERIES OF HOUSE-TO-HOUSE SEARCHES IN WHICH PEOPLE WERE TORTURED OR MURDERED

Below: *Nezar Hindawi, the Syrian who planned to destroy a Jumbo Jet full of passengers – using his pregnant girlfriend as a human bomb.*

Bottom: *Part of Hindawi's terror kit, including a gun, a calculator made into a bomb timer and a fake passport.*

Below: *Anne-Marie Murphy, Hindawi's girl-friend. She was stopped before taking a bomb onto the Israeli plane.*

the full force of the army; heavy artillery shells rained down on the civilian population, children and women were gang raped, property was looted and men were slaughtered, their bodies thrown into mass graves. At the end of three weeks some 30,000 men, women and children were dead, parts of the 1,000-year-old city destroyed forever. 'Death to the Moslem Brother!' roared Assad in a speech from his palace in Damascus the month following the massacre. 'Death to those who tried to play havoc with the homeland! Death to the Moslem Brothers who were hired by U.S. intelligence, reaction and Zionism!' Assad, who had started out on his political career as a respected strongman, was now viewed firmly by his people as a butcher to be deeply feared.

In 1986, any remaining pretensions he may have had to statesman-ship were ripped away. At 9a.m. on April 17 an Israeli security guard at London's Heathrow Airport discovered 1.5 kilogrammes of the explosive Semtex in the false bottom of a bag being carried by pregnant Irishwoman Ann Murphy as she was about to board an El-Al plane to Tel Aviv. Murphy was engaged to a Jordanian named Nezar Hindawi.

Hindawi, 32, had given her the bomb which she believed contained his personal effects. She, her five-month-old unborn child and some 350 passengers would have been blown sky high had it not been for the security guard. Hindawi, who was booked on a flight to Damascus later that day, headed instead for the Syrian Embassy in London – because it was Syria that had masterminded the diabolical plot in the first place. He had a Syrian secret service passport and told police after his capture how the entire affair had been plotted in Syria at the highest levels. Britain broke off diplomatic relations with Syria and it stood condemned in the eyes of the world.

He remains in power. He remains dominant in the region. He remains a very, very dangerous man.

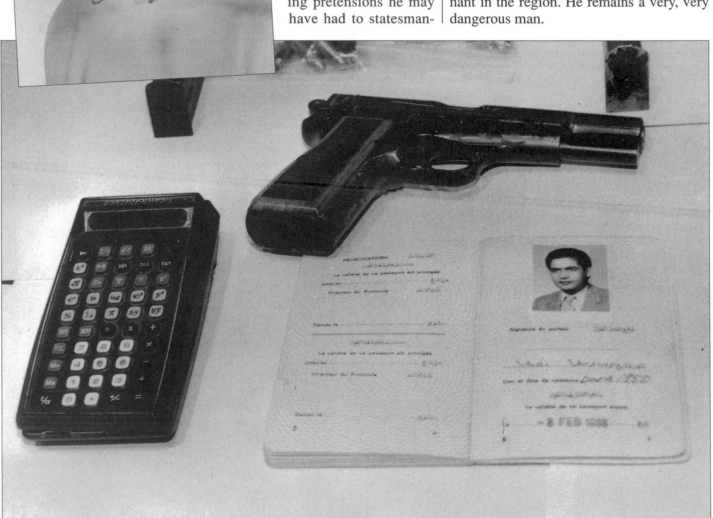